Grammar Joy
중등 영문법

2b

 **POLY BOOKS**

저자 **이 종 저**

이화여자대학교 졸업
Longman Grammar Joy 1, 2, 3, 4권
Longman Vocabulary Mentor Joy 1, 2, 3권
I am Grammar 1, 2권
Grammar & Writing Level A 1, 2권 / Level B 1, 2권
문법을 잡아주는 영작 1, 2, 3, 4권
기본을 잡아주는 중등 영문법 1a, 1b, 2a, 2b, 3a, 3b권
Grammar joy & Writing 1, 2, 3, 4권
Bridging 초등 Voca 1, 2권
Joy 초등 Voca 1, 2, 3권

저자 **박 영 교**

서울대학교 졸업
IVY 영어학원장

감수 **Jeanette Lee**

Wellesley college 졸업

Grammar Joy 중등 영문법 2b

지은이 | 이종저, 박영교
펴낸곳 | POLY books
펴낸이 | POLY 영어 교재 연구소
기 획 | 박정원
편집디자인 | 박혜영

초판 1쇄 인쇄 | 2015년 10월 30일
초판 6쇄 인쇄 | 2022년 11월 5일

POLY 영어 교재 연구소
경기도 성남시 분당구 황새울로 200번길 28 (수내동, 오너스타워)
전 화 070-7799-1583 Fax (031) 262-1583

ISBN | 979-11-86924-81-5
　　　979-11-86924-77-8 (세트)

Grammar Joy 중등 영문법

2b

먼저 그 동안 Grammar Joy Plus를 아껴 주시고 사랑해 주신 분들께 감사를 드립니다. 본 책의 저자는 Grammar Joy Plus를 직접 출간하게 되었습니다. 저자가 직접 출간하게 된 만큼 더 많은 정성과 노력을 들여 미흡하였던 기존의 Grammar Joy Plus를 완전 개정하고 내신문제를 추가하였으며, 책 제목을 Grammar Joy 중등영문법으로 바꾸어 여러분께 선보이게 되었습니다.

모든 교재에서 키포인트는 저자가 학생들의 눈높이를 아는 것입니다. 같은 내용의 문법을 공부하더라도 그 내용을 저자가 어떻게 쉽게 풀어 나가느냐 하는 것이 가장 중요하며, 이에 비중을 두어 만든 교재야말로 최상의 교재라고 생각합니다. Grammar Joy 중등영문법은 저희가 오랜 현장 경험을 바탕으로 이 부분에 초점을 맞추어 만들었습니다.

첫째, 본 교재는 비록 처음 접하는 어려운 내용의 문법일지라도 학생들에게 쉽게 학습효과를 얻을 수 있도록 설명하였습니다. 학생들이 small step으로 진행하면서 학습 목표에 도달할 수 있도록 쉬운 내용부터 시작하여 어려운 내용까지 단계별로 구성하였습니다.

둘째, 시각적으로 용이하게 인식할 수 있도록 문제의 틀을 만들었습니다. 문장의 구조를 도식화하여 설명과 문제 유형을 만들었으므로, 어렵고 복잡한 내용도 쉽게 이해하고 기억에 오래 남을 수 있습니다.

셋째, 쉬운 단어로 구성했습니다. 학습자들이 문장 중에 어려운 단어가 많으면 정작 배워야 할 문법에 치중하지 못하고 싫증을 내고 맙니다. 따라서 학습자 누구나 단어로 인한 어려움 없이 공부할 수 있도록 단어를 선별하였습니다.

넷째, 생동감 있는 문장들을 익힐 수 있도록 하였습니다. 실생활에서 사용되어지는 문장들을 가지고 공부함으로써 현장에 적용시킬 수 있습니다.

다섯째, 풍부한 양의 문제를 제공합니다. 최대의 학습 효과를 얻기 위해서는 학생 스스로가 공부하는 시간을 많이 가지는 것입니다. 또한 많은 문제를 제공함으로 학생 스스로 문제를 풀어 가면서 문법 내용을 본인도 모르는 사이에 저절로 실력 향상을 이룰 수 있습니다.

본 교재를 비롯하여 Grammar Joy Start, Grammar Joy, Grammar Joy 중등영문법을 연계하여 공부한다면 Grammar는 완벽하게 이루어질 것입니다.

특히 저자가 직접 출간한 교재는 타사의 본 교재를 흉내낸 교재들이 따라 올 수 없는 차이점을 느끼실 수 있습니다. 아무쪼록 이 시리즈를 통하여 여러분의 영어 공부에 많은 발전이 있기를 바라며 함께 고생해 주신 박혜영, 박정원께도 감사를 드립니다.

저자 이종거 박영교

Contents

Series Contents

Guide to **This Book**

이 책의 구성과 특징을 파악하고 본 책을 최대한 여러분의 시간에 맞춰 공부 계획을 세워 보세요.

1 Unit별 핵심정리

예비 중학생들이 반드시 알아 두어야 할 문법들을 체계적으로 간단 명료하게 unit별로 정리하였습니다.

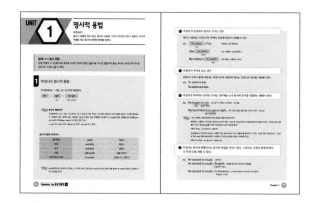

2 핵심 정리

좀 더 심화된 문법을 배우기전 이미 학습한 내용을 정리하여 쉽게 복습할 수 있도록 하였습니다.

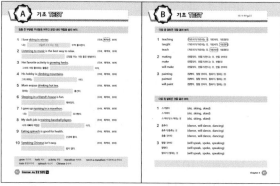

3 기초 test

각 unit별 필수 문법을 잘 이해하고 있는지 기초적인 문제로 짚어 보도록 합니다.

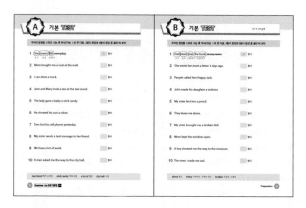

4 기본 test

기초 test 보다 좀 더 어려운 문제를 풀어 봄으로써 핵심 문법에 좀 더 접근해 가도록 하였습니다.

5

실력 test

좀 더 심화된 문제를 통하여 문법을 완성시켜 주도록 하였습니다.

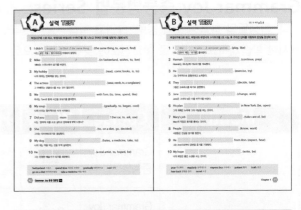

6

내신대비

지금까지 배운 내용을 내신에 적용할 수 있도록 문제 유형을 구성하였고 이를 통해 시험 대비 능력을 키울 수 있도록 하였습니다.

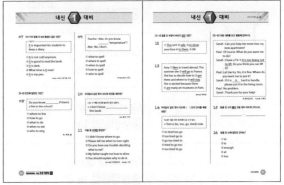

7

종합 문제

본 책에서 공부한 내용을 총괄하여 문제를 구성하였으므로 이를 통하여 학습 성과를 평가할 수 있습니다.

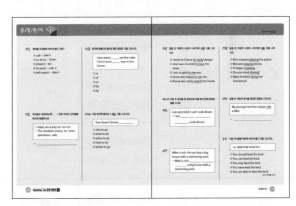

8

영단어 Quizbook

본 책의 학습에 필요한 단어들을 사전에 준비시켜 어휘가 문법을 공부하는데 걸림돌이 되지 않도록 하고 학생들의 어휘 실력을 향상시킬 수 있도록 준비하였습니다.

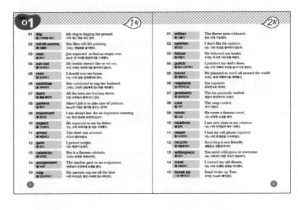

How to Use This Book

Grammar Joy 중등영문법 Series는 총 6권으로 각 권당 6주 총 6개월의 수업 분량으로 이루어져 있습니다. 학생들의 학업 수준과 능력, 그리고 학습 시간에 따라 각 테스트를 과제로 주어 교육 과정 조정이 가능합니다. 아래에 제시한 학습계획표를 참고로 학교진도에 맞춰 부분적으로 선별하여 학습을 진행할 수도 있습니다.

Month	Course	Week	Hour	Part	Homework/Extra
1st Month	Grammar Joy 중등영문법 1a	1st	1 2 3	문장의 구성 부정사 A	▶chapter별 단어 test는 과제로 주어 수업 시작 전에 test
	Grammar Joy 중등영문법 1a	2nd	1 2 3	부정사 B 동명사	▶각 chapter별 내신대비는 과제로 주거나 각 chapter 수업 후 test
	Grammar Joy 중등영문법 1a	3rd	1 2 3	분사	
	Grammar Joy 중등영문법 1a	4th	1 2 3	조동사	
2nd Month	Grammar Joy 중등영문법 1a	1st	1 2 3	수동태	
	Grammar Joy 중등영문법 1a	2nd	1 2 3	현재완료	
	Grammar Joy 중등영문법 1b	3rd	1 2 3	명사와 관사	
	Grammar Joy 중등영문법 1b	4th	1 2 3	대명사	
3rd Month	Grammar Joy 중등영문법 1b	1st	1 2 3	형용사와 부사	
	Grammar Joy 중등영문법 1b	2nd	1 2 3	비교 전치사	
	Grammar Joy 중등영문법 1b	3rd	1 2 3	명사절과 상관 접속사	
	Grammar Joy 중등영문법 1b	4th	1 2 3	부사절	▶종합 test는 각 권이 끝난 후 evaluation 자료로 사용한다

Month	Course	Week	Hour	Part	Homework/Extra
4th Month	Grammar Joy 중등영문법 2a	1st	1 2 3	부정사 A	▶chapter별 단어 test는 과제로 주어 수업 시작 전에 test
	Grammar Joy 중등영문법 2a	2nd	1 2 3	부정사 B	▶각 chapter별 내신대비는 과제로 주거나 각 chapter 수업 후 test
	Grammar Joy 중등영문법 2a	3rd	1 2 3	동명사	
	Grammar Joy 중등영문법 2a	4th	1 2 3	분사 구문	
5th Month	Grammar Joy 중등영문법 2a	1st	1 2 3	조동사 수동태	
	Grammar Joy 중등영문법 2a	2nd	1 2 3	완료	
	Grammar Joy 중등영문법 2b	3rd	1 2 3	비교 명사절	
	Grammar Joy 중등영문법 2b	4th	1 2 3	부사절과 접속부사	
6th Month	Grammar Joy 중등영문법 2b	1st	1 2 3	관계대명사 A	
	Grammar Joy 중등영문법 2b	2nd	1 2 3	관계대명사 B	
	Grammar Joy 중등영문법 2b	3rd	1 2 3	시제의 일치와 화법	
	Grammar Joy 중등영문법 2b	4th	1 2 3	가정법	▶종합 test는 각 권이 끝난 후 evaluation 자료로 사용한다

Month	Course	Week	Hour	Part	Homework/Extra
7th Month	Grammar Joy 중등영문법 3a	1st	1 2 3	부정사	▶chapter별 단어 test는 과제로 주어 수업 시작 전에 test
	Grammar Joy 중등영문법 3a	2nd	1 2 3	동명사	▶각 chapter별 실전Test는 과제로 주거나 각 Chapter 수업 후 test
	Grammar Joy 중등영문법 3a	3rd	1 2 3	분사	
	Grammar Joy 중등영문법 3a	4th	1 2 3	분사구문	
8th Month	Grammar Joy 중등영문법 3a	1st	1 2 3	조동사	
	Grammar Joy 중등영문법 3a	2nd	1 2 3	수동태 명사와 관사	
	Grammar Joy 중등영문법 3b	3rd	1 2 3	대명사	
	Grammar Joy 중등영문법 3b	4th	1 2 3	형용사와 부사	
9th Month	Grammar Joy 중등영문법 3b	1st	1 2 3	비교	
	Grammar Joy 중등영문법 3b	2nd	1 2 3	관계사	
	Grammar Joy 중등영문법 3b	3rd	1 2 3	가정법	
	Grammar Joy 중등영문법 3b	4th	1 2 3	전치사 특수 구문	▶종합 Test는 각 권이 끝난 후 evaluation 자료로 사용한다

Chapter 1

비교란?

1 기본 비교

원급(동등)비교 : as 원급 as ~: ~만큼 ~ 한

비교하는 두 개의 정도가 같을 때 사용한다.

ex. **She is as tall as I (am).** 그녀는 나만큼 키가 크다.

비교급(우등)비교 : 비교급 than ~: ~보다 더 ~ 한

비교하는 둘 중의 하나가 그 정도가 더 할 때 쓴다.

ex. **She is taller than I (am).** 그녀는 나보다 더 키가 크다.

최상급비교 : the 최상급 in/of ~: 가장 ~ 한

세 개 이상 중에서 가장 최고의 뜻을 나타낼 때 쓴다.

ex. **She is the tallest in our class.** 그녀는 우리 반에서 가장 키가 크다.

* 최상급 in + 장소, 범위 / 최상급 of + 복수명사

ex. **She is the tallest in her team.** 그녀는 그녀의 팀에서 가장 키가 크다.

ex. **She is the tallest of the three.** 그녀는 셋 중에서 가장 키가 크다.

2 비교급의 강조, 원급을 이용한 비교급, 비교 구문을 이용한 표현

비교급의 강조 : 훨씬 더 ~ 하게

비교급 앞에 much, even, far, still, a lot 등을 써서 비교급을 강조하고 '훨씬'의 뜻이 있다.

ex. **She is much taller than I.** 그녀는 나보다 훨씬 더 키가 크다.

원급을 이용한 비교급 표현

원급의 부정으로 비교급 표현을 할 수 있다.

ex. **She is not as tall as I.** 그녀는 나만큼 키가 크지 않다. = **I am taller than she.** 나는 그녀보다 더 키가 크다.

비교 구문을 이용한 표현

• as 원급 as one can : 가능한 한 ~한   • 비교급 and 비교급 : 점점 더 ~하다
• the 비교급 ~, the 비교급... : ~하면 할수록 더 ....하다
• 배수사 + 원급 : ~의 ...배 만큼 ~한

1

급의 전환과 최상급의 다른 표현

1 급의 전환

비교급과 원급으로 최상급을 나타낼 수 있다. 이를 급의 전환이라 한다.

🔷 비교급으로 최상급을 나타내는 방법

ex. Bill is **the strongest boy** in my school. (최상급) Bill은 나의 학교에서 가장 힘이 센 소년이다.

= Bill is **stronger than any other boy** in my school. (비교급)

Bill은 나의 학교에서 어떤 다른 소년보다 더 힘이 세다.

= **No (other) boy** in my school is **stronger than Bill**. (비교급)

나의 학교에서 어떤 다른 소년도 Bill 보다 더 힘이 세지 않다.

* any other + 단수명사, no other + 단수명사

🔷 원급으로 최상급을 나타내는 방법

ex. Bill is **the strongest boy** in my school. (최상급) Bill은 나의 학교에서 가장 힘이 센 소년이다.

= **No (other) boy** in my school is **as strong as Bill**. (원급)

나의 학교에서 어떤 다른 소년도 Bill 만큼 힘이 세지 않다.

2 최상급의 다른 표현

🔷 one of the 최상급 + 복수명사

'가장 ~한 것 중의 하나'라는 뜻을 가진다.

ex. She is **one of the most popular singers** in Korea.

그녀는 한국에서 가장 인기 있는 가수 중의 한 명이다.

* 'one of the 최상급 + 복수명사'가 문장의 주어로 사용 시 단수 취급한다.

ex. One of the tallest boys in my school is Jack. 나의 학교에서 가장 키가 큰 소년 중의 한 명이 Jack이다.

🔷 the 최상급 + 명사 (that) 주어 + have ever P.P

'이제 까지~한 것 중에서 가장 ~한'이라는 뜻을 가진다.

ex. This is **the most exciting game that I have ever seen**.

이것은 내가 이제까지 본 것 중에서 가장 흥미진진한 경기이다.

A 기초 TEST

주어진 문장을 우리말로 바꾸어 옮겨 보자.

1 Jane is the wisest girl in my class.

= Jane is wiser than any other girl in my class.

Jane은 나의 반에서 *어떤 다른 소녀보다 더 현명하다* .

= No other girl in my class is wiser than Jane.

나의 반에서 .

= No other girl in my class is as wise as Jane.

나의 반에서 .

2 Edison is one of the greatest inventors in the world.

에디슨은 세상에서 이다.

3 This is the longest bridge that I have ever crossed.

이것은 이다.

4 This is the oldest tree in Korea.

= No other tree in Korea is older than this.

한국에 있는 .

= No other tree in Korea is as old as this.

한국에 있는 .

= This is older than any other tree in Korea.

이것은 한국에 있는 .

5 This is the nicest bag that she has ever seen.

이것은 이다.

6 Brian is one of the most popular actors in the country.

Brian은 그 나라에서 이다.

---

great 위대한   **inventor** 발명가   **cross** 건너가다   **old** 오래된, 나이가 많은   **popular** 인기있는   **actor** (남자)배우

주어진 문장과 같은 뜻의 문장이 되도록 알맞게 배열해 보자.

1 Susan is the smartest girl in my class.

= Susan is *smarter than any other girl* in my class.
(girl, other, any, than, smarter)

= _____ in my class is _____ Susan.
(other, girl, no, than, smarter)

= _____ in my class is _____ Susan.
(other, girl, no, as, as, smart)

2 Aprok River is the longest river in Korea.

= _____ in Korea is _____ Aprok River.
(than, longer, no, river, other)

= _____ in Korea is _____ Aprok River.
(long, no, as, as, river, other)

= Aprok River is _____ in Korea.
(any, river, other, than, longer)

3 The elephant is the largest animal on land.

= _____ on land is _____ the elephant.
(no, animal, than, larger, other)

= The elephant is _____ on land.
(animal, any, other, than, larger)

= _____ on land is _____ the elephant.
(as, large, animal, as, no, other)

on land 육지에서

A 기본 TEST

다음 주어진 단어를 우리말에 알맞게 나열해 보자.

1 Paul is *one of the most diligent workers* in the factory.

(the most, diligent, workers, of, one)

Paul은 그 공장에서 가장 부지런한 일꾼들 중의 한 명이다.

2 This is in the city.

(the tallest, one, of, buildings)

이것은 이 도시에서 가장 높은 빌딩 중의 하나이다.

3 A rose is in the world.

(of, the most, one, flowers, beautiful)

장미는 세상에서 가장 아름다운 꽃들 중의 하나이다.

4 Jane has in the class.

(one, ideas, of, the best)

Jane은 반에서 가장 좋은 아이디어 중 하나를 가지고 있다.

다음 주어진 단어를 우리말에 알맞게 나열해 보자.

1 This is *the most delicious pizza that I have ever eaten* .

(I, ever, have, eaten, pizza, that, the most delicious)

이것은 내가 이제까지 먹어 본 중에서 가장 맛있는 피자이다.

2 This is .

(the cleverest, we, have, kept, that, ever, dog)

이것은 우리가 이제까지 길러 본 중에서 가장 영리한 개이다.

3 This was .

(she, that, the most interesting, ever, movie, has, watched)

이것은 그녀가 이제까지 본 중에서 가장 재미있는 영화였다.

4 This is .

(the longest, he, passed, through, tunnel, ever, has, that)

이것은 그가 이제까지 통과 한 것 중에서 가장 긴 터널 이다.

---

diligent 부지런한   clever 영리한   pass through 통과하다

B 기본 TEST

정답 및 해설 p.2

( ) 안의 지시대로 같은 뜻의 문장이 되도록 문장을 완성해 보자.

1 New York is the biggest city in America.

= New York is *bigger than any other city* in America. (비교급)

= _____ in America is _____ New York. (비교급)

= _____ in America is _____ New York. (원급)

2 Jake is the oldest barber in the town.

= _____ in the town is _____ Jake. (원급)

= _____ in the town is _____ Jake. (비교급)

= Jake is _____ in the town. (비교급)

3 This is the most expensive cap in this shop.

= This is _____ in this shop. (비교급)

= _____ in this shop is _____ this. (원급)

= _____ in this shop is _____ this. (비교급)

4 Peter is the fastest swimmer in the country.

= _____ in the country is _____ Peter. (원급)

= Peter is _____ in the country. (비교급)

= _____ in the country is _____ Peter. (비교급)

barber 이발사

주어진 단어를 이용하여 우리말에 알맞게 문장을 완성해 보자.

1 Picasso is _one of the most famous painters_ in the world. (famous, painter)

피카소는 세상에서 가장 유명한 화가 중의 하나이다.

2 This is _____. (big, watermelon)

이것은 내가 이제까지 본 것 중에서 가장 큰 수박이다.

3 Siberia is _____ on the earth. (cold, place)

시베리아는 지구상에서 가장 추운 장소중의 하나이다.

4 It was _____. (sweet, music)

그것은 그가 이제까지 들어 본 중에서 가장 감미로운 음악이었다.

5 He is _____. (honest, person)

그는 내가 이제까지 만난 (사람)중에서 가장 정직한 사람이다.

6 She is _____ in Korea. (well-known, singer)

그녀는 한국에서 가장 잘 알려진 가수 중의 하나이다.

7 Mr. Lee is _____ in our school. (strict, teacher)

이 선생님은 우리 학교에서 가장 엄격한 선생님들 중 한 명이다.

8 This monkey is _____ in the zoo. (funny, animal)

이 원숭이는 그 동물원 안에서 가장 우스꽝스러운 동물들 중의 하나이다.

9 She is _____. (wise, person)

그녀는 우리가 이제까지 알고 있는 (사람)중에서 가장 현명한 사람이다.

10 Bungee jumping is _____.

번지점프는 내가 이제까지 가져본 것 중에서 가장 특별한 경험이다.　　　(special, experience)

Siberia 시베리아　　sweet 감미로운　　well known 잘 알려진　　strict 엄격한　　Bungee jump 번지점프
special 특별한　　experience 경험

01 다음 최상급을 비교급으로 나타낼 때 빈칸에 알맞은 것은?

> Tom is the smallest boy in my school.
> = Tom is smaller than _____ in my school.

① any other boys
② any other boy
③ no other boy
④ no other boys
⑤ any boy

02 다음 최상급을 원급으로 나타낼 때 빈칸에 알맞은 것은?

> Jane is the prettiest girl in her class.
> = _____ in her class is as pretty as Jane.

① Any other girls
② Any other girl
③ No other girl
④ No other girls
⑤ Any girl

03 다음 밑줄 친 중에서 틀린 곳을 바르게 고치시오.

> He is one of the greatest scientist in Korea.
> 그는 한국에서 가장 위대한 과학자 중 한 명이다.

_____ → _____

04 다음을 우리말에 맞게 배열하시오.

> This is _____
> _____ .
> (I, have, seen, ever, the most beautiful, that, flower)
> 이것은 내가 이제까지 본 중에서 가장 아름다운 꽃이다.

05 다음 최상급을 비교급으로 나타낼 때 빈칸을 알맞게 채우시오.

> That is the longest bridge in the world.
> = No other bridge in the world is _____ .

06 다음에서 틀린 문장을 고르시오.

① No other mountain in Japan is as high as Mt. Fuji.

② Mt. Fuji is higher than any other mountain in Japan.

③ Mt. Fuji is higher than any mountain in Japan.

④ No other mountain in Japan is higher than Mt. Fuji.

⑤ No mountain in Japan is higher than Mt. Fuji.

09 다음 비교급을 최상급으로 바꾸어 쓰시오.

No other jewel in the world is more expensive than diamond.

= Diamond is _____

_____.

jewel 보석

07 다음 밑줄 친 중에서 어법상 어색한 곳을 고르시오.

① One of ② the nicest ③ buildings in Korea ④ are 63 ⑤ building.

10 빈칸에 공통으로 알맞은 말을 쓰시오.

· Have you _____ been to China?
너는 중국에 가본 적이 있니?

· This is the smallest car that I have _____ seen.
이것은 내가 이제까지 본 중에서 가장 작은 자동차다.

→ _____

08 다음 우리말에 맞게 밑줄 친 곳에 쓰시오.

No other tower in Seoul is _____
_____ Namsan tower.
서울에서 어떤 타워도 남산 타워 만큼 높지 않다.

[11–13] 다음을 ( ) 안의 지시대로 바꾸어 쓰시오.

> This dictionary is the thickest book in the library.

hick 두꺼운

11 〈비교급〉

This dictionary is _____ _____ in the library.

12 〈비교급〉

_____ in the library is _____ this dictionary.

13 〈원급〉

_____ in the library is _____ this dictionary.

14 다음에서 생략 할 수 있는 것을 고르시오.

> ① No ② other bird on the ③ earth is ④ as big ⑤ as a condor.
> 지구상에서 어떤 다른 새도 콘도르만큼 크지는 않다.

[15–16] 다음 문장에서 밑줄친 곳이 올바르지 않은 것을 고르시오.

15 ① This is the oldest <u>temple</u> in India.
② This is one of the oldest <u>temple</u> in India.
③ No other <u>temple</u> in India is older than this.
④ No <u>temple</u> in India is as old as this.
⑤ This is the oldest <u>temple</u> that she has ever seen.

temple 절, 사원

16 ① One of the most diligent workers in the factory <u>are</u> Paul.
② No other worker in the factory <u>is</u> as diligent as Paul.
③ Paul <u>is</u> one of the most diligent workers in the factory.
④ Paul <u>is</u> the most diligent worker that we have ever known.
⑤ No worker in the factory <u>is</u> more diligent than Paul.

factory 공장

[17–18] 다음 글을 읽고 물음에 답하시오.

One day there lived an ugly duckling in the lake.
His siblings said, 'You are strange.
ⓐ You are the ugliest duckling in the lake.'
Though ⓑ no other duckling in the lake was bigger than he, he always ran away.

ugly 못생긴   duckling 오리새끼   sibling 형제, 자매

17 밑줄 친 ⓐ를 같은 뜻의 비교급으로 바꾸어 쓴 것 중 틀린 것은?

① You are uglier than any other duckling in the lake.
② Any other duckling in the lake is uglier than you.
③ No duckling in the lake is uglier than you.
④ No other duckling in the lake is uglier than you.
⑤ 없음

18 밑줄 친 ⓑ를 같은 뜻의 최상급으로 바꾸어 쓰시오.

→ He was _____ .

[19–20] 다음 글을 읽고 물음에 답하시오.

Mom : It is too late. Where have you been, Jake?
Jack : I read a storybook at the school library. My friend said, ⓐ 'That is one of the most interesting storybook in the library'. It was really so.
Mom : I see. And you are hungry, aren't you?
Jack : Yes, I'm starving.
Mom : Here are bread, milk and strawberries for supper.
(a few minutes later)
Jack : Mom, ⓑ 이것들은 내가 먹어본 중에서 가장 달콤한 딸기예요.
(I, have, eaten, ever, the sweetest, strawberries, that).

starve 굶주리다

19 밑줄 친 ⓐ에서 틀린 곳을 찾아 바르게 고치시오.

_____ → _____

20 밑줄 친 ⓑ를 우리말에 맞게 배열해 보시오

→ These are _____
_____ .

[11–13] 다음 빈칸에 알맞은 것을 고르시오.

01

Tom is taller than _____ in his school.

Tom은 그의 학교에서 어떤 다른 소년보다 더 키가 크다.

① any boy
② any other boy
③ any boys
④ any other boys
⑤ other boys

02

No other boy in his class is _____ Ron.

그의 반에서 어떤 다른 소년도 Ron만큼 똑똑하지 않다.

① as smart as
② smarter of
③ most smart
④ the smartest
⑤ the most smart

03

_____ in my school is slimmer than Lauren.

나의 학교에서 어떤 다른 소녀도 Lauren 보다 더 날씬하지 않다.

① No girls
② No other girls
③ Other girls
④ No girl
⑤ Other girl

04 다음 빈 칸에 들어갈 말이 알맞게 짝지어진 것은?

Beyonce is _____ of the most popular _____ in the world.

Beyonce는 세계에서 가장 인기 있는 가수 중의 한 명이다.

① a singer - one
② singers - ones
③ singers - ones
④ one - singers
⑤ one – singer

05 다음 문장의 괄호 안에서 알맞은 것에 O표 해보시오.

One of the most expensive (car / cars) in this store (is / are) the red one.

이 매장에서 가장 비싼 차 중의 하나가 저 빨간 차이다.

[06–07] 다음 괄호 안의 단어를 우리말에 맞게 배열하시오.

06

This is the most delicious food that _____ .
(have, eaten, I, ever)

이것은 내가 이제까지 먹어본 것 중에서 가장 맛있는 음식이다.

07

This is _____

_____ .

(in Korea, the oldest, churches, of, one)

이것은 한국에서 가장 오래된 교회중에 하나이다.

08 다음 우리말에 맞게 밑줄 친 곳에 쓰시오.

No other river in Seoul is _____ Han River.

서울에서 어떤 강도 한강만큼 길지 않다.

09 다음 원급을 최상급 표현으로 바꾸어 쓸 때, 빈 칸에 들어갈 알맞은 말을 쓰시오.

No other man in the world is as rich as Bill.
= Bill is _____ in the world.

10 다음 최상급을 비교급으로 나타낼 때 빈 칸에 알맞게 쓰시오.

This is the tallest building in the world.
= No other building in the world is _____ this.

11 다음 문장을 바르게 영작한 것을 고르시오.

이것은 내가 이제까지 본 것 중에서 가장 흥미진진한 경기이다.

① This is the most exciting game that I have ever seen.
② This is the most exciting game that I have never seen.
③ This is the excitest game that I have ever seen.
④ This is the excitest game that I have never seen.
⑤ This is the excitest game that I have seen.

12 다음 우리말에 알맞게 밑줄 친 곳에 쓰시오.

> Jane is _____ the youngest members in the company.
> Jane은 회사에서 가장 젊은 직원 중 한 명이다.

13 다음 밑줄 친 단어와 바꿔 쓸 수 <u>없는</u> 것을 고르시오.

> He is <u>much</u> kinder than his friend.

① so
② even
③ far
④ still
⑤ a lot

[14–15] 다음 글을 읽고 물음에 답하시오.

> My friend, Rachel was the tallest student in my class. ⓐ _____ in my class is taller than she. (나의 반에서 어떤 다른 학생도 그녀보다 더 키가 크지 않았다.)
> Some boys used to make fun of her, but Rachel did not mind. After graduating school, Rachel became a fashion model. ⓑ Now, she is one of the <u>famous model</u> in the world.
> (지금, 그녀는 세상에서 가장 유명한 모델들 중의 한 명이다.)

14 다음 ⓐ의 빈칸에 들어갈 알맞은 말을 고르시오. (답 2개)

① Any other student
② Any student
③ No other student
④ No student
⑤ No other students

15 ⓑ 문장에서 밑줄 친 부분을 바르게 고치시오.

ⓑ famous model → _____

16 다음 두 문장의 뜻이 같도록 빈칸에 알맞은 것을 골라 보시오.

> Bill is the strongest boy in my school.
> = No other boy is _____ Bill.

① strong than
② strongest than
③ as strong as
④ as stronger as
⑤ as strongest as

17 다음 문장에서 <u>틀린</u> 곳을 찾아 바르게 고치시오.

> Einstein is one of the greatest scientist of all time.
> 아인슈타인은 역대 가장 위대한 과학자 중 한 명이다.

_____ → _____

of all time 역대/ 역사상

18 다음을 우리말에 맞게 배열하시오.

> This is (I, have, visited, ever, the most beautiful, that, castle)
> 여기는 내가 방문한 곳 중에서 가장 아름다운 성이다.

castle 성

This is _____

_____ .

19 다음 중 어법상 알맞지 <u>않은</u> 것은?

① This is the oldest tree in Korea.
② This is one of the oldest tree in Korea.
③ No other tree in Korea is older than this.
④ No tree in Korea is as old as this.
⑤ This is the oldest tree that I have ever seen.

20 다음 밑줄 친 곳 중에서 어법상 어색한 곳을 고르시오.

> ① One of ② the nicest ③ places in Korea ④ are ⑤ COEX.

Chapter 2

명사절

명사절이란?

문장 안에서 명사역할을 하는 절을 말하며
접속사 that, whether(= if), 의문사 등이 절을 이끈다.

1 접속사 that이 이끄는 명사절

🔳 우리말로는 '~라는 것, ~라고'에 해당한다.

〈주어〉 *ex.* **That he is honest** is true. 그가 정직하다는 것은 사실이다.
　　　　　　　주어

〈목적어〉 *ex.* I think **that he is honest**. 나는 그가 정직하다고 생각한다.
　　　　　　　　　　목적어

〈보어〉 *ex.* The fact is **that he is honest**. 사실은 그가 정직하다는 것이다.
　　　　　　　　　　　보어

2 가주어 it과 that의 생략

🔳 that으로 시작되는 명사절은 주어로 문장 앞에 잘 쓰지 않는다. 그러므로 가주어 it으로 바꾸어 쓰는 것이 보통이다.

ex. **That he is smart** is true. 그가 똑똑하다는 것은 사실이다.
= **It** is true **that he is smart**.
　　가주어　　　　　진주어

🔳 that으로 시작되는 명사절이 목적어로 쓰일 때는 접속사 that을 생략할 수 있다.

ex. I think **that she is wise**. 나는 그녀가 현명하다고 생각한다.
= I think 　 she is wise.

Tip! that이 이끄는 명사절의 어순은 : that 주어 + 동사 ~ 이다.

1

whether, if가 이끄는 명사절

1 whether, if가 이끄는 명사절

◆ whether~ (or not) : ~인지 아닌지

ex. I wonder **whether** it is true. 나는 그것이 사실인지 아닌지 궁금하다.

◆ if~ (or not) : ~인지 아닌지

ex. I know **if** the rumor is true. 나는 그 소문이 사실인지 아닌지 안다.

ⓐ **if**(~인지 아닌지)가 이끄는 명사절은 의미가 미래이면 미래로 나타낸다.

    ex. I don't know <u>if he will **come**</u>. 그가 올지 안 올지 나는 모르겠다.
                       명사절

ⓑ **if**(만일~라면)가 이끄는 부사절은 그 의미가 미래라도 현재로 나타낸다.

    ex. <u>If he **comes**</u>, I will be happy. 만일 그가 온다면, 나는 행복할 것이다.
         부사절

◆ whether와 if의 차이

ⓐ **whether**가 이끄는 명사절은 주어, 목적어, 보어로 쓰이지만 **if** 는 목적어가 되는 명사절만 이끈다.

    ex. **Whether he comes or not** doesn't matter. 그가 오던지 말던지 상관없다.

    ex. I wonder **if he will come**.

    ~~If he will come doesn't matter.~~

ⓑ **whether / if~or not**은 둘 다 가능하고, **whether or not~** 은 가능하나 **if or not~** 은 쓰지 않는다.

    ex. I don't know **whether or not** it works. 그것이 작동하는지 아닌지 나는 모른다.

    ~~I don't know if or not it works.~~

    ex. I don't know **whether(if)** it works **or not**.

ⓒ **whether**는 to부정사를 이끌 수 있다.

    ex. We can't decide **whether to** leave or stay. 우리는 떠나야할지 머물러야할지 결정할 수 없다.

A 기초 TEST

다음에서 명사절을 찾아 ○표 하고 우리말로 써 보자. 문장에서의 쓰임도 골라 보자.

1 He wonders (whether Jane likes meat or not). (주어, 보어, (목적어))

그는 ~~Jane이 고기를 좋아하는지 아닌지~~ 궁금해 한다.

2 Whether she loves him or not isn't certain. (주어, 보어, 목적어)

확실치 않다.

3 I don't know if she will come here. (주어, 보어, 목적어)

나는 알지 못한다.

4 The question is whether we may drink this water or not. (주어, 보어, 목적어)

문제는 이다.

5 I am not sure if it will be fine tomorrow. (주어, 보어, 목적어)

나는 확신할 수 없다.

다음에서 명사절과 부사절을 찾아 ○표 하고 우리말로 써보자. 절의 종류도 구별해 보자.

1 The kid asked her mom (if there is a monster under her bed).

그 아이는 ~~그녀의 침대아래 괴물이 있는지 없는지~~ 그녀의 엄마에게 물었다. ((명사절), 부사절)

2 We will go on a picnic if the weather is good.

우리는 소풍을 갈 것이다. (명사절, 부사절)

3 Sarah doesn't decide if she should wear the blue dress or the red one.

Sarah는 결정하지 못한다. (명사절, 부사절)

4 He will never spend his money if he is a miser.

그는 그의 돈을 결코 쓰지 않을 것이다. (명사절, 부사절)

5 He is not sure if she will be helpful for him or not.

그는 확신하고 있지 않다. (명사절, 부사절)

---

certain 확실한, 틀림없는   **sure** 확신하는, 확실히 아는   **monster** 괴물   **miser** 구두쇠   **helpful** 도움이 되는

B 기초 TEST

정답 및 해설 **p.4**

우리말에 알맞은 것을 골라 보자.

1 I can't see if he (will look, looks) at me from that distance.

나는 그가 저 멀리서 나를 쳐다볼지 아닐지 알 수가 없다.

2 We will not wait if the line (will be, is) long.

만일 줄이 길다면 우리는 기다리지 않을 것이다.

3 I don't know if Susan (meet, will meet) him.

나는 Susan이 그를 만날지 아닐지 모르겠다.

4 If he (survives, will survives), he will be very lucky.

그가 생존한다면, 그는 행운일 것이다.

5 She wonders if Brian (will be, is) a famous cook.

그녀는 Brian이 유명한 요리사가 될지 안 될지 궁금해 한다.

6 You can arrive there in time if you (start, will start) now.

네가 지금 출발한다면 너는 제 시간에 거기 도착할 수 있다.

7 People will love him if he (will be, is) honest.

그가 정직하다면 사람들은 그를 좋아할 것이다.

8 You may watch TV if you (will finish, finished) your homework.

네가 숙제를 끝마쳤다면 너는 TV를 보아도 좋다.

9 I'm not sure if Paul (works, will work) with them or not.

나는 Paul이 그들과 함께 일을 할지 아닐지 확실히는 모르겠다.

10 Whether or not she (answers, will answer) is the key point.

그녀가 대답할지 아닐지가 요점이다.

---

from that distance 그만큼 떨어진 곳에서(멀리서)   **line** 줄   **survive** 생존하다   **lucky** 행운의
key point 요점   **can't see** 알 수 없다

다음 주어진 단어를 이용하여 우리말에 알맞게 써 보자.

1 She wants to know if Jimmy _____is_____ at school or not. (be)

그녀는 Jimmy가 학교에 있는지 없는지 알기를 원한다.

2 You will be cool if you _____ the air-conditioner. (turn on)

만일 네가 에어컨을 켠다면 너는 시원해질 것이다.

3 I am wondering if she _____ really sick. (be)

나는 그녀가 정말로 아픈지 아닌지 궁금해 하고 있다.

4 They will not go camping if it _____ tomorrow. (rain)

만일 내일 비가 온다면 그들은 캠핑을 가지 않을 것이다.

5 We will help them if they _____ wounded. (be)

만일 그들이 부상당해 있다면, 우리는 그들을 도울 것이다.

6 Jane wonders if he _____ in life. (succeed)

Jane은 그가 인생에서 성공할지 못할지 궁금해 한다.

7 Nobody knows if Linda _____ here. (come)

아무도 Linda 가 여기로 올지 안 올지 모르고 있다.

8 You should be a creative guy if you _____ to be famous. (want)

만일 네가 유명해 지기를 바란다면, 너는 창의적인 사람이 되어야 한다.

9 We don't know if she _____ it. (like)

우리는 그녀가 그것을 좋아할지 아닐지 모르겠다.

10 Let me know if you _____ my help. (need)

만일 네가 나의 도움이 필요하면, 나에게 알려줘.

---

really 정말   **wound** (상처) 부상을 입히다   **creative** 창의적인   **need** 필요하다

다음 중 알맞은 것을 골라 보자. (두 개 가능)

1 I can't tell (if, whether) she is sick or not.

2 I am not sure (whether, if) Ana is here yet.

3 (Whether, If) he will do it is up to you.

4 Tom didn't know (if, whether) he should take off his shoes in the house.

5 (Whether, If) she comes to the party is of no account to me.

6 He thinks (if, whether) to see a doctor.

7 They can't decide (whether, if) or not Bill should get the award.

8 We didn't know (whether, if) to laugh or cry.

9 (If, Whether) she is in danger is not clear.

10 Nobody knows (whether, if) Bill will win the prize or not.

11 I didn't decide (whether, if) or not to buy it.

12 He didn't decide (whether, if) he should drive to work or walk.

13 Mary thinks (whether, if) to move to other city.

14 (Whether, if) she was blind was not crucial.

15 We will consider (whether, if) or not we should accept the applicant.

be of no account 대수롭지 않다   award 상   be in danger 위험에 처하다   crucial 결정적인, 중대한
consider 고려하다   accept 받아들이다   applicant 신청자

whether와 if 중에 알맞은 것을 골라 써 넣어 보자. (두 개 가능)

1 I wasn't sure _whether, if_ I should watch a DVD or read a book.

2 They can't tell _____ the park is closed at this hour or not.

3 I can't decide _____ to order pizza or hamburger for him.

4 We will have to figure out _____ or not we are lost.

5 _____ he is tall or not is not important.

6 I'm not sure _____ the air conditioner is on now.

7 _____ Annie is in her room is not sure.

8 _____ the traffic light is green or red is very important.

9 They are debating _____ to study or play.

10 We couldn't decide _____ we should meet at my house or his.

figure out ~을 생각해내다   **the air conditioner is on** 냉방중   **traffic light** 교통 신호등   **debate** 토론하다

F 기초 TEST

정답 및 해설 **p.4**

---

whether와 if 중에서 알맞은 것을 골라 써 넣어 보자. (두 개 가능)

1 Dad didn't know   *whether*   or not mom got a perm.

아빠는 엄마가 파마를 했는지 안했는지 몰랐다.

2 I asked him _____ the train would be delayed or not.

나는 그에게 기차가 연착할지 아닐지 물어보았다.

3 She is considering _____ to keep working.

그녀는 일을 계속해야 할지말지 숙고하고 있다.

4 I can't tell _____ or not it will rain tomorrow.

나는 내일 비가 올지 안 올지 말할 수 없다.

5 She asked the teacher _____ the answer was correct or not.

그녀는 선생님께 그 답이 맞는지 아닌지 여쭤 보았다.

6 _____ to hire Jack is a great difficulty for my boss.

Jack을 고용할지 아닐지는 나의 상사에게 큰 어려움이다.

7 I don't know _____ to live here.

나는 여기 살아야 할지 아닌지 모르겠다.

8 He is curious _____ or not his son is happy at school.

그는 그의 아들이 학교에서 즐거운지 아닌지 알고 싶다.

9 Jim has to choose _____ he should buy a basketball.

Jim은 농구공을 사야할지 말아야 할지 선택해야만 한다.

10 My parents don't remember _____ they met Joe, my friend.

나의 부모님은 나의 친구Joe를 만났는지 아닌지를 기억하지 못하신다.

---

get a perm 파마를 하다   delay 미루다, 연기하다   correct 옳은   curious 궁금한, 호기심이 많은

우리말 뜻과 같도록 주어진 단어를 나열해 보자.

1 *Whether(or not) he is honest or not* is very important.
(he, whether, honest, is, or not)
그가 정직한지 아닌지는 매우 중요하다.

2 I don't know   .
(she, Tom's auntie, whether, is)
나는 그녀가 Tom의 이모인지 아닌지 모르겠다.

3   is not certain.
(Susan, a dog, likes, whether)
Susan이 개를 좋아하는지 아닌지는 확실하지 않다.

4 Jane didn't decide   .
(if, the backpack, would buy, she)
Jane은 그 배낭을 살지 말지를 결정하지 못했다.

5 Dad asked me   .
(I, if, homework, finished)
아빠는 내가 숙제를 끝마쳤는지 아닌지를 나에게 물어보았다.

6   is my concern.
(Paul, whether, me, will call, or not)
Paul이 나에게 전화할지 아닐지가 나의 관심거리이다.

7 My worry is   .
(the gas, if, turned off, my younger sister, or not)
나의 걱정은 여동생이 가스 불을 껐는지 아닌지이다.

8   doesn't matter.
(poor, is, or not, whether, he)
그가 가난한지 아닌지는 문제가 되지 않는다.

---

backpack 배낭   concern 관심거리, 관심사   worry 걱정   matter 중요하다, 문제되다

주어진 단어를 사용하여, 우리말과 같도록 문장을 완성해 보자.

1   *Whether(or not) Tom wears a suit (or not)*   to dinner is not certain. (suit)

Tom이 저녁식사에 정장을 입는지 아닌지는 확실하지 않다.

2   I can't tell   . (hungry)

나는 그 개가 배고픈지 아닌지 말할 수 없다 (알 수 없다).

3   is his problem. (mail)

그 우편물이 배달될지 아닐지가 그의 문제이다.

4   She is not sure   . (present)

그녀는 네가 그녀의 선물을 좋아하는지 아닌지 확신하지 못하고 있다.

5   is not my concern. (text)

나의 친구가 나에게 문자를 했는지 아닌지는 나의 관심이 아니다.

6   She asked me   . (fine)

그녀는 뉴욕의 날씨가 좋은지 아닌지를 나에게 물어보았다.

7   Dad is always worried about   . (sick)

아빠는 할아버지가 아픈지 아닌지에 대해서 항상 걱정하신다.

8   is up to the chief. (end)

그들이 그 회의를 끝낼지 아닐지는 장(우두머리)에게 달려 있다.

9   Please ask   . (ready)

저녁이 준비되었는지 물어봐 주세요.

10   I had to decide   . (go)

나는 그 파티에 가야 할지 결정해야만 했다.

---

mail 우편물   **deliver** 배달하다   **weather** 날씨   **N.Y.** 뉴욕   **be up to** ~에게 달려있다

동격을 나타내는 명사절

> ⬢ the 추상명사 + that이 이끄는 명사절 : ~라는 ....

ex. **The fact** <u>**that he is rich**</u> is well known. 그가 부자라는 사실은 잘 알려져 있다.
    └── = ──┘

ex. I heard <u>**the news**</u> <u>**that she passed the exam**</u>. 나는 그녀가 시험에 합격했다는 소식을 들었다.
       └── = ──┘

- 동격에 사용되는 추상명사

  fact 사실, **news** 소식, **idea** 생각, **hope** 희망, **report** 보고 ....

  주의! 동격으로 사용된 명사절은 that을 생략하지 않는다.
        ex. The fact that he is rich is well known.
        ~~The fact   he is rich is well known.~~

동격을 나타내는 명사와 명사절을 ○표 하고 우리말로 바꿔 보자.

1 ⟨The dream⟩⟨that she sees her son again⟩ may come true.

→ 　그녀가 그녀의 아들을 다시 만난다는 그 꿈은　 이루어질지도 모른다.

2 I heard the news that he won a gold medal.

→ 나는 　　　　　　　　　　　　　　　　　　　　들었다.

3 The fact that the teacher is strict is not known.

→ 　　　　　　　　　　　　　　　　　　　　　알려져 있지 않다.

4 All agreed with the idea that new bridge should be built over the river.

→ 모두가 　　　　　　　　　　　　　　　　　　에 동의 했다.

5 The report that we were at war in the west sea was sent to the general.

→ 　　　　　　　　　　　　　　　　　　　　가 장군에게 보내졌다.

주어진 말이 들어갈 자리를 ✓표 해 보자.

1 Nobody knows ✓that he stole the jewel. (the fact)

아무도 그가 보석을 훔쳤다는 사실을 모른다.

2 All of us have that we will be reunified in the near future. (the hope)

우리 모두는 가까운 미래에 통일될 것이라는 희망을 가지고 있다.

3 Everybody were surprised at that the building was destroyed by air-crash. (the news)

모든 사람이 그 빌딩이 비행기 충돌에 의해 파괴되었다는 소식에 놀랐다.

4 The official announced that the accident was the driver's fault. (the report)

공무원은 그 사고가 운전자의 과실이었다는 보고서를 발표했다.

5 That he should make an electric car came to his mind. (the idea)

그는 전기차를 만들겠다는 생각이 그의 마음에 떠올랐다.

---

be at war 교전중인　　**reunify** 통일하다　　**official** 공무원　　**jewel** 보석　　**announce** 발표하다

driver's fault 운전자 과실　　**come to one's mind** (생각이) ~의 머리(마음)에 떠오르다　　**electric** 전기의

UNIT 3

의문사가 이끄는 명사절

1 역할

⬢ 우리말로는 '누가 / 언제 / 어디에서 / 무엇을 / 어떻게 / 왜 ~할지'의 뜻을 가지며 문장 내에서 주어, 목적어, 보어 역할을 한다.

〈주어〉 *ex.* **Where he lives** is not sure. 그가 어디 사는지는 확실하지 않다.
　　　　　　　주어

〈목적어〉 *ex.* He doesn't know **when she will come**. 그는 그녀가 언제 올지를 모르고 있다.
　　　　　　　　　　　　　　　목적어

〈보어〉 *ex.* Her worry is **how she should live**. 그녀의 걱정은 그녀가 어떻게 살아야 하는지 이다.
　　　　　　　　　　　　보어

2 어순

⬢ '의문사(구) + 주어 + 동사'이다.

ex. I don't know **why** **she** **is** angry. 나는 그녀가 왜 화가 나있는지 모르겠다.
　　　　　　　의문사　주어　동사

ex. I don't know **how old** **she** **is**. 나는 그녀가 몇 살인지 모르겠다.
　　　　　　　　의문사구　　주어 동사

단, 의문사가 명사절의 주어로 사용되었을 때는 '의문사 + 동사'의 어순을 갖는다.

ex. I don't know **who broke** the window. 나는 누가 그 창문을 깨뜨렸는지 모르겠다.
　　　　　　　의문사 + 동사

3 가주어 it

⬢ 의문사로 시작되는 명사절은 가주어 it으로 바꾸어 쓸 수 있다.

ex. **Who he is** isn't known. 그가 누구인지는 알려져 있지 않다.
= **It** isn't known **who he is** .
　가주어　　　　　　　진주어

A 기초 TEST

다음에서 명사절을 찾아 ○표 하고 우리말로 써 보자. 또, 문장에서의 쓰임을 (   ) 안에서 골라 보자.

1 He asked his son (what he wanted to be).   (주어, 목적어, 보어)

그는 그의 아들에게 _그가 무엇이 되기를 원하는지_ 물었다.

2 She wonders why he is here.   (주어, 목적어, 보어)

그녀는 _____ 궁금해 한다.

3 What he is making is not sure.   (주어, 목적어, 보어)

_____ 확실하지 않다.

4 His question is how old this cathedral is.   (주어, 목적어, 보어)

그의 질문은 _____ 이다.

5 I don't remember where I lost my umbrella.   (주어, 목적어, 보어)

나는 _____ 기억이 나지 않는다.

다음 두 문장을 한 문장으로 바꿔 보자.

1 I don't know. + How much does it cost?

I don't know _how much it costs_ .

2 She may know. + Where is Tom playing now?

She may know _____ .

3 I am wondering. + What is he working for?

I am wondering _____ .

4 Jenny can't remember. + When did the carnival begin?

Jenny can't remember _____ .

5 Please tell me. + How did you get it?

Please tell me _____ .

cathedral 성당   carnival 카니발

주어진 문장을 같은 뜻이 되도록 만들어 보자.

1 Who broke the vase is not sure.

= *It is not sure who broke the vase.* .

2 It isn't known how deep the cave is.

= .

3 It is doubtful where he comes from.

= .

4 When I take this medicine is very important.

= .

5 It is clear what she will ask for me at Christmas.

= .

우리말에 알맞은 말을 만들어 보자.

1 그녀가 왜 시카고로 이사했는지는 불분명하다.

= It isn't clear *why she moved to Chicago* .

2 나의 아들이 무엇을 원하는지 확실하다.

= It is sure .

3 네가 어떻게 그것을 만들었는지 미스터리이다.

= It is mysterious .

4 그의 회사가 얼마나 멀리 있는지는 상관없다.

= It doesn't matter .

doubtful 의심스러운   **Chicago** 시카고   **mysterious** 기이한, 이해하기 힘든   **company** 회사

명사절에 ○표 하고 주어진 단어를 우리말에 알맞게 배열해 보자.

1 Do you know _what Susan likes_ ?
(Susan, what, likes)
너는 (Susan이 무엇을 좋아하는지) 알고 있니?

2 I wonder _____ .
(how, well, skates, Nancy)
나는 Nancy가 얼마나 스케이트를 잘 타는지 궁금하다.

3 Do you know _____ ?
(David, Africa, when, left for)
너는 David가 언제 아프리카로 떠났는지 알고 있니?

4 She doesn't remember _____ .
(made of, the cake, what, was)
그녀는 그 케이크가 무엇으로 만들어 졌는지 기억하지 못한다.

5 _____ is not important.
(is, planning, what, Bill)
Bill이 무엇을 계획하고 있는지는 중요치 않다.

6 He wonders _____ today.
(how many people, the meeting, will, attend)
그는 오늘 얼마나 많은 사람이 그 모임에 참석할지 궁금하다.

7 She doesn't know _____ .
(when, end, will, this movie)
그녀는 이 영화가 언제 끝날지 모른다.

8 They wonder _____ on the ground.
(drawing, is, what, Sam)
그들은 Sam이 땅위에 무엇을 그리고 있는지 궁금해 한다.

Africa 아프리카   **ground** 땅

명사절에 ○표 하고 주어진 단어를 이용하여 우리말에 알맞게 써 보자.

1 I can't remember *where I put my ring* . (put)

나는 내가 나의 반지를 어디에 두었는지 기억할 수 없다.

2 Did you ask him   ? (make)

너는 그에게 그가 어떻게 파스타를 만들었는지 물었니?

3 Ann didn't know   . (laugh at)

Ann은 그가 왜 그녀를 보고 웃는지를 몰랐다.   laugh at: ~에 웃다

4 It is not sure   . (begin)

그 회의가 언제 시작할지는 확실하지 않다.

5 He forgot   . (say)

그는 그의 아내가 무엇이라고 말했는지 잊었다.

6 We want to know   . (be)

우리는 준결승전이 어땠는지 알기를 원한다.

7 The question is   . (start)

의문은 그 지진이 어디서 시작되었는지이다.

8 We all wonder   . (be)

우리 모두는 회장이 누구인지 궁금하다.

9 I know   . (love)

나는 나의 부모님이 나를 얼마나 많이 사랑하시는지 안다.   how much 얼마나 많이

10 Nobody knows   . (build)

아무도 그 우주선이 어떻게 만들어졌는지 모른다.

---

pasta 파스타   semifinal 준결승   earthquake 지진   chairman 회장   spaceship 우주선

01 다음을 우리말에 맞게 할 때 빈칸에 알맞은 말은?

> 그가 올지 안 올지 궁금하다.
> I wonder _____ he will come.

① what
② as
③ and
④ if
⑤ that

02 빈칸에 공통으로 알맞은 말을 고르시오.

> • _____ she is still alive is not certain.
> • I am not sure _____ he can arrive there in time.

① whether
② if
③ what
④ where
⑤ when

alive 살아있는

03 다음 중 밑줄친 곳을 바르게 고쳐 보시오.

> Nobody knows if or not he is honest.

→ _____

04 두 문장을 하나의 문장으로 만들 때 옳은 것은?

> I don't know.
> Where did he live?

① I don't know where did he live.
② I don't know where he lives.
③ I don't know where he lived.
④ Where I don't know he live.
⑤ Where I don't know he lived.

05 다음을 가주어 it을 사용하여 바꾸어 쓰시오.

> What he wants to say is not certain.
> → _____
> _____

06 다음 밑줄 친 곳에 들어갈 적당한 말을 고르시오.

> Tom : Do you know _____ she will go there?
> Billy : Maybe tomorrow.

① what
② where
③ when
④ how
⑤ who

07 빈칸에 들어갈 가장 알맞은 것을 고르시오.

> I don't know _____ it is right or not.

① where
② what
③ that
④ whether
⑤ which

right 옳은

08 다음 문장들 중 바르지 <u>않은</u> 것을 고르시오.

① Whether Jane will go there is not certain.
② If Tom is diligent is not known.
③ I don't know if Jimmy can play soccer.
④ The problem is whether the baby will cry or not.
⑤ I am wondering whether Jenny is at home or not.

09 우리말을 영문으로 바르게 바꾼 것을 고르시오.

> 너는 누가 그녀에게 그 책을 줬는지 알고 있니?

① Who do you know gave the book her?
② Who do you know gave her the book?
③ Do you know who gave her the book?
④ Who do you know did she give the book?
⑤ Who do you know give her the book?

10 빈칸에 들어갈 알맞은 말을 고르시오.

> I don't know whether it will rain _____ not.

① and
② but
③ or
④ as
⑤ to

11 다음 밑줄친 부분중 어법에 맞지 <u>않는</u> 것을 고르시오.

> I ① <u>called</u> Jenny 1 hour ② <u>ago</u>.
> She ③ <u>didn't</u> answer my phone.
> Maybe she is very busy ④ <u>now</u>.
> I don't know when she ⑤ <u>finishes</u>
> her work.

12 어법상 옳은 문장을 고르시오.

① Do you know what does she make?
② Do you know what she makes?
③ What do you know she makes?
④ What do you know she does make?
⑤ What do you know she make?

13 두 문장을 바르게 연결하여 한 문장으로 바꿔 보시오.

> Did you forget?
> Where did you park your car?

→ _____

_____ ?

14 주어진 문장을 우리말로 바꿔 보시오.

> He was shocked at the news
> that his dad passed away.

→ 그는 _____
충격을 받았다.

passed away 돌아가시다

15 다음 문장에서 올바르지 <u>않은</u> 것을 고르시오.

① I wonder if my son is playing the
piano now.
② I wonder whether my son is playing
the piano now.
③ Whether my son is playing the
piano now is not sure.
④ If my son is playing the piano now
is not sure.
⑤ My question is whether my son is
playing the piano now.

16 다음 ( ) 안의 단어를 우리말에 맞게 배열하시오.

> Did you ask me _____
> _____ ?
> (this bridge, was, how, old)
> 너는 나에게 이 다리가 얼마나 오래 되었냐고 물었니?

[17–18] 다음 대화를 읽고 물음에 답하시오.

> *Josh* : How do you like my house?
> *Luke* : Very nice! ⓐ <u>Do you know? Who is the boy?</u>
> *Josh* : He is my little brother.
> *Luke* : I see. Your mom doesn't care ⓑ <u>whether or not</u> he plays all day?
> *Josh* : She only lets him play for an hour. Then he has to do his homework.

little brother 남동생   care 관심을 갖다

17 밑줄 친 ⓐ를 하나의 문장으로 만들어 보시오.

→ _____ .

18 밑줄 친 ⓑ와 바꿔 쓸 수 있는 말을 고르시오.

① what
② if
③ that
④ how
⑤ when

[19–20] 다음 대화를 읽고 물음에 답하시오.

> *A* : My best friend ① <u>moved</u> to N.Y. last month.
> *B* : ⓐ <u>Do you know? How long will he live there?</u>
> *A* : I don't know ② <u>if</u> he ③ <u>will come</u> back to Korea.
> I'll be glad ④ <u>if</u> I ⑤ <u>will see</u> him again.

19 ①~⑤ 번 중 어법에 맞지 <u>않는</u> 것을 골라 바르게 고치시오.

_____ → _____

20 밑줄 친 ⓐ를 하나의 문장으로 만들어 보시오.

→ _____
_____

정답 및 해설 p.7

01 다음 중 어색한 문장을 고르시오.

① I wonder whether the story is true.
② I wonder if the story is true.
③ I am not sure if he will come.
④ She will be happy if he will come.
⑤ She wonders whether he will come.

02 다음 중 빈칸에 if가 들어가지 않는 문장을 고르시오.

① ___ he is honest or not isn't sure.
② I don't know ___ he is still in school.
③ ___ she doesn't arrive on time, he will get angry.
④ I want to know ___ she is married.
⑤ We are not sure ___ John is a doctor or not.

03 다음 중 맞는 표현에 O표하시오.

I am not sure (whether / if) or not he told a lie to me.
나는 그가 나에게 거짓말을 했는지 안 했는지 확신할 수 없다.

04 다음 문장의 빈칸에 whether와 if 둘 다 사용할 수 있는 것을 고르시오.

① _____ she was a singer doesn't matter.
② _____ he knows it or not is important.
③ I don't know _____ or not it is mine.
④ I can't decide _____ to leave or stay.
⑤ I don't know _____ it will help or not.

05 다음 ( )안의 단어를 우리말에 맞게 배열하시오.

I don't know _____
_____ . (she, if, me, or not, likes)
나는 그녀가 나를 좋아하는지 아닌지 모르겠다.

06 다음 문장에서 틀린 부분(한 단어)을 찾아 바르게 고치시오.

If she will do it or not is up to you.
그녀가 그것을 할지 안할지는 너에게 달려있다.

_____ → _____

07 다음 빈칸에 공통으로 들어갈 말을 고르시오.

> · We should decide_____ to leave or stay.
> · I don't know _____ or not he is a teacher.

① where
② when
③ whether
④ if
⑤ how

[08–09] 다음 우리말에 맞게 빈칸에 들어갈 올바른 말을 고르시오.

08

> The _____ that she is talkative is well known.
> 그녀가 수다스럽다는 사실은 잘 알려져 있다.

① idea
② fact
③ report
④ hope
⑤ news

talkative 수다스러운

09

> I heard the _____ that Yuna Kim won the gold medal.
> 우리는 김연아가 금메달을 땄다는 소식을 들었다.

① idea
② fact
③ report
④ hope
⑤ news

[10–11] 다음 ( )안의 단어를 우리말에 맞게 배열하시오.

10 빈칸에 들어갈 알맞은 말을 고르시오.

> _____ is not known.
> (he, where, from, is)
> 그가 어디 출신인지는 알려져 있지 않다.

11 빈칸에 들어갈 알맞은 말을 고르시오.

> She wonders _____ .
> (he, old, is, how)
> 그녀는 그가 몇 살이지 궁금해 한다.

12 다음 중 없어야 할 단어를 고르시오.

> ① Who ② you ③ broke the vase
> ④ is ⑤ not sure.
> 누가 그 꽃병을 깨뜨렸는지 확실하지 않다.

13 다음 두 문장의 뜻이 같도록 가주어 it을 사용하여 빈칸을 채워보시오.

> Who he is is not clear.
> = _____ is not clear _____ he is.

[14–15] 다음 대화를 읽고 물음에 답하시오.

> *Dan* : Will your friend, Blair come to
>   the party?
> *Serena* : I am not sure ⓐ_____ she will
>   come or not. I hope she will
>   come.
> *Dan* : ⓑ If she will not come, will you
>   be very disappointed? (만일 그녀가
>   오지 않는다면, 너는 아주 실망하겠지?)
> *Serena* : Yes.

14 ⓐ에 들어갈 알맞은 접속사를 쓰시오.

> ⓐ : _____

15 어법에 맞게 ⓑ의 밑줄 친 부분을 바르게 고쳐보시오.

> ⓑ If she will not come
> → If she _____

16 다음 문장을 올바르게 영작한 것을 고르시오.

> The report that Korean soccer
> team won against Brazil surprised
> people.

① 사람들은 한국 축구팀이 브라질을 이겼다고 보고했다.
② 한국 축구팀이 브라질을 이겼다고 보고되었다.
③ 한국 축구팀이 브라질을 이겼다는 놀라운 보고가 있었다.
④ 한국 축구팀이 브라질을 이겼다는 보고가 잘못된
   것으로 알려졌다.
⑤ 한국 축구팀이 브라질을 이겼다는 보고가 사람들을
   놀라게 했다.

17 다음 괄호 안의 단어를 우리말에 맞게 배열하시오.

> It is not polite to ask people
> (are, or not, if, married, they)
> 사람들에게 그들이 결혼했는지 안 했는지를 묻는 것은
> 예의바르지 않다.

→ It is not polite to ask people _____
_____ .

18 두 문장을 하나의 문장으로 만들 때 옳은 것은?

> The police don't know.
> What did the thief steal?

① The police don't know what did the thief steal.

② The police don't know what the thief stole.

③ The police don't know what stole the thief.

④ The thief doesn't know what the police stole.

⑤ The thief doesn't know what stole the police.

19 다음 빈칸에 공통으로 들어갈 말을 고르시오.

> · ____ he doesn't come, I will be sad.
> · We don't know yet ____ he will come to the party or not.

① whether

② if

③ that

④ how

⑤ when

20 다음 밑줄 친 부분 중 생략 가능한 것을 고르시오.

① I understand <u>why</u> she is angry.

② <u>How</u> he got there is still a mystery.

③ Do you know <u>where</u> she is from.

④ I don't know <u>whether</u> it will snow or not.

⑤ I think <u>that</u> she is very talented.

Chapter 3

부사절 및 접속부사

부사절이란?

문장 안에서 부사 역할을 하는 절을 말하며 접속사 when, after, before 등이 절을 이끈다.

◆ 시간을 나타내는 접속사

ⓐ when : ～할 때

ex. **When** he was young, he was a teacher.

그가 젊었을 때, 그는 선생님이었다.

ⓑ after : ～한 후에

ex. **After** she graduated from college, she got a job.

그녀는 대학을 졸업한 후에, 일자리를 구했다.

ⓒ before : ～하기 전에

ex. **Before** you eat dinner, you should wash your hands.

너는 저녁 먹기 전에, 손을 씻어야만 한다.

ⓓ while : ～하는 동안

ex. **While** mom cleans the house, I do the dishes.

엄마가 집을 청소하는 동안, 나는 설거지를 한다.

ⓔ until / till : ～할 때 까지

ex. You can't drive a car **until** you become 20 years old.

너는 20살이 될 때까지 너는 운전을 할 수 없다.

ⓕ since : ～이래로 / ～부터

ex. I have lived here **since** I was born. 나는 태어난 이래로 여기서 살아 왔다.

주의!

• 시간을 나타내는 부사절 (since 제외)은 뜻이 미래를 나타낼지라도 미래 시제 대신 현재시제를 쓴다.

ex. **When** Anna comes home, I will go shopping with her.

Anna가 집에 올 때, 나는 그녀와 함께 쇼핑하러 갈 것이다.

• since가 이끄는 시간을 나타내는 부사절은, 대개 부사절은 과거, 주절은 현재완료를 쓴다.

ex. Jack has worked for the bank **since** he moved to Seoul.

Jack은 서울로 이사 온 이후로 그 은행에서 근무해왔다

🔷 이유를 나타내는 접속사

ⓐ because : ～때문에

ex. **Because I had a headache, I went to the drug store.**

나는 두통이 있었기 때문에, 약국으로 갔다.

ⓑ as : ～이므로 / ～해서

ex. **As Tom is too fat, he can't pass the door.**

Tom은 너무 뚱뚱해서 그 문을 통과할 수 없다.

🔷 결과를 나타내는 접속사

ⓐ so : 그래서, 그 결과

ex. **Jack caught a cold, so he went to see a doctor.**

Jack은 감기에 걸렸다 그래서 그는 의사를 보러 갔다

🔷 조건을 나타내는 접속사

ⓐ if : (만일) ～이라면 / ～한다면

ex. **If you work hard, you will succeed.**

(만일) 네가 열심히 일한다면, 너는 성공할 것이다.

조건을 나타내는 부사절도 문맥상 미래를 나타낼지라도 미래시제대신 현재시제를 쓴다.

ex. **If it is hot tomorrow, I'll go to the beach.**

(만일) 내일 덥다면, 나는 해변으로 갈 것이다.

ⓑ unless : (만일) ～하지 않으면, ～하지 않는 한

ex. **Unless you hurry, you will be late.**

(만일) 서두르지 않는다면, 너는 늦을 것이다.

*unless는 '만일 ～하지 않으면'의 자체 부정의 뜻을 가지고 있으므로 부정문에 사용하지 않는다.

🔷 양보를 나타내는 접속사

ⓐ though : (비록) ～이지만 / 일지라도

ex. **Though Mr. Bush is old, he enjoys drinking coffee.**

(비록) Mr. Bush는 나이가 많으시지만, 커피 마시기를 즐기신다.

UNIT 1

시간을 나타내는 부사절, 이유 / 결과를 나타내는 부사절, 조건 / 양보를 나타내는 부사절

1 시간을 나타내는 접속사

as soon as~ (=on~ing) : ~하자마자

부사절과 주절의 주어가 같을 때, 'On ~ing'로 바꾸어 쓸 수 있다.

ex. **As soon as** he saw me, he ran away. 그는 나를 보자마자, (그는) 도망갔다.
= **On seeing** me, he ran away.

every time~ (=each time~) : ~할 때 마다

ex. **Every time** he needs help, he calls me. 그는 도움이 필요할 때마다 나에게 전화한다.
= **Each time** he needs help, he calls me.

2 이유/결과를 나타내는 접속사

because~ (=since, as~) : ~때문에, ~이므로

ex. **Because** he is honest, we like him. 그가 정직하기 때문에, 우리는 그를 좋아한다.
= **Since** he is honest, we like him.
= **As** he is honest, we like him.

...., so~ : ...., 그래서~

ex. He is honest, **so** we like him. 그는 정직하다. 그래서 우리는 그를 좋아한다.
Because, Since, As, for와 바꾸어 쓸 수 있다.

ex. He is honest, **so** we like him.
= **Because** he is honest, we like him.

◆ ....,(comma) for ~ : ....,왜냐하면 ~이기 때문에

'(comma) for ~'는 because, since, as와 유사한 뜻의 접속사로서, 문장의 뒤에 온다.

ex. **Because** he is honest, we like him. 그가 정직하기 때문에, 우리는 그를 좋아한다.

= We like him, **because** he is honest.   우리는 그를 좋아한다. 왜냐하면 그가 정직하기 때문이다.

= We like him, **for** he is honest.

Tip! 대부분의 부사절은 주절과 위치를 바꾸어 쓸 수 있다.

3 조건 / 양보를 나타내는 접속사

▶조건을 나타내는 접속사

◆ If ~not ~ (=Unless ~) : (만일) ~하지 않으면

'If ~ not~'의 문장은 'Unless ~'로 바꾸어 쓸 수 있다.

ex. **If** you don't study harder, you'll fail in the test.

= **Unless** you study harder, you'll fail in the test.

(만일) 네가 더 열심히 공부하지 않는다면. 너는 시험에 떨어질 거야.

▶양보를 나타내는 접속사

◆ though (=although, =even though, =even if) : (비록) ~이지만/(비록) ~일지라도

ex. **Though** Mr. Bush is old, he enjoys drinking coffee.

(비록) Mr. Bush는 나이가 많으시지만, 커피 마시기를 즐기신다.

though는 although, even though, even if로 바꿔 쓸 수 있다.

ex. **Though** Yuna is a gold medalist, she practices everyday.

= **Although** Yuna is a gold medalist, she practices everyday.

= **Even though** Yuna is a gold medalist, she practices everyday.

= **Even if** Yuna is a gold medalist, she practices everyday.

(비록) 연아는 금메달리스트일지라도, 그녀는 매일 연습한다.

A 기초 TEST

다음 밑줄 친 부분을 우리말로 바꾸어 써 보자.

1 As soon as she came home, she drank a cup of water.

그녀는 집에 오자마자 , 그녀는 물 한잔을 마셨다.

2 Every time I call him. he doesn't answer the phone.

, 그는 전화를 받지를 않는다.

3 He got a bad cold, so he didn't go to work.

그는 심한 감기에 걸렸다, .

4 I sat on the bench, for I walked too much.

나는 벤치에 앉았다, .

5 Though they are not rich, they are happy.

, 그들은 행복하다.

6 If it doesn't rain, we will go fishing.

, 우리는 낚시하러 갈 것이다.

7 Because Jane wanted to wear the shirt, mom bought it.

, 엄마는 그것을 샀다.

8 As soon as Bill finished homework, he started to play PC games.

, 그는 PC 게임을 하기 시작했다.

9 Though she is young, she is not shy.

, 그녀는 수줍어하지 않는다.

10 Every time Sam tells a lie, he blinks his eyes.

, 그는 눈을 깜빡거린다.

---

go to work 일하러 가다   shy 수줍어 하는   blink 깜빡거리다

B 기초 TEST

주어진 접속사의 뜻과 같은 의미로 쓰이는 접속사(또는 부사구)를 보기에서 골라 써 넣어 보자. (중복사용 가능)

| 보기 |

- A. .... 그래서 ~
- B. 만일 ~ 하지 않으면
- C. ~할 때마다
- D. 비록 ~일지라도
- E. ~ 하자 마자
- F. (왜냐하면) ~때문에, 이므로

a.	although	b.	since
c.	even if	d.	....., for ~
e.	as	f.	on~ing
g.	unless	h.	even though
i.	....., so ~	j.	each time

1 as soon as   *E* — *f*

2 every time   ___ — ___

3 because   ___ — ___ / ___ / ___

4 so   ___

5 if ~not   ___ — ___

6 though   ___ — ___ / ___ / ___

A 기본 TEST

다음 빈칸에 들어갈 수 있는 접속사를 보기에서 골라 모두 써 보자.

| 보기 |

as soon as   every time   because
so   for   if   though

1 Jimmy felt boring, _so_ he tried calling Bob.

2 A_____ she heard the story, she burst into laughter.

3 She has few friends in Korea, _f_____ she lived in Paris till last month.

4 B_____ it is cloudy now, you don't need to wear the sunglasses.

5 I_____ you don't avoid eating fast food, you may get fatter.

6 E_____ Jane needs pocket money, she asks dad for help.

7 A_____ it started raining, Linda opened the umbrella.

8 T_____ Korea is small, it is an advanced country in many ways.

9 You made a mistake, _s_____ the situation got worse.

10 B_____ Ann was ill, she missed her mom.

---

burst 터트리다   laughter 웃음   pocket money 용돈   be proud of ~을 자랑스러워하다
advanced country 선진국   in many ways 여러 가지 면에서   avoid 피하다, 그만두다   situation 상황
get worse 더 나빠지다   miss 그리워하다

우리말에 알맞은 접속사(또는 부사구)를 써 넣어 보자.

| 보기 |
| on arriving   each time   as   even though |
| although   even if   so   since   unless |

1 My mom was angry at me, *as* I fought my brother.

2 U the meeting is canceled, I can't go home early.

3 Bill is successful in his business, s he has creative thinking.

4 O in Paris, she called her auntie.

5 Tom liked his school, s he did well at school.

6 A Mrs. Brown is busy, she keeps her promise.

7 U he trusts Jane, he won't deposit his bankbook with her.

8 E I asked her some questions, she answered kindly.

9 E I didn't want to see him, I often faced him on my way home.

10 There was no answer, s Jimmy hung up the phone.

cancel 취소하다   creative 창의적인   keep a promise 약속을 지키다   trust 믿다, 신뢰하다
deposit 맡기다   bankbook 통장   face 마주치다   on my way home 내가 집에 가는 길에
hang(hung-hung) up (전화를) 끊다

주어진 문장을 같은 의미의 문장으로 바꿔 써 보자.

1 Because he is smart, he can solve the riddle.

= He can solve the riddle, *for* he is smart.

= _____ he is smart, he can solve the riddle.

= _____ he is smart, he can solve the riddle.

= He is smart, _____ he can solve the riddle.

2 If you don't mind, I will stay here.

= _____ you mind, I will stay here.

3 Everytime I listen to his song, I feel sad.

= _____ I listen to his song, I feel sad.

4 They are very different, so they can't understand each other.

= _____ they are very different, they can't understand each other.

= _____ they are very different, they can't understand each other.

= They can't understand each other, _____ they are very different.

= _____ they are very different, they can't understand each other.

5 Though it is not important, I tried to do it.

= _____ it is not important, I tried to do it.

= _____ it is not important, I tried to do it.

= _____ it is not important, I tried to do it.

6 Unless you hurry up, there will be no tickets for the game.

= _____ you don't hurry up, there will be no tickets for the game.

riddle 수수께끼   solve 풀다

D 기본 TEST

정답 및 해설 **p.8**

주어진 문장을 같은 의미의 문장으로 바꿔 써 보자.

1 If you are not patient, you will not succeed.

= *Unless you are patient* , you will not succeed.

2 Each time I looked at him, he was napping.

= _____ , he was napping.

3 Unless you eat breakfast, you may lose your health.

= _____ , you may lose your health.

4 Since the child was too short, he didn't ride a bike.

= The child was too short, _____ .

= The child didn't ride a bike, _____ .

= _____ , he didn't ride the bike.

= _____ , he didn't ride the bike.

5 Even though he doesn't watch TV, he knows all of the TV drama.

= _____ , he knows all of the TV drama.

= _____ , he knows all of the TV drama.

= _____ , he knows all of the TV drama.

be patient 인내심을 갖다   **nap** 졸다   **support** 지지하다

Chapter 3 63

UNIT 2

여러 가지 뜻으로 쓰이는 접속사 as와 since, while, if

1 as

 ~이므로 : = because, since

> *ex.* **As** he was young, he couldn't understand it.
> 그는 어렸으므로, 그는 그것을 이해 할 수 없었다.
> = **Because** he was young, he couldn't understand it.

 ~하는 동안에 : = while

> *ex.* **As** mom cooked dinner, I did my homework.
> = **while** mom cooked dinner, I did my homework.
> 엄마가 저녁식사를 만드시는 동안, 나는 숙제를 했다.

 ~하면서 : = while

> *ex.* She sings **as** she goes on a walk.
> 그녀는 산책하면서 노래를 부른다.
> = She sings **while** she goes on a walk.

2 since

 ~부터

> *ex.* I have known her since she was a child. 그녀가 아이였을 때부터 나는 그녀를 알고 있다.
> 현재완료   과거
>
> 주절은 현재완료, since 로 시작하는 부사절은 과거를 사용하는 것이 보통이다.

● ~이므로 : = as, because

> *ex.* **Since** he was old, he could understand it.
> 그는 나이가 들었으므로, 그는 그것을 이해할 수 있었다.
>
> = **As** he was old, he could understand it.
> = **Because** he was old, he could understand it.

3 while

● ~하는 동안에 : = as

> *ex.* **While** you were out, she came here. 네가 밖에 있는 동안에, 그녀가 왔다.
> = **As** you were out, she came here.

● ~하면서 : = as

> *ex.* She sings **as** she goes on a walk. 그녀는 산책하면서 노래를 부른다.
> = She sings **while** she goes on a walk.

4 If

● 만일 ~라면 (부사절)

> *ex.* If she comes to the party, everybody will be happy.
> (만일) 그녀가 파티에 온다면, 모두 기쁠 것이다.

● ~인지 아닌지 (= 명사절) : = whether

> *ex.* Nobody knows **if** she will come to the party.
> = Nobody knows **whether** she will come to the party.
> 아무도 그녀가 그 파티에 올지 안 올지 모르고 있다.

A 기초 TEST

다음 접속사에 알맞은 우리말을 골라 보자.

1 As I have no money, I cannot buy the pen.
((~이므로), ~하는 동안, ~하면서)

2 As he was walking along the road, he saw his friend.
(~이므로, ~하는 동안, ~하면서)

3 I have lived in Seoul since I was 7 years old.
(~부터, ~이므로)

4 If he is confident, he will not be nervous.
(만일~라면, ~인지 아닌지)

5 It has been 7 years since I started to learn English.
(~부터, ~이므로)

6 I don't know if I can make it.
(만일~라면, ~인지 아닌지)

7 As we ate popcorn, we watched the movie.
(~이므로, ~부터, ~하면서)

8 Since it was snowing, they went out.
(~부터, ~이므로)

9 She knows if the story is true.
(만일~라면, ~인지 아닌지)

10 As mom was out, Bill cleaned up the house.
(~이므로, ~하는 동안, ~하면서)

---

confident 자신감 있는   nervous 불안해하는   popcorn 팝콘

다음 접속사에 알맞은 우리말을 골라 보자.

1 As mom drives a car, she listens to music.
(〜이므로, 〜인지 아닌지, (〜하면서))

2 Since Jane got a cold, she didn't go out.
(〜부터, 〜이므로)

3 While Tom was riding a horse, I sat on the bench.
(〜하는 동안, 〜하면서)

4 If you don't care about the dog, it will get weak.
(만일〜라면, 〜인지 아닌지)

5 As this coat is too small, I cannot wear it.
(〜이므로, 〜하는 동안, 〜하면서)

6 While we were having dinner, someone rang the doorbell.
(〜하는 동안, 〜하면서)

7 Since he lived in America, he speaks English well.
(〜부터, 〜이므로)

8 While Susan was waiting for a bus, she met her teacher.
(〜하는 동안, 〜하면서)

9 Do you know if Bill studied for the test?
(만일〜라면, 〜인지 아닌지)

10 She has worked for a bank since she graduated from high school.
(〜부터, 〜이므로)

---

care about 〜에 관심을 두다 **doorbell** 초인종 **gradute** 졸업하다 **high school** 고등학교

주어진 문장을 같은 의미의 문장으로 바꿔 보자.

1 As she felt hungry, she dropped by the snack-bar nearby.

= _Because_ she felt hungry, she dropped by the snack-bar nearby.

= _Since_ she felt hungry, she dropped by the snack-bar nearby.

2 I don't know if the weather will be fine this weekend.

= I don't know _____ the weather will be fine this weekend.

3 Since he wants me to be here, I'll not leave.

= He wants me to be here, _____ I'll not leave.

= I'll not leave, _____ he wants me to be here.

4 While Jack has meals, he says nothing.

= _____ Jack has meals, he says nothing.

5 I'm wondering if mom is upset at my grade.

= I'm wondering _____ mom is upset at my grade.

6 Because James was careless, he fell down the stairs.

= _____ James was careless, he fell down the stairs.

= _____ James was careless, he fell down the stairs.

7 While she does the dishes, she runs water.

= _____ she does the dishes, she runs water.

---

drop by ~에 들르다 **nearby** 가까이 **fall down** 떨어지다 **stairs** 계단 **careless** 부주의한 **run water** 물을 틀어놓다

다음 빈칸에 들어갈 수 있는 접속사를 보기에서 골라 써 보자. (두 개 이상 가능)

| 보기 |
as   because   while   since   if   whether

1   *As (While)*   he washes the car, he sings in a hushed voice.

그는 차를 닦으면서, 그는 낮은 목소리로 노래를 부른다.

2   you don't exercise, you will get unhealthy.

만일 네가 운동하지 않는다면, 너는 건강하지 않게 될 것이다.

3   she was sick, she went to hospital with mom.

그녀는 아팠으므로, 그녀는 엄마와 함께 병원에 갔다.

4   Jane has played the cello   she was 5.

Jane은 그녀가 5살 때부터 첼로를 연주하고 있다.

5   I skipped lunch, I'm starving.

나는 점심을 걸러서, 지금 매우 배가 고프다.

6   I am not sure   Susan will like this present for her birthday.

나는 Susan이 이 생일 선물을 좋아할지 안 좋아할지 확신이 안 선다.

7   I was sleeping, Tom texted to me four times.

내가 자고 있던 동안에, Tom이 나에게 4번 문자를 보냈다.

8   the story was so funny, all of us couldn't help laughing.

그 이야기는 너무 웃겨서, 우리 모두는 웃지 않을 수 없었다.

unhealthy 건강하지 않은   **starve** 굶주리다, 매우 배가 고프다   **text** 문자를 보내다

UNIT 3 접속부사

문장과 문장을 연결시켜주는 부사(구)를 말한다.

◈ 앞의 내용에 대한 첨가

in fact	사실	in addition	게다가
besides	게다가	moreover	게다가

ex. Bob is good at math. **Besides**, he is kind to his friends.
Bob은 수학을 잘한다. 게다가, 그는 친구들에게 친절하기 까지 하다.

◈ 앞의 내용에 대한 결과

therefore	그러므로	instead	그 대신에

ex. You are getting fat. **Therefore**, you should exercise.
너는 살이 찌고 있구나. 그러므로, 너는 운동을 해야 만 해.

ex. I missed the school bus this morning. **Instead**, I took a subway.
나는 오늘 아침 스쿨버스를 놓쳤어. 그 대신에 지하철을 탔어.

◈ 앞의 내용과 대조

however	하지만	by the way	그런데
otherwise	그렇지 않으면	nevertheless	그럼에도 불구하고

ex. He made a kite. **However**, it didn't fly well.
그는 연을 만들었어. 하지만, 그것은 잘 날지 못했어.

ex. I am hungry. **In fact**, I didn't have lunch today.
나는 배가 고프다. 사실, 나는 오늘 점심을 못 먹었어.

A 기초 TEST

다음에 해당하는 접속사를 보기에서 골라 써 보자.

| 보기 |

therefore	in addition	in fact	however
moreover	instead	otherwise	by the way
besides	nevertheless		

1 그럼에도 불구하고   *nevertheless*

2 게다가   b

3 그러므로

4 사실

5 그 대신에

6 하지만

7 그런데

8 그렇지 않으면

9 게다가   i

10 게다가   m

다음 중 알맞은 것을 골라 보자.

1 He is strong.

(By the way, In addition), he is intelligent.

2 It takes 30 minutes to the place.

(Therefore, moreover), we must start right now to get there on time.

3 I have studied English for many years.

(Instead, However), I cannot speak English well.

4 I'm kind to Henry.

(In fact, In addition), I love him.

5 He has a good daughter.

(Otherwise, Moreover), she is a great doctor.

6 You should start at once.

(In fact, Otherwise), you will be late.

7 They were hungry and thirsty.

(Besides, However) it was too cold.

8 We were out of rice this morning.

(Instead, Besides) mom cooked noodle for us.

9 We have a lot of homework to do this weekend, don't we?

(Moreover, By the way), do you know where Jack is now?

10 He works hard. (Moreover, Nevertheless) we don't need him here.

그럼에도 불구하고

---

on time 제 시간에   **noodle** 국수   **be out of** ~이 다 떨어지다

B 기본 TEST

다음 보기에서 알맞은 접속사를 골라 빈칸에 써 넣어 보자.

| 보기 |

| instead | moreover | however | therefore | besides |
| otherwise | in fact | in addition | nevertheless | by the way |

1 The movie isn't well-known. *Nevertheless* it moved me.

2 He asked her to vote for the plan. H , she voted against it.

3 Be quiet. O , you will be scolded by the teacher.

4 I am very tired today. B I have a lot of work.

5 Uncle ordered beefsteak. I , he likes beef best.

6 All the flowers are sold out. T , she closed her flower shop.

7 I am so busy that I cannot attend the meeting today.
I , my assistant will attend the meeting.

8 They are poor. I their son is sick.

9 B , who is he?

10 I'm strong. And m I'm three years older than you.

move 감동시키다   vote for ~에 찬성투표하다   vote against ~에 반대투표하다   scold 야단치다, 꾸짖다
sold out 다 팔린   assistant 조수

A 실력 TEST

다음 보기에서 알맞은 접속사를 골라 빈칸에 써 넣어 보자. (두 개 이상 가능)

| 보기 |

therefore	however	besides	nevertheless	moreover
instead	in fact	in addition	by the way	otherwise

1 Jane should help her mom do the laundry today.

Besides, Moreover, In addition , she has a lot of homework to do.

2 He proposed a marriage to her.

she refused it.

3 I could see the movie star.

, I took a picture of him.

4 She speaks like a teacher.

, she was a teacher before.

5 It was getting dark and cold.

, they needed the place to stay at night.

6 People told him not to climb up the tree.

he tried climbing it up to the top.

7 It is very hot today.

, where is the art center?

8 Do your homework before dinner.

you will go hungry.

---

do the laundry 세탁하다   **art center** 아트센터   **go hungry** 굶주리다

[01–02] 다음 밑줄 친 곳과 같은 뜻으로 알맞은 것을 고르시오.

01

> <u>As soon as she saw us</u>, she hid behind a tree.
>
> 그녀는 우리를 보자마자 나무 뒤로 숨었다.

① Seeing us
② In seeing us
③ To seeing us
④ On seeing us
⑤ For seeing us

02

> <u>Every time</u> I watch a movie, I eat popcorn.

① Each time
② From time
③ This time
④ Next time
⑤ Next time

03 다음 밑줄 친 곳과 바꾸어 쓸 수 있는 것을 모두 고르시오.

> <u>Since</u> Tom studied hard, he got a good grade.

① Because
② As
③ So
④ Before
⑤ From

04 다음을 같은 뜻으로 바꾸어 쓴 문장 중 <u>틀린</u> 문장을 고르시오.

> As it is foggy, we cannot see anything.

① Because it is foggy, we cannot see anything.
② We cannot see anything, for it is foggy.
③ So it is foggy, we cannot see anything.
④ Since it is foggy, we cannot see anything.
⑤ We cannot see anything, because it is foggy.

foggy 안개가 낀

[05–06] 다음을 같은 뜻의 문장으로 바꿀 때 빈칸에 알맞은 말을 쓰시오.

05

> If you don't walk faster, you will miss the last train.
>
> = _____ you walk faster, you will miss the last train.

06

> I don't know if he is right or wrong.
>
> = I don't know _____ he is right or wrong.

07 다음 밑줄 친 곳과 바꾸어 쓸 수 있는 것을 고르시오.

> <u>As</u> Susan listens to music, she does her homework.

① Because
② Since
③ If
④ While
⑤ Though

08 다음 밑줄 친 곳과 바꾸어 쓸 수 <u>없는</u> 것을 모두 고르시오.

> <u>Though</u> he was tired, he finished his homework.

① Although
② Even though
③ Even if
④ Even although
⑤ if though

09 문맥상 알맞은 말을 고르시오.

> Mrs. Brown is weak. _____ she does a lot of housework.

① Instead
② Moreover
③ In addition
④ Nevertheless
⑤ In fact

[10–12] 빈칸에 알맞은 접속부사(구)를 보기에서 골라 쓰시오.

| 보기 |

moreover   otherwise
by the way

10

You should study harder, _____ you will fail in the exam.

11

You look healthy. _____ , when does summer vacation start?

12

It is raining heavily here.
_____ , it is windy.

13 다음 (   ) 안의 단어를 우리말에 맞게 배열하시오.

나는 택시를 탔다, 왜냐하면 내가 너무 늦게 일어났기 때문이다.

_____

_____

(a taxi, took, I, I, too late,
got up, for)

[14–15] 다음을 (   ) 안의 말을 사용하여 바꾸어 쓰시오.

14

Because they were brave, they won the battle. (so)
= _____

15

As it was hot, we went to the beach.(for)
= _____

_____

battle 전투

16 다음을 같은 뜻으로 바꿀 때 빈칸에 알맞은 말을 쓰시오.

As soon as she arrived here, she started crying.
= On _____ here,
   she started crying.

[17–18] 다음 대화를 읽고 물음에 답하시오.

> *Tom* : Look at these prices. The teddy bear is 5 dollars.
>
> *Jane* : How much is the robot?
>
> *Tom* : It is 20 dollars. ⓐ If you don't have enough money, I'll lend you some.
>
> *Jane* : Thanks. But, ⓑ as the robot is too expensive for me, I will buy the teddy bear.

17 다음 밑줄 친 ⓐ를 같은 뜻으로 바꾸어 쓰시오.

→ Unless _____

_____

18 다음 밑줄 친 ⓑ를 같은 뜻으로 <u>틀리게</u> 바꾸어 쓴 것은?

① I will buy the teddy bear, because the robot is too expensive for me.

② the robot is too expensive for me, so I will buy the teddy bear.

③ the robot is too expensive for me, for I will buy the teddy bear.

④ because the robot is too expensive for me, I will buy the teddy bear.

⑤ since the robot is too expensive for me, I will buy the teddy bear.

[19–20] 다음 대화를 읽고 물음에 답하시오.

> *Grandma* : Tom, It's time for lunch. Come inside.
>
> *Tom* : I like to have some meat, ___ⓐ___ I'll order bacon and ham.
>
> *Grandma* : They are not good for health. ___ⓑ___ we will have tuna sandwich with sprouts. And you can have pretzels after meal.
>
> *Tom* : Thanks, grandma.

19 다음 밑줄 친 ⓐ에 알맞은 것을 고르시오.

① in fact

② by the way

③ for a long time

④ therefore

⑤ otherwise

20 다음 ⓑ에 들어갈 말로 알맞은 접속부사를 고르시오.

> ___ⓑ___ we will have tuna sandwich with sprouts.

① Instead

② Moreover

③ In addition

④ Besides

⑤ By the way

tuna 참치   sprouts 채소 새싹   pretzel 비스킷의 일종

[01-03] 다음 밑줄 친 부분과 바꿔 쓸 수 있는 것을 고르시오.

01

> As soon as the thief saw the police, he ran away.
> = _____ , the thief ran away.
> 도둑은 경찰을 보자마자 도망갔다.

① As seeing the police
② On seeing the police
③ To seeing the police
④ Since seeing the police
⑤ So seeing the police

02

> Every time I need help, I think of my parents.
> 나는 도움이 필요할 때마다 부모님을 생각한다.

① As soon as
② Whether or not
③ Even if
④ In fact
⑤ Each time

03

> Because he is polite, people like him.
> 그가 예의바르기 때문에, 사람들은 그를 좋아한다.

① Though
② So
③ As
④ If
⑤ To

04 다음 중 빈칸에 들어갈 알맞은 말을 고르시오.

> I was thirsty, (as / so) I bought some water to drink.

05 다음 빈칸에 들어갈 수 없는 것을 고르시오.

> _____ she is pretty and kind, she is popular with the boys.

① Because
② Since
③ As
④ So
⑤ 없음

06 다음 문장과 뜻이 같은 보기를 고르시오.

> If you don't apologize to her, she'll be very angry.

① Unless you don't apologize to her, she'll be very angry.
② Unless you apologize to her, she'll be very angry.
③ Though you apologize to her, she'll be very angry.
④ As you apologize to her, she'll be very angry.
⑤ Even if you apologize to her, she'll be very angry.

07 다음 밑줄 친 단어와 바꿔 쓸 수 있는 단어를 고르시오.

> <u>Though</u> Yang is a very rich woman, she always works hard.

① Even if
② Because
③ Unless
④ If not
⑤ Since

08 다음 빈칸에 알맞지 <u>않은</u> 단어를 고르시오.

> _____ my grandmother is very old, she is still healthy.
> 비록 우리 할머니는 나이가 많으시지만, 그녀는 아직 건강하시다.

① Though
② Although
③ Even though
④ Even if
⑤ Even since

09 다음 빈칸에 as를 사용할 수 <u>없는</u> 것을 고르시오.

① ___ he was fat, he tried to lose weight.
② ___ mom cooked, I did my homework.
③ He listens to music ___ he studies.
④ I watched TV ___ I waited for my sister.
⑤ I have known her ___ we were children.

10 다음 중 밑줄 친 부분과 바꿔 쓸 수 있는 접속사를 고르시오.

> <u>While</u> I stayed at his house, he cooked for me everyday.

① Since
② Because
③ As
④ Though
⑤ During

[11–13] 다음 빈칸에 들어갈 알맞은 접속부사를 고르시오.

11

> She ate too much last night.
> _____ , she is going to skip breakfast this morning.

skip 건너뛰다, (식사를) 먹지 않다

① by the way
② besides
③ moreover
④ therefore
⑤ nevertheless

12

> You have to start early.
> _____ , you will be late.

① otherwise
② nevertheless
③ in addition
④ in fact
⑤ however

13

> I told her not to apply red lipstick.
> _____ , she did it.

apply lipstick 립스틱을 바르다

① otherwise
② besides
③ nevertheless
④ moreover
⑤ by the way

[14–15] 다음 대화를 읽고 물음에 답하시오.

> Waiter : What would you like to order?
> I : A ham pizza and coke, please.
> Waiter : We are sorry that ham pizza is not available now.
> I : In that case, ⓐ_____ (그 대신에), I would order a cheese pizza and coke.
> Waiter : All right, sir. If you have any other request, push the bell please.

available 이용 가능한

14 ⓐ에 들어갈 접속부사를 적으시오.

ⓐ : _____

15 다음 대화의 내용과 맞은 것을 고르시오.

① 나는 햄 피자와 콜라를 주문해서 먹었다.
② 다른 요청이 있으면, 벨을 누르면 된다.
③ 다른 손님들은 햄 피자를 주문할 수 있다.
④ 나는 결국 치즈 피자만 주문했다.
⑤ 나는 직접 손을 들고 웨이터를 부르면 된다.

16 다음 빈 칸에 공통으로 들어갈 단어를 고르시오.

> • _____ last year, I have lived in Tokyo.
> • He couldn't understand the question ____ he never learned it before.

① since
② because
③ while
④ though
⑤ if

17 다음을 같은 뜻으로 바꾸어 쓴 문장 중 **틀린** 문장을 고르시오.

> As it is raining heavily, we can't go camping.

① Because it is raining heavily, we can't go camping.

② We can't go camping, for it is raining heavily.

③ We can't go camping, so it is raining heavily.

④ Since it is raining heavily, we can't go camping.

⑤ We can't go camping, as it is raining heavily.

18 다음 ( )안의 단어를 우리말에 맞게 배열하시오.

> (I, embarrassed, I, was, made, for, a mistake)
>
> 나는 당황스러웠다. 왜냐하면 내가 실수를 했기 때문이다.

embarrassed 당황스러운

→ _____

_____ .

[19~20] 다음 대화를 읽고 올바른 답을 고르시오.

> *Jack* : Amy, look outside!
>
> *Amy* : Oh, the weather is wonderful!
>
> *Jack* : I think we should not go to the movies. ⓐ_____ , why don't we go to the park?
>
> *Amy* : It sounds perfect. Can you wait for me ⓑ_____ I change my clothes?
>
> *Jack* : Sure.

19 다음 대화 내용과 일치하지 <u>않는</u> 것을 고르시오.

① 날씨가 좋다.

② Jack과 Amy는 원래 영화를 보러 가려 했다.

③ Jack은 Amy에게 새로운 제안을 했다.

④ Amy는 옷을 갈아입을 것이다.

⑤ Amy는 Jack의 새로운 제안을 좋아하지 않았다.

20 빈칸 ⓐ, ⓑ에 들어갈 말이 알맞게 짝지어진 것을 고르시오.

① instead - since

② instead - while

③ in addition - as

④ otherwise - while

⑤ otherwise - as

Chapter 4

관계대명사A

관계대명사 who, which, whose

관계대명사란?
두 문장에서 같은 말의 반복을 피하고 이 두 문장을 이어주는 접속사와 대명사의
역할을 하는 것을 말하며 우리말로는 '~ 하는, ~인'등에 해당한다.

1 관계대명사와 선행사

관계대명사가 이끄는 절은 명사(선행사)를 꾸며주는 형용사 역할을 하므로 '형용사절'이 된다. 이 때 수식을 받는
명사를 선행사라고 한다.

ex. I have **a friend**. **She** is a model.

I have **a friend** **who is a model**. 나는 모델인 친구가 있다.
선행사   관계대명사 (she)

형용사절

2 형용사절 안에서의 관계대명사의 격

관계대명사는 형용사절 안에서 그 쓰임에 따라 주격, 목적격, 소유격의 역할을 한다.

〈주격〉 The girl is slim. + She is coming here.

= The girl <u>who **is coming here**</u> is slim. 여기로 오고 있는 소녀는 날씬하다.
형용사 절

Tip! 관계대명사가 형용사절 안에서 주어의 역할을 하므로, '주어'가 따로 없다.
ex. <u>who</u> 주어 is coming here
주어

〈목적격〉 The student is diligent. + I know him.

= The student <u>who(m) **I know**</u> is diligent. 내가 알고 있는 그 학생은 부지런하다.
형용사 절

Tip! 관계대명사가 형용사절 안에서 목적어 역할을 하므로, 관계대명사절 안에 주어가 있다.
ex. <u>who(m)</u>   <u>I</u>   know
목적어   주어

〈소유격〉 He has a sister. + Her friend is a lawyer.

= He has a sister **whose friend is a lawyer.** 그는 (그녀의) 친구가 변호사인 여동생이 있다.

형용사 절

Tip! 소유격은 명사를 수식하므로, 'whose + 명사'의 형태를 가지고 있다.

3 선행사의 종류

선행사는 사람과 사물/동물의 2가지로 나누어지며, 관계대명사는 선행사의 종류에 따라 달라진다.

선행사	주격	목적격	소유격	역할
사람	who	who(m)	whose	형용사절
사물/동물	which	which	whose	형용사절

ⓐ 선행사가 사람이면서 목적격일 때, whom과 who 둘 다 사용할 수 있다.

ex. He has a son **whom** everybody likes.

= He has a son **who** everybody likes.

Tip! 선행사가 사람이면서 목적격일 때, 사용하는 whom은 who로 자주 쓰인다.

ⓑ 선행사가 사물/동물일 때는 소유격 관계대명사 whose는 'of which the 명사', 또는 'the 명사 of which' 로 바꿔 쓸 수 있다.

I have a doll	whose	eyes	are big.
I have a doll	of which	the eyes	are big.
I have a doll	the eyes	of which	are big.

~~I have a doll of which eyes are big.~~

이때 선행사는 eyes가 아니고 a doll이다.

두 문장에서 같은 뜻의 단어들을 각각 찾아 ○표 하고, 아래의 문장에서 선행사는 '□', 관계대명사는 '△'로 표시해 보자.

1 He likes my sister. + She is shy.

→ He likes my sister who is shy.

2 The sky is blue. + Jinny is drawing it.

→ The sky which Jinny is drawing is blue.

3 This is a basket. + We can use it for our picnic.

→ This is a basket which we can use for our picnic.

4 We saw a girl. + She was walking slowly.

→ We saw a girl who was walking slowly.

5 She wears a ring. + It is very expensive.

→ She wears a ring which is very expensive.

6 The soup tastes salty. + He cooked it.

→ The soup which he cooked tastes salty.

7 I know the boy. + His father is a doctor.

→ I know the boy whose father is a doctor.

8 Jenny has a sister. + Her dream is to be a car designer.

→ Jenny has a sister whose dream is to be a car designer.

---

picnic 소풍   car designer 자동차 설계사

관계대명사로 시작하는 형용사 절을 찾아 밑줄을 친 후 우리말로 옮겨 보고, 관계대명사의 격도 골라 보자.

1 The cashier <u>who works here</u> is Jane's brother.　　　　(주격, 목적격, 소유격)

　　　여기서 일하는　　　　　　계산원은 Jane의 오빠이다.

2 I know the boy whose arms are very long.　　　　(주격, 목적격, 소유격)

나는　　　　　　　　　　　소년을 알고 있다.

3 The apples which they are selling are fresh.　　　　(주격, 목적격, 소유격)

　　　　　　　　사과들은 신선하다.

4 I saw a lot of Koreans whose shirts were red.　　　　(주격, 목적격, 소유격)

나는　　　　　　　　　　　많은 한국인들을 보았다.

5 Is this the park which is called Central Park?　　　　(주격, 목적격, 소유격)

이곳이　　　　　　　　　　공원이니?

6 She is the woman who Tom married three months ago.　　　　(주격, 목적격, 소유격)

그녀는　　　　　　　　　　여자이다.

7 Nick showed me a robot which he made during vacation.　　　　(주격, 목적격, 소유격)

Nick은 나에게　　　　　　　　로봇을 보여주었다.

8 He met a friend whose cell-phone looked nice.　　　　(주격, 목적격, 소유격)

그는　　　　　　　　　　　친구를 만났다.

9 The exam which she passed was not easy.　　　　(주격, 목적격, 소유격)

　　　　　　　　시험은 쉽지 않았다.

10 She goes to the school which is near the post office.　　　　(주격, 목적격, 소유격)

그녀는　　　　　　　　　　학교에 다닌다.

cashier 계산원　　　Central Park 센트럴 파크　　　near 근처에, 가까이에

기초 TEST

관계대명사로 시작하는 형용사 절과 선행사를 찾아 밑줄을 친 후 우리말로 옮겨 보고, 관계대명사의 격도 골라 보자.

1 Pass me <u>the salt which are on the table</u>. (주격) 목적격, 소유격)

　나에게 　식탁위에 있는 소금을　 건네 줘.

2 This is the book which he read yesterday. (주격, 목적격, 소유격)

　이것은 　　　　　　　　　　　　　　　이다.

3 John borrowed a book whose cover was really old. (주격, 목적격, 소유격)

　John은 　　　　　　　　　　　　　　　빌렸다.

4 This is a painting which was drawn by my mom. (주격, 목적격, 소유격)

　이것은 　　　　　　　　　　　　　　　이다.

5 Tom is one of my friends who are interested in music. (주격, 목적격, 소유격)

　Tom은 　　　　　　　　　　　　　　　이다.

6 That is the woman whose interest is beauty. (주격, 목적격, 소유격)

　저 사람은 　　　　　　　　　　　　　　　이다.

7 He has a son who is older than you. (주격, 목적격, 소유격)

　그는 　　　　　　　　　　　　　　　가지고 있다.

8 We looked at the kite which was flying in the sky. (주격, 목적격, 소유격)

　우리는 　　　　　　　　　　　　　　　바라보았다.

9 I have a nephew whose job is too hard. (주격, 목적격, 소유격)

　나는 　　　　　　　　　　　　　　　있다.

10 They visited a house whose garden was beautiful. (주격, 목적격, 소유격)

　그들은 　　　　　　　　　　　　　　　방문했다.

---

cover 겉표지　　**interest** 관심　　**beauty** 미, 아름다움

선행사를 찾아 O표시를 한 후, 다음 중 알맞은 관계대명사를 골라 보자. (두 개 가능)

1 The man is (the cook) ((who), whom, which, whose) is excellent at Chinese food.

2 The pigs (who, whom, which, whose) she grows are all fat.

3 The girl (who, whom, which, whose) is smiling in this picture is my sister.

4 Have you seen the old lady (who, whom, which, whose) hat is round?

5 Mike is a musician (who, whom, which, whose) I have met once.

6 This is the cup (who, whom, which, whose) I used.

7 There lived a rich man (who, whom, which, whose) life was unhappy.

8 Tommy likes the chair (who, whom, which, whose) legs are short.

9 My brother (who, which, whose) doesn't like to study is sleeping on the couch.

10 The movie (who, whom, which, whose) was directed by Karl is fun.

11 I know the baby (who, whom, which, whose) mom is a teacher.

12 The dishes (who, whom, which, whose) she cooked smell sweet.

13 Kate saw a fish (who, whom, which, whose) teeth were sharp.

14 She is with my friend (who, whom, which, whose) wallet was stolen in the bus.

15 Bill is the person (who, whom, which, whose) we can trust.

couch 소파   direct 감독하다   dish 요리, 접시   trust 신뢰하다

A 기본 TEST

다음 중 알맞은 관계대명사를 골라 보자. (두 개 가능)

1 The boy ((who), whom, which, whose) is studying hard is my cousin.

2 She is the painter (who, whom, which, whose) drew the picture.

3 These are the subjects (who, whom, which, whose) you should learn.

4 I'm not a man (who, whom, which, whose) you are talking about.

5 I go to the church (who, whom, which, whose) bell is on the tower.

6 It is the puppy (who, whom, which, whose) Ana saw at the pet shop.

7 He likes the cap (who, whom, which, whose) was made in China.

8 Take care of a baby (who, whom, which, whose) is crying in the room.

9 The calendar (who, whom, which, whose) was made by the man is used now.

10 He met an actress (who, whom, which, whose) I like.

11 These are the shoes (who, whom, which, whose) were mended by John.

12 Peter is an assistant (who, whom, which, whose) he is looking for.

13 She has a bracelet (who, whom, which, whose) price is high.

14 There lived an old man (who, whom, which, whose) son was an architect.

15 This is the car (who, whom, which, whose) I bought yesterday.

---

subject 과목   mend 수선하다   actress 여배우   assistant 조수   price 가격   architect 건축가

다음 중 알맞은 관계대명사를 골라 보자. (두 개 가능)

1 I like a girl (who, which, whom, whose) lives next door.

2 I know the man (who, which, whom, whose) name is Jack.

3 Bill is a boy (who, which, whom, whose) wish is to be a movie star.

4 He found a special recipe (who, which, whom, whose) was in his mom's old drawer.

5 Mathematics is the subject (who, which, whom, whose) many students don't want to study.

6 She has a book (who, which, whom, whose) is written by Robert.

7 She likes a house (who, which, whom, whose) ceiling is very high.

8 Do you know the store (who, which, whom, whose) is open at night?

9 A woman (who, which, whom, whose) I mentioned in my novel is my girlfriend.

10 My dad has an old friend (who, which, whom, whose) has been sick since 2014.

11 She met a girl (who, which, whom, whose) talent is amazing.

12 The dog (who, which, whom, whose) my sister brought yesterday is a poodle.

13 He bought a sneakers (who, which, whom, whose) came with shoelaces.

14 The umbrella (who, which, whom, whose) handle was broken is my son's.

15 He has a daughter (who, which, whom, whose) weight is over 100 kg.

recipe 조리법　　drawer 서랍　　talent 재능　　mention 언급하다　　amaze 놀라게 하다
shoelaces 신발끈　　weight 무게

C 기본 TEST

다음 빈칸에 알맞은 관계대명사를 써 넣어 보자. (두 개 가능)

| 보기 |
who   whom   which   whose

1 I have a sister ___whose___ friend went abroad to study.

2 Jun-ho is a student ___ speaks Chinese well.

3 The food ___ the chef makes is fantastic.

4 We happened to meet a wolf ___ eyes were blue.

5 Jim picked up the pear ___ fell from the tree.

6 The lady ___ I saw in the subway was very pretty.

7 There is a president ___ speech is wonderful.

8 The barber ___ a lot of customers like is my uncle.

9 Wednesday is the day ___ comes after Tuesday.

10 A dolphin is an animal ___ is really clever.

---

fantastic 환상적인   happened to 우연히 ~하다   pear 배   abroad 해외   speech 연설
barber 이발사   customer 고객

다음 빈칸에 알맞은 관계대명사를 써 넣어 보자. (두 개 가능)

1 He sells meat ____which____ is imported from America.

2 There is a monkey _____ nose is big.

3 The student _____ she called just now is Brian's sister.

4 The man _____ he took home yesterday is very poor.

5 Here is the tree _____ is over 500 years old.

6 The desk _____ my dad bought me last year is still good.

7 Tennis is the sport _____ my brother enjoys playing.

8 They are the fire-fighters _____ we never forget.

9 They have a TV set _____ size is large.

10 That is my brother's backpack _____ weighs 15 pounds.

---

import 수입하다　　just now 방금 전에　　over ~이상　　weigh ~의 무게가 나가다

다음 빈칸에 알맞은 관계대명사를 써 넣어 보자. (두 개 가능)

1 He can't forget the girl _who, whom_ he met at the party last night.

2 I read a book _____ title was Titanic.

3 Eat the food _____ is on the table.

4 I know a man _____ dream is to travel through space.

5 She is my best friend _____ helps me anytime.

6 This is a baby _____ I have to look after.

7 The dog _____ had been lost yesterday was found.

8 Jane has a friend _____ hobby is the same as hers.

9 Birds _____ can't fly are penguins and hens.

10 Spider man is a hero _____ people look up to.

space 우주   anytime 언제든지   look after 돌보다   penguin 펭귄   look up to 존경하다

소유격 관계대명사를 이용한 문장이다. 같은 표현으로 바꿔 보자.

1 He lives in the house whose backyard is wide.

= He lives in the house **of which the backyard** is wide.

= He lives in the house **the backyard of which** is wide.

2 Grandma likes the chair whose legs are short.

= Grandma likes the chair   are short.

= Grandma likes the chair   are short.

3 We go to the church of which the bell is on the tower.

= We go to the church   is on the tower.

= We go to the church   is on the tower.

4 I saw a bird the beak of which was sharp.

= I saw a bird   was sharp.

= I saw a bird   was sharp.

5 This is the coat whose material is wool.

= This is the coat   is wool.

= This is the coat   is wool.

---

backyard 뒷마당   wide 넓은   beak 부리   sharp 날카로운   material 소재   wool 양모

2

관계대명사의 수의 일치,
관계대명사를 이용한 문장 만들기

● 관계대명사의 수의 일치

ⓐ 주격 관계대명사의 동사는 선행사의 수에 일치시켜야 한다.

ex. I know the **girl(s)** <u>who is(are)</u> dancing. 나는 춤추고 있는 소녀(들)를 안다.
　　　　　　　　　　주어

ⓑ 관계대명사절의 선행사가 문장의 주어인 경우 문장의 동사는 선행사의 수에 일치시켜야 한다.

　주어　＋ 관계대명사절 ＋ 　동사
　└→　　　수의 일치　　　←┘

ex. **The boy(s) who sing(s) with Bill is(are) my brother(s).**
　　　　　　　　　　주어

Bill과 함께 노래하는 소년들은 나의 남동생(들)이다.

● 주격 관계대명사

ex. The boy is coming here. + He likes Jane.

step 1　두 문장에서 같은 뜻의 단어를 찾아 O표시를 하고 대명사를 없앤다.

　　　　The boy is coming here. + ~~He~~ likes Jane.

step 2　없앤 대명사대신 알맞은 관계대명사를 넣는다.

　　　　The boy is coming here. + who likes Jane.

step 3　관계대명사가 붙어있는 문장 전체를 같은 뜻의 단어 바로 뒤에 넣는다.

　　　　The boy who likes Jane is coming here. Jane을 좋아하는 소년이 여기로 오고 있다.

🟦 목적격 관계대명사

ex. A boy is coming here. + I hate him.

step 1   두 문장에서 같은 뜻의 단어를 찾아 O표시를 하고 대명사를 없앤다.

  A boy is coming here. + I hate ~~him~~ .

step 2   없앤 대명사대신 알맞은 관계대명사를 앞에 넣는다.

  A boy is coming here. + whom I hate .

step 3   관계대명사가 붙어있는 문장 전체를 같은 뜻의 단어 바로 뒤에 넣는다.

  A boy whom I hate is coming here.   내가 싫어하는 소년이 여기로 오고 있다.

🟦 소유격 관계대명사

ex. I have a dog. + Its tail is very long.

step 1   두 문장에서 같은 뜻의 단어를 찾아 O표시를 하고 대명사를 없앤다.

  I have a dog . + ~~Its~~ tail is very long.

step 2   없앤 대명사대신 알맞은 관계대명사를 넣는다.

  I have a dog . + whose tail is very long.

step 3   관계대명사가 붙어있는 문장 전체를 같은 뜻의 단어 바로 뒤에 넣는다.

  I have a dog whose tail is very long.   나는 꼬리가 매우 긴 개가 있다.

A 기초 TEST

1 "D" is (the letter) which (come, comes) after "C".

2 I bought two watermelons which (was, were) very fresh.

3 We don't know the boy who (is, are) drinking milk.

4 Tom wants to marry someone who (understand, understands) him well.

5 Here are some candies which Jane (like, likes) best.

6 This is the work which (makes, make) me tired everyday.

7 The cars which (go, goes) by diesel fuel (is, are) made at this factory.

선행사를 찾아 ○표시를 한 후, ( ) 안의 동사를 알맞게 바꿔서 빈칸에 써 넣어 보자. (현재형)

1 There are (some bears) which _____eat_____ fish in the zoo. (eat)

2 He lives in a house which _____ a big window. (have)

3 I have two daughters who _____ good at music. (be)

4 The season which _____ before spring _____ winter. (come, be)

5 Look at the cathedral whose windows _____ stained colorfully. (be)

---

diesel fuel 디젤유   **cathedral** 성당   **stain** (유리에) 착색하다. 채색하다   **colorfully** 다채롭게

두 문장에서 같은 뜻의 단어를 찾아 ○표시를 하고, 관계대명사를 사용하여 한 문장으로 만들어 보자.

1 step 1 : This is ⬡a runner⬡ + ⬡He⬡ won the race today.

step 2 : This is a runner. + *who* won the race today.

step 3 : This is *a runner* *who* won the race today.

이 사람이 오늘 경주에서 우승한 달리기 선수이다.

2 step 1 : Here is the place. + We will visit it tomorrow.

step 2 : Here is the place. + we will visit tomorrow.

step 3 : Here is we will visit tomorrow.

여기가 내일 우리가 방문 할 장소이다.

3 step 1 : Dad has an old book. + its cover is worn.

step 2 : Dad has an old book. + cover is worn.

step 3 : Dad has cover is worn.

아빠는 표지가 닳아빠진 책 한권을 가지고 있다.

4 step 1 : The man is a lawyer. + His office is near the post office.

step 2 : The man is a lawyer. + office is near the post office.

step 3 : The man is office is near the post office.

그남자는 그의 사무실이 우체국 근처에 있는 변호사이다.

5 step 1 : The building is tall. + It is her uncle's.

step 2 : The building is tall. + is her uncle's.

step 3 : is her uncle's is tall.

그녀 삼촌의 소유인 그 빌딩은 높다.

worn 닳아빠진

두 문장에서 같은 뜻의 단어를 찾아 ○표 하고 관계대명사를 사용하여 한 문장으로 만들어 보자.

1 step 1 : Do you know [the woman]? + [She] is talking with Tom.

step 2 : Do you know   *the woman*   +   *who*   is talking with Tom.

step 3 : Do you know   *the woman who*   is talking with Tom?

2 step 1 : This is a pet pig. + Its nose is pink.

step 2 : This is   +   nose is pink.

step 3 : This is   nose is pink.

3 step 1 : An old man is waiting outside. + He wants to see you.

step 2 :   is waiting outside. +   wants to see you.

step 3 :   wants to see you is waiting outside.

4 step 1 : This is the plane. + I flew it for the first time.

step 2 : This is   +   I flew for the first time.

step 3 : This is   I flew for the first time.

5 step 1 : There are two boys. + They are good at math.

step 2 : There are   +   are good at math.

step 3 : There are   are good at math.

outside 밖에서   fly (a plane) 비행기를 조종하다   for the first time 난생 처음으로

정답 및 해설 p.12

두 문장에서 같은 뜻의 단어를 찾아 ○표 하고 관계대명사를 사용하여 한 문장으로 만들어 보자.

1   step 1 : ⬚The clerk⬚ is kind. + ⬚She⬚ is standing at the lobby.

     step 2 : The clerk is kind. + *who is standing at the lobby* .

     step 3 : *The clerk who is standing at the lobby* is kind.

2   step 1 : This kitten is very cute. + Mary brought it.

     step 2 : This kitten is very cute. + .

     step 3 : is very cute.

3   step 1 : The boy is too shy. + His cheeks turned red.

     step 2 : The boy is too shy. + .

     step 3 : is too shy .

4   step 1 : The woman is my aunt. + She is picking peaches.

     step 2 : The woman is my aunt. + .

     step 3 : is my aunt.

5   step 1 : The cell-phone looks nice. + My dad bought it for me.

     step 2 : The cell-phone looks nice. + .

     step 3 : looks nice.

shy 수줍은   cheek 뺨 · turn 바뀌다   peach 복숭아

C 기본 TEST

다음 두 문장을 관계대명사를 사용하여 한 문장으로 만들어 보자.

1 We like the boy. + He sings well.

= We like the boy _____*who sings well*_____ .

2 The student lives here. + His dad is a dentist.

= The student _____ .

3 She wears the hairpin. + I don't like it.

= She wears the hairpin _____ .

4 These are the orphans. + Andy takes care of them.

= These are the orphans _____ .

5 The old lady teaches math. + Her daughter works at this library.

= The old lady _____ teaches math.

6 The bears sleep in winter. + They live in Alaska.

= The bears _____ sleep in winter.

7 I bought a ruler. + It was made in Japan.

= I bought a ruler _____ .

8 My uncle drives a truck. + Its wheels are very big.

= My uncle drives a truck _____ .

9 The rifles look cool. + The soldiers carry them.

= The rifles _____ look cool.

10 Do you know the banker? + Jim has seen him before.

= Do you know the banker _____ ?

---

dentist 치과의사   **orphan** 고아   **Alaska** 알라스카   **wheel** (차) 바퀴   **rifle** 장총   **banker** 은행가

다음 두 문장을 관계대명사를 사용하여 한 문장으로 만들어 보자.

1 The boy is my cousin. + He is quarreling with Sam.

= The boy _who is quarreling with Sam_ is my cousin.

2 James has a brother. + He goes to the elementary school.

= James has a brother _____ .

3 The puppy is Susan's. + Its tail is short.

= The puppy _____ is Susan's.

4 The engineer is very skillful. + He studied in Germany.

= The engineer _____ is very skillful.

5 The girl is his daughter. + Her face is small.

= The girl _____ is his daughter.

6 Kate saw some peacocks. + Their feathers were wonderful.

= Kate saw some peacocks _____ .

7 Jin-ho sent her a letter. + He wrote it in English.

= Jin-ho sent her a letter _____ .

8 I bought a T-shirt. + Its size is 90.

= I bought a T-shirt _____ .

9 The dishes smell sweet. + The chef cooked them.

= The dishes _____ smell sweet.

10 These are the toys. + Jenny wanted them so badly.

= These are the toys _____ .

---

quarrel 말다툼하다　**skillful** 숙련된　**peacock** 공작새　**feather** (새) 깃털　**badly** 간절히

주어진 단어를 이용하여 우리말에 알맞게 문장을 완성해 보자.

1 그가 좋아하는 음료수는 콜라이다. (like)

The drink *which he likes* is Coke.

2 빨간 모자를 쓰고 있는 소년은 Sam이다. (wear)

The boy   a red cap   is Sam.

3 그것은 내가 한번 본 적이 있는 영화이다. (watch)

It is the movie   once   .

4 이 마을에 살고 있는 저 아이는 나의 친구이다. (live)

The child   in this village   is my friend.

5 그녀가 가지고 다니는 가방은 세련되어 보인다. (carry)

The bag   looks chic.

6 나는 벤치 아래에서 자고 있는 고양이를 발견했다. (sleep)

I found a cat   under the bench   .

7 그가 오늘 공부해야 하는 과목은 과학이다. (study)

The subject   today   is science.

8 나는 그녀의 아버지가 택시를 운전하는 소녀를 알고 있다. (drive)

I know the girl   a taxi   .

9 저것은 아빠에 의해서 지어진 집이다. (build)

That is the house   by dad   .

10 Judy는 그것의 눈이 빨간 토끼 한 마리를 기르고 있다. (have)

Judy keeps a rabbit   red   .

drink 음료수   chic 세련된

주어진 단어를 이용하여 우리말에 알맞게 문장을 완성해 보자.

1 여기에 우리가 지난해에 심었던 많은 나무들이 있다. (plant)

Here are many trees _____ *which we planted* _____ last year _____ .

2 그녀는 Karen이 LA로부터 보낸 이 메일을 읽었다. (send)

She read an e-mail _____ from L.A _____ .

3 그는 그가 함께 일했던 소녀를 좋아한다. (work)

He likes the girl _____ with _____ .

4 Emile는 그의 날개가 큰 새를 보았다. (be)

Emile saw a bird _____ big _____ .

5 그녀가 만들고 있는 웨딩드레스는 정말 아름답다. (make)

The wedding dress _____ is really beautiful.

6 Mary가 그린 그림은 매우 독특하다. (draw)

The painting _____ is very unique.

7 Denny는 미국에서 인기 있는 가수이다. (be)

Denny is a singer _____ in America _____ .

8 그는 그것의 털이 매우 부드러운 고양이를 보고 미소지었다. (be)

He smiled at a cat _____ very soft _____ .

9 James는 고등학교에 다니는 누나가 있다. (go)

James has a sister _____ to high school _____ .

10 그녀가 어제 (착용)했던 목걸이는 나의 것이었다. (wear)

The necklace _____ yesterday _____ was mine.

wing 날개   wedding dress 웨딩드레스   unique 독특한   popular 인기있는   fur 털, 모피   wear 착용하다

실력 TEST

정답 및 해설 p.13

주어진 단어를 이용하여 우리말에 알맞게 문장을 완성해 보자.

1 나는 공부를 열심히 하는 남동생이 있다. (be)

I have a brother _____*who is studious*_____ .

2 저것은 어제 나를 놀라게한 개이다. (frighten)

That is the dog _____ .

3 Jane은 그의 직업이 수의사인 남자를 안다. (be)

Jane knows a man _____ .

4 그녀는 젊은이들이 무척 좋아하는 연예인이다. (love)

She is a celebrity _____ .

5 나는 내가 만나기를 원했던 나의 옛 선생님을 만났다. (want)

I met my old teacher _____ .

6 그는 축구를 잘하는 소년이다. (play)

He is the boy _____ .

7 7월은 8월 전에 오는 달이다. (come)

July is the month _____ .

8 Susan은 (그녀의) 아빠가 소방관인 소녀이다. (be)

Susan is the girl _____ .

9 이 곳은 내가 아는 식당이다. (know)

This is the restaurant _____ .

10 내 조카는 (그것의) 눈이 큰 인형을 가지고 있다. (be)

My niece has a doll _____ .

---

studious 공부를 열심히 하는   frighten 놀라게 하다   vet 수의사   celebrity 유명인

[01–04] 다음 빈칸에 알맞은 말을 |보기|에서 골라 쓰시오.

| 보기 |

who   whom   which   whose

01 She is the girl _____ brother is my friend.

02 The kid _____ is running over there is Sally's nephew.

03 Ted works for a company _____ makes computers.

04 The woman _____ I talked to was very kind.

05 다음 우리말에 맞게 ( ) 안의 단어를 배열하여 문장을 완성하시오.

이것은 그들의 모국어가 영어가 아닌 부모들을 위한 것이다.

This is for the parents (mother tongue, not, English, is, whose)

→ This is for the parents _____
_____ .

mother tongue 모국어

06 다음 두 문장을 바르게 연결한 것은?

· The bag is not mine.
· It is on the chair.

① The bag which on the chair is not mine.
② The bag who is on the chair is not mine.
③ The bag which is on the chair is not mine.
④ The bag is on the chair not mine.
⑤ The bag is not mine which on the chair.

07 빈칸에 알맞은 것을 고르시오.

The boy whose friend won the prize _____ excited.

① be
② is
③ are
④ were
⑤ being

O8 빈칸에 공통으로 들어갈 말로 알맞은 것을 고르시오.

> · Who ate the cake _____ was in the fridge?
> · This is the house _____ he wants to stay in all this summer.

① who
② whom
③ what
④ which
⑤ whose

fridge 냉장고

O9 ( ) 안의 관계대명사가 들어갈 위치를 고르시오.

> He is ① a great ② writer ③ got ④ the Nobel Prize ⑤ 2 years ago.
> (who)

10 다음 문장에서 어법상 어색한 부분을 하나만 고르시오.

> The ① boys ② who ③ have just ④ arrived at the school ⑤ is Korean.

11 다음 중 밑줄 친 부분의 쓰임이 나머지와 다른 것은?

① I like the boy who wears a red cap.
② Emile is the girl who likes a yellow skirt.
③ Joseph is the boy who works in the Japanese restaurant.
④ She knows the man who lives next door.
⑤ Peter knows who ate the rice-cake.

12 빈칸에 들어갈 알맞은 말을 고르시오.

> Frances went to the garden _____ full of flowers.

① who were
② which were
③ who was
④ which was
⑤ whose was

be full of ~으로 가득하다

13 다음 밑줄 친 부분 중 어법상 어색한 것은?

① Do you know the man <u>whose</u> sister is a ballerina?
② There are some children <u>who</u> study at night.
③ The book <u>which</u> is on the desk is mine.
④ Look at the man <u>whom</u> is running along the beach.
⑤ He loves the girl <u>who</u> we met yesterday.

14 다음 밑줄 친 부분 중에 어색한 것을 고르시오.

My best friend ① <u>whose</u> name is Mary ② <u>lives</u> in America. She has a dog ③ <u>who</u> is very cute and brave. I like dogs, ④ <u>too</u>. I really want to ⑤ <u>have</u> a dog like hers.

15 다음 우리말을 영어로 옮긴 것 중 알맞은 것을 고르시오.

나는 이탈리아에서 만들어진 가방 하나를 가지고 있다.

① I have a bag who was made in Italy.
② I have a bag which was made in Italy.
③ I have a bag whom was made in Italy.
④ I have a bag whose was made in Italy.
⑤ A bag was made in Italy is mine.

16 밑줄 친 부분의 용법이 <u>다른</u> 하나는?

① Is this the computer <u>which</u> you saw yesterday?
② Jimmy bought a laptop <u>which</u> they sold at the store.
③ I will give you a pen <u>which</u> I have.
④ Winter is the season <u>which</u> I like best.
⑤ <u>Which</u> is the best item?

item 상품

[17-18] 다음 대화를 읽고 물음에 답하시오.

> *Walter* : Where is my pen?
> *Karen* : I don't know. I have a friend
>   ⓐ can lend you another
>   one.
> *Walter* : No, I need to find my pen.
>   ⓑ I love the pen. It means a lot
>   to me.
> *Karen* : I see. I will help you look for it.
> *Walter* : Thanks. Where should we start
>   looking?
> *Karen* : Why don't we try looking under
>   your desk first?
> *Walter* : Good idea.

mean 의미가 있다

17 밑줄 친 ⓐ에 알맞은 관계대명사를 고르시오.

① who
② which
③ whose
④ whom
⑤ what

18 밑줄 친 ⓑ를 관계대명사를 사용하여 한 문장으로 연결하시오.

→ _____

_____ .

[19-20] 다음 글을 읽고 물음에 답하시오.

> Jessica is planning to spend the weekend at a ski resort. She is looking for someone ⓐ will watch and feed her dog. She has asked all of her friends if they would do it. Most of them, however, are too busy. ⓑ Jessica's friends know a man. His daughter would be willing to do the job. She is very kind and loves a dog ⓒ name is Ben. Jessica will hire her on the spot.

on the spot 즉시

19 밑줄 친 ⓐ와 ⓒ에 들어갈 알맞은 관계대명사를 차례로 짝지은 것을 고르시오.

① who - who
② which - who
③ whose - who
④ who - which
⑤ who - whose

20 밑줄 친 ⓑ를 한 문장으로 연결할 때, 빈칸을 채우시오.

> Jessica's friends know a man
> _____ daughter would
> be willing to do the job.

be willing to ～기꺼이 ～하다

[01–03] 다음 빈칸에 알맞은 관계대명사를 고르시오.

01

> Math is the subject _____ I like best.

① who
② which
③ when
④ why
⑤ how

02
(답 2개)

> The girl is diligent. + I know her.
> = The girl _____ I know is diligent.

① who
② which
③ whose
④ whom
⑤ what

03

> She has a boyfriend. + His dad is a vet.
> = She has a boyfriend _____ dad is a vet.

① who
② whom
③ whose
④ which
⑤ what

04 다음 중 틀린 문장을 고르시오.

① The girl who is in the room is my sister.
② I like the earrings which Susan is wearing.
③ The boy who you met looked very cute.
④ This is the purse which I bought yesterday.
⑤ She has a sister whose her hair is brown.

05 관계대명사를 이용하여 다음 두 문장을 한 문장으로 바르게 합친 것을 고르시오.

> The girl is sad. + She lost her cell phone. 핸드폰을 잃어버린 소녀는 슬프다.

① The girl is sad who she lost her cell phone.
② The sad girl lost whose her cell phone.
③ The girl who is sad lost her cell phone.
④ The girl whom lost her cell phone is sad.
⑤ The girl who lost her cell phone is sad.

06 다음 중 없어야 할 단어를 고르시오.

> ① The man ② who ③ he ④ is wearing a grey jacket ⑤ is my uncle.
> 회색 재킷을 입고 있는 남자가 내 삼촌이다.

07 밑줄 친 부분을 whom으로 바꿔 쓸 수 있는 것은?

① He is the singer <u>who</u> young people like.
② The boy <u>who</u> broke the window is my brother.
③ The girl has a brother <u>who</u> became a pianist.
④ I bought a pen <u>which</u> was made in China.
⑤ She is the English teacher <u>who</u> is from Canada.

[08–09] 다음 ( ) 안에서 알맞은 것을 고르시오.

08

> The boy who (is, are) dancing on the stage (is, are) my brother.

09

> The rings which Kate (is, are) wearing (is, are) not so luxurious.

luxurious 사치스러운

10 다음 보기 중 밑줄 친 부분과 바꿔 쓸 수 있는 것을 고르시오.

> He hunted a fox <u>whose tail</u> was silver.

① which tail
② of which tail
③ who the tail
④ of which the tail
⑤ whom the tail

11 다음 밑줄 친 것이 알맞지 <u>않은</u> 것은?

① I know the boy <u>whose</u> ears are big.
② This is the cat <u>which</u> I told you about.
③ She has a book of <u>which</u> the cover is red.
④ I have a friend of <u>which</u> the dream is to be a pilot.
⑤ He has a sister <u>whom</u> everybody loves.

[12–13] 다음 빈칸에 들어갈 단어가 올바르게 짝지어진 것을 고르시오.

12

> My family has a dog. + ____ tail is very short. = My family has a dog _____ tail is very short.

① his - which
② his - who
③ its - which
④ its - of whom
⑤ its - whose

13

> The girl is coming here. + Tony likes ____ . = The girl _____ Tony likes is coming here.

① her - whom
② her - of which
③ her - which
④ she - who
⑤ she - whom

[14–15] 다음 글을 읽고 물음에 답하시오.

> *Rick* : Katy, did you see my ring?
> *Katy* : No, I did not. Is the ring important for you?
> *Rick* : Yes, very much. ⓐThe ring means a lot. My girlfriend gave it to me.
> *Katy* : I see. I will help you find it.
> *Rick* : Thank you so much.

14 위의 글의 내용과 일치하지 않는 것을 고르시오.

① Rick은 반지를 잃어버렸다.
② Rick은 여자 친구에게 선물로 반지를 줬다.
③ Rick에게 반지는 매우 중요하다.
④ Katy는 Rick이 반지를 찾는 것을 도와주기로 했다.
⑤ Katy는 Rick의 반지를 못 보았다.

15 밑줄 친 ⓐ를 관계대명사를 사용하여 한 문장으로 연결할 때, 빈칸을 알맞게 채우시오.

The ring _____
_____ means a lot.

16 다음 두 문장을 바르게 연결한 것은?

> · The necklace is not mine.
> · It is made with gold.

① The necklace which made with gold is not mine.
② The necklace who is made with is not mine.
③ The necklace which is made with gold is not mine.
④ The necklace is made with gold, but not mine.
⑤ The necklace is not mine which made with gold.

17 다음 문장에서 어법상 어색한 부분을 고르시오.

> ① People ② who ③ have just ④ got off the plane ⑤ is Americans.

18 다음 우리말에 맞게 괄호 안의 단어를 배열하여 문장을 완성하시오.

> This book is for the children
> (abilities, good, English, are, whose)
> 이 책은 그들의 영어 실력이 좋은 아이들을 위한 것이다.

ability 능력, 실력

→ This book is for the children
_____.

19 빈칸에 공통으로 들어갈 말로 알맞은 것을 고르시오.

> · Tom ate the cake _____ was in the fridge.
> · This is the house _____ he wants to stay in all this summer.

fridge 냉장고

① who
② whom
③ what
④ which
⑤ whose

20 ( )안의 관계대명사가 들어갈 위치를 고르시오.

> He is ① the famous ② actor ③ won ④ the Academy Awards ⑤ last year. (who)

Chapter 5

관계대명사B, 관계부사

UNIT 1 관계대명사 that, 관계대명사의 생략

1 관계대명사 that

● 주격 관계대명사와 목적격 관계대명사 who, whom, which는 that으로 바꿔 쓸 수 있다.

ex. He is the teacher who(that) we like. 그는 우리가 좋아하는 선생님이다.

ex. The house which(that) was built in 1854 is famous. 1854년에 지어진 그 집은 유명하다.

* 소유격 관계대명사 whose는 that으로 바꾸어 쓸 수 없다.

● 선행사가 '사람+사물'인 경우 that만 사용한다.

ex. I know a boy and his dog that are running in the park.
　　　나는 공원에서 달리고 있는 소년과 그의 개를 알고 있다.

* 선행사에 아래와 같은 말이 포함되어 있을 경우 주로 that을 사용한다.

> every, all, any, some, no
>
> the only 유일한, the very 바로 그, the same 똑 같은, the last 마지막
>
> 최상급, 서수

ex. Tom is the only boy that I know. Tom은 내가 아는 유일한 소년이다.

2 관계대명사의 생략

● 목적격 관계대명사 'who(m), which, that'은 생략 할 수 있다.

ex. Tom called the policeman ~~(whom)~~ I knew. Tom은 내가 아는 경찰관에게 전화했다.

This is the computer ~~(which)~~ I bought yesterday. 이것이 내가 어제 산 컴퓨터이다.

● '주격 관계대명사 + be동사 + 분사구'의 경우 '관계대명사 + be동사'는 함께 생략할 수 있다.

ex. The woman ~~(who is)~~ cooking in the kitchen is Maria. 부엌에서 요리하고 있는 여자는 Maria이다.
　　　　　　　　　　　　현재분사구

ex. She can read a letter ~~(which is)~~ written in English. 그녀는 영어로 써진 편지를 읽을 수 있다.
　　　　　　　　　　　　　과거분사구

Tip! 우리는 명사를 꾸며주는 현재분사와 과거분사가 수식어구가 있을 때 명사 뒤로 오는 이유를 이해할 수 있다.

ex. The woman (who is) cooking in the kitchen is Maria. = The woman cooking in the kitchen is Maria.

A 기초 TEST

선행사를 찾아 ○표시를 한 후, 다음 중 알맞은 관계대명사를 모두 골라 보자.

1 She is the only daughter (who, whom, that) he has.

2 That is the same pen (which, who, that) we saw yesterday.

3 The pen (whose, which, that, whom) I bought yesterday is green.

4 All trees (which, that, whose) grow here are tall.

5 The boy (who, whom, that) Jane likes lives next door to me.

6 No food (which, whose, that) she cooks tastes good.

7 This is the very dress (who, which, that) I am looking for.

8 The book (whose, which, that) cover is blue is Jimmy's.

9 Look at the boy and wolf (which, who, that) are playing together.

10 The largest animal (who, which, that) lives in the sea is a whale.

11 This is the map (who, which, that) leads me to your apartment.

12 It was the last tiger (who, which, that) lived in Korea.

13 This is my boyfriend (who, whose, that) uncle is an exellent engineer.

14 They are the man and his monkey (who, which, that) performed in the circus.

15 This is a sleeping bag (who, which, that) you can use tonight.

---

whale 고래   **lead** 이끌다   **circus** 서커스

B 기초 TEST

알맞은 관계대명사를 써 넣어 보자.

1 He is the only doctor _that_ will save my husband.

2 The wind _____ is blowing makes it hard for me to walk.

3 She got a haircut _____ made her look young.

4 Everybody _____ he met in Korea was kind to him.

5 I have no answer _____ I can give to my friend.

6 That is the girl _____ mom is a math teacher.

7 That is the same sweater _____ Jane bought 2 hours ago.

8 The driver _____ eyes are big drives too slow.

9 The manager _____ I respect is very strict.

10 We know the woman and cats _____ have lived in the old house since 1999.

save 구하다   respect 존경하다   strict 엄격한

다음에서 생략할 수 있는 '관계대명사'와 '주격 관계대명사 + be동사'를 지워보자. (생략할 수 없는 것은 그대로 둘 것)

1 That is the car ~~which~~ my son likes.

2 This is the boat that was made in America.

3 The boy who likes my sister is my best friend.

4 This is the rule that we should follow.

5 The girl who is playing the cello is his niece.

6 The man who is chasing the thief is my friend's father.

7 A bird which sat on the tree flew away.

8 Math and science are the subjects that we learned today.

9 She dried her hair which had gotten wet with rain.

10 She is the hair-dresser whose shop is famous in Paris.

11 The old man who is holding a cane is Mr. Bond.

12 The tree which my dad planted 10 years ago is now tall.

13 February is the month that comes after January.

14 The island that the man found is very beautiful.

15 The robot which she made was amazing.

---

rule 규칙   fly away 날아가버리다   cane 지팡이   island 섬   amaze 놀라게하다

UNIT 2

관계대명사의 용법, 전치사 + 관계대명사, 관계대명사 what

1 관계대명사의 계속적 용법

관계대명사 앞에 '(comma)'를 써서 선행사에 대한 추가 설명을 해주는 것을 말한다.

● **'who(m)/ which'는 'and(또는 but) + 대명사'로 바꾸어 쓸 수 있다.**

~. + who(m) / which	and / but + 대명사	그런데 / 그러나 (대명사는, 대명사를)

ⓐ 선행사가 사람인 경우

   ex. She has a son, **who** became a teacher.
      = She has a son, **and he** became a teacher.
         그녀는 아들이 한 명 있다. 그런데 그는 선생님이 되었다.

ⓑ 선행사가 사물인 경우

   ex. He bought a pen, **which** was made in China.
      = He bought a pen, **and it** was made in China.
         그는 펜 하나를 샀다. 그런데 그것은 중국에서 만들어졌다.

● **제한적용법과 계속적용법의 차이**

ⓐ **제한적 용법** : 관계대명사 앞에 comma(,)가 없는 경우를 말한다.

   ex. He has two caps **which** are red.   그는 빨간색인 모자 2개를 가지고 있다.
       (다른 색 모자도 있을 수 있다 → 그는 모자가 2개 이상일 수 있음)

ⓑ **계속적 용법** : 관계대명사 앞에 comma(,)가 있는 경우를 말한다.

   ex. He has two caps, **which** are red.
      = He has two caps, **and they** are red.   그는 모자 2개를 가지고 있다. 그런데 그것들은 빨간색이다.
       (둘 다 빨간색이다 → 그는 모자가 단지 2개밖에 없음)

● **계속적용법에서는 관계대명사 who(m), which 대신 that을 사용하지 못한다.**

   ex. He has two caps, which are red.
      = ~~He has two caps, that are red.~~

2 전치사 + 관계대명사

목적격 관계대명사가 이끄는 형용사절에서, 뒤에 남아 있는 전치사를 관계대명사 앞으로 보낼 수 있다.

🔷 선행사가 사람인 경우 : 전치사 + whom

ⓐ 전치사가 형용사절 뒤에 있을 때는 who(m), that 모두 가능하다.

ex. She needs a boyfriend **who(m)** she will talk **with**.

= She needs a boyfriend **that** she will talk **with**.

그녀는 같이 얘기할 남자친구가 필요하다.

ⓑ 전치사가 관계대명사 앞으로 위치할 때는 '전치사 + whom'만 가능하다.

ex. She needs a boyfriend **with whom** she will talk.

~~She needs a boyfriend with who she will talk.~~

~~She needs a boyfriend with that she will talk.~~

🔷 선행사가 사물인 경우 : 전치사 + which

ⓐ 전치사가 형용사절 뒤에 있을 때는 which, that 모두 가능하다.

ex. This is the house **which** Tom lives **in**. 이곳이 Tom이 살고 있는 집이다.

= This is the house **that** Tom lives **in**.

ⓑ 전치사가 관계대명사 앞으로 위치할 때, '전치사 + which'만 가능하다.

ex. This is the house **in which** Tom lives.

~~This is the house in that Tom lives.~~

Tip! 실제로는 대개의 경우 전치사를 문장 뒤에 두는 경우를 사용한다.

3 관계대명사 what

🔷 우리말 : '~하는 것(들)'

선행사 the thing(s)과 관계대명사 that(which)가 하나로 합쳐진 것을 말한다.

> **the thing(s) + that(which) = what**

ex. I got **the thing(s) that** I wanted. 나는 내가 원했던 것(들)을 얻었다.

= I got **what** I wanted.

다음 밑줄 친 부분을 알맞은 우리말로 써 넣어 보자.

1 I met two ladies <u>who were beautiful and kind.</u>

나는 　　　　　　　*아름답고 친절한*　　　　　　　 두 명의 숙녀를 만났다.

I met two ladies, <u>who were beautiful and kind.</u>

나는 두 명의 숙녀를 만났다. 　　　*그런데 그들은 아름답고 친절했다*　　　 .

2 She has five pens <u>which were made in China.</u>

그녀는 　　　　　　　　　　　　　　　　　 5개의 펜을 가지고 있다.

She has five pens, <u>which were made in China.</u>

그녀는 5개의 펜을 가지고 있다. 　　　　　　　　　　　　 .

3 Tom has three close friends, <u>who live far apart.</u>

Tom은 3명의 친한 친구가 있다. 　　　　　　　　　　　 .

Tom has three close friends <u>who live far apart.</u>

Tom은 　　　　　　　　　　　　　　　　 3명의 친한 친구가 있다.

4 Jane likes the boy <u>who doesn't care about her.</u>

Jane은 　　　　　　　　　　　　　　　 .

Jane likes the boy, <u>who doesn't care about her.</u>

Jane은 　　　　　　　　　　　　　　　 .

5 We <u>have two teachers who are from Canada.</u>

우리는 　　　　　　　　　　　　　　 .

We <u>have two teachers, who are from Canada.</u>

우리는 　　　　　　　　　　　　　　 .

---

close 가까운　　**far apart** 멀리 떨어져　　**care about** ~에게 관심이 있다　　**be from** ~에서 왔다, ~출신이다

다음 중 알맞은 것을 골라 보자.

1 The chair has one leg which is a little short.

그 의자는 다리가 (1개뿐임, 1개 이상일 수 있음)

2 Jim has three friends who are smart and gentle.

Jim은 친구가 (3명뿐임, 3명 이상일 수 있음)

3 Jane uses 3 pens, which are black.

Jane은 펜이 (3자루뿐임, 3자루 이상일 수 있음)

4 In the school, there are 3 teachers who teach science.

그 학교에는, 선생님이 (3명뿐임, 3명 이상일 수 있음)

5 The farmer raises fifty cows, which are all black and white.

그 농부는 암소가 (50마리뿐임, 50마리 이상일 수 있음)

6 In the class, there are 7 students who can speak in English.

그 반에는 학생이 (7명뿐임, 7명 이상일 수 있음)

7 Sam has two uncles whom he lives with.

샘은 삼촌이 (2명뿐임, 2명 이상일 수 있음)

8 He bought five candies, which he gave to her.

그가 산 사탕은 (5개뿐임, 5개 이상일 수 있음)

9 Jason has three cousins, who go to the same school.

Jason은 사촌이 (3명뿐임, 3명 이상일 수 있음)

10 He wrote 5 books which are selling well.

그가 쓴 책이 (5권뿐임, 5권 이상일 수 있음)

---

leg 다리   **gentle** 신사적인

다음을 같은 문장으로 바꿀 때 ( ) 안에 알맞은 말을 써 넣어 보자. (두 개 가능)

1 She taught math to the boy, who failed the exam.

= She taught math to the boy, *but* *he* failed the exam.

2 People like my uncle, who is also fond of others.

= People like my uncle, is also fond of others.

3 I don't like the singers, whom my sister loves.

= I don't like the singers, my sister loves .

4 We borrowed a video tape, which we could not watch last night.

= We borrowed a video tape, we could not watch last night.

5 He has a niece, whom he should take care of.

= He has a niece, he should take care of .

6 Lora likes her son, who doesn't do well at school.

= Lora likes her son, doesn't do well at school.

7 James wants to see the doctor, who is the only one that can cure him.

= James wants to see the doctor, is the only one that can cure him.

8 I keep a black cap, which I rarely wear.

= I keep a black cap, I rarely wear .

be fond of ~을 좋아하다   niece 조카(여자)   do well at school 학교성적이 좋다   cure 치료하다   rarely 드물게

다음을 같은 문장으로 바꿀 때 다음 중 알맞은 관계대명사를 모두 골라 보자.

1 He is the barber that I am fond of.
= He is the barber of (that, who, (whom), which) I am fond.

2 These are the earrings that you are looking for.
= These are the earrings for (that, who, whom, which) you are looking.

3 Is this the bed that the baby sleeps on?
= Is this the bed (who, whom, which) the baby sleeps on?

4 We need a place that we will take a rest in.
= We need a place (who, whom, which) we will take a rest in.

5 This is the day that they parted on.
= This is the day on (that, who, whom, which) they parted.

6 The lady who he told the story to is his aunt.
= The lady to (that, who, whom, which) he told the story is his aunt.

7 They bought a couch that they would sit on.
= They bought a couch (who, whom, which) they would sit on.

8 I need a knife that I will cut the steak with.
= I need a knife with (that, who, whom, which) I will cut the steak.

9 Here is a patient that we should take care of.
= Here is a patient (who, whom, which) we should take care of.

10 She is the teacher that I'd like to talk with.
= She is the teacher with (that, who, whom, which) I'd like to talk.

fond 좋아하는   part 헤어지다

A 기본 TEST

주어진 문장을 같은 뜻의 문장으로 만들어 보자.

1 Tom is his brother <u>whom he plays soccer with</u>.

= Tom is his brother | *who he plays soccer with* | .

= Tom is his brother | *that he plays soccer with* | .

= Tom is his brother | *with whom he plays soccer* | .

2 That is the swing <u>which we played on</u>.

= That is the swing _____ .

= That is the swing _____ .

3 She is the lady <u>whom I told you about</u>.

= She is the lady _____ .

= She is the lady _____ .

= She is the lady _____ .

4 It is the hat <u>that she paid 20 dollars for</u>.

= It is the hat _____ .

= It is the hat _____ .

---

swing 그네   pay (paid-paid) 지불하다

다음 영어를 우리말로 옮겨 보자.

1 This is what I bought yesterday.

이것이 　*내가 어제 산 것*　 이다.

2 Those are the things that he wants.

저것들은 　　　　　　　　　　　　　　이다.

3 She can buy what she likes.

그녀는 　　　　　　　　　　　　　　 살 수 있다.

4 The letter that the mailman delivered has a good news.

　　　　　　　　　　　　 기쁜 소식을 가지고 있다.

5 What I need is a picture book.

　　　　　　　　　　　　 그림책이다.

6 They can't believe what they saw.

그들은 　　　　　　　　　　　　 믿을 수 없다.

7 What is important is to do your best.

　　　　　　　　　　　　 너의 최선을 다하는 것이다.

8 The paper-boat that she made is very nice.

　　　　　　　　　　　　 매우 멋지다.

9 Show me what you have in your bag.

　　　　　　　　　　　　 나에게 보여줘.

10 That is the necklace that mom is looking for.

저것이 　　　　　　　　　　　　 이다.

delivery 배달하다　　picture book 그림책　　look for ~를 찾다

C 기본 TEST

다음 that과 what 중에서 알맞은 것을 골라 보자.

1 This is the thing ((that), what) I lost.

This is (that, (what)) I lost.

2 These are (that, what) she collected.

These are the things (that, what) she collected.

3 This is (that, what) he made.

This is the thing (that, what) he made.

4 The meal (that, what) the chef cooks is delicious.

(That, What) the chef cooks is delicious.

5 Do you understand (that, what) he said?

Do you think (that, what) she is rude?

6 Everybody knows (that, what) he is a liar.

Nobody knows (that, what) he is.

7 (That, What) he left for Paris is true.

(That, What) he left in the bus is his paper.

8 The river (that, what) they swam in is the Han-river.

(That, What) Jane is wearing is a life-vest.

---

collect 모으다   what he is 그의 직업이 무엇이지   leave 떠나다/ 놓고 내리다   life-vest 구명조끼

that, what 중에서 알맞은 것을 골라 써 넣어 보자.

1 This is the meat ___that___ I burned.

2 _____ David reads are comic books.

3 The park _____ we played in is over there.

4 It is the big fish _____ I missed 1 hour ago.

5 This toy is _____ children like to play with.

6 _____ he got driver's licence is false.

7 This bike is _____ his sister rode yesterday.

8 _____ Tom wants is a notebook PC.

9 Look at my sweater _____ shrank in the dryer.

10 I can't understand _____ he says.

burn 태우다   false 거짓인, 가짜인   shrink(shrink-shrank) 오그라들다   dryer 건조기

UNIT 3 관계부사

관계부사는 관계대명사처럼 문장을 연결하는 접속사 역할을 하며 자신이 이끄는 절에서 부사 역할을 한다. '관계부사 = 전치사 + 관계대명사' 이다.

where : 선행사가 장소를 나타낼 때

관계부사 where는 장소를 나타내는 명사를 선행사로 가지며 'in, at, on + which' 대신 사용한다.

ex. This is **the house**.+ I was born in **the house**.

= This is the house **which** I was born **in**.
  <small>관계대명사</small>

= This is the house **in which** I was born.
  <small>전치사 + 관계대명사</small>

= This is the house **where** I was born. 이곳이 내가 태어난 집이다.
  <small>관계부사 (in + which)</small>

when : 선행사가 시간을 나타낼 때

관계부사 when은 시간을 나타내는 명사를 선행사로 취하며 'in, at, on + which' 대신 사용한다.

ex. I remember **the day**. + I first met him **on the day**.

= I remember the day **which** I first met him **on**.

= I remember the day **on which** I first met him.

= I remember the day **when** I first met him. 나는 내가 처음 그를 만났던 날을 기억하고 있다.

Tip! 실제로는 대개의 경우 전치사를 관계대명사 앞에 두는 경우보다 전치사를 문장 뒤에 두는 경우를 사용하며 전치사를 관계대명사 앞에 두는 경우에 관계부사를 이용한다고 생각하면 된다.

◆ why : 선행사가 이유를 나타낼 때

관계부사 why는 이유를 나타내는 명사를 선행사로 가지며 'for + which' 대신 사용한다.

ex. He knows **the reason**. + She is late for **the reason**.

= He knows the reason **which** she is late **for**.

= He knows the reason **for which** she is late.

= He knows the reason **why** she is late. 그는 그녀가 늦은 이유를 알고 있다.

◆ how : 선행사가 방법을 나타낼 때

관계부사 how는 방법을 나타내는 명사를 선행사로 가지며 'in + which' 대신 사용한다. 단, the way how는 사용하지 않고 the way that을 사용하거나 또는 하나를 생략하여 the way 나 how 둘 중의 하나만을 쓴다.

ex. We don't know **the way**. + He made it in **the way**.

= We don't know **the way which** he made it **in**.

= We don't know **the way in which** he made it.

= We don't know **the way that** he made it. 우리는 그가 그것을 만든 방법을 알지 못한다.

= We don't know **the way** he made it.

= We don't know **how** he made it.

= ~~We don't know the way how he made it.~~

선행사에 따른 관계부사

	선행사	전치사 + 관계대명사	관계부사
장소	the place...	in, at, on+ which	where
시간	the time...	in, at, on+ which	when
이유	the reason	for which	why
방법	the way	in which	(how)

A 기초 TEST

다음 두 문장에서 같은 단어를 찾아 ○표시를 하고, 빈칸에 알맞은 말을 써 넣어 보자.

1 This is (the hotel). + I stayed at (the hotel).

= This is the hotel   *which*   I stayed   *at*   .

= This is the hotel   *at*   *which*   I stayed.

= This is the hotel   *where*   I stayed.

2 I remember the year. + The accident happened in the year.

= I remember the year   the accident happened   .

= I remember the year   the accident happened.

= I remember the year   the accident happened.

3 That is the reason. + She hurries for the reason.

= That is the reason   she hurries   .

= That is the reason   she hurries.

= That is the reason   she hurries.

4 I know the way. + He solved the problem in the way.

= I know the way   he solved the problem   .

= I know the way   he solved the problem.

= I know the way   he solved the problem.

= I know   he solved the problem.

= I know   he solved the problem.

---

accident 사고   happen 발생하다   hurry 서두르다   reason 이유

정답 및 해설 p.15

다음 두 문장에서 같은 단어를 찾아 ○표시를 하고, 빈칸에 알맞은 말을 써 넣어 보자.

1 (The day) was very cold. + They married on (the day).

= The day ___which___ they married ___on___ was very cold.

= The day ___on___ ___which___ they married was very cold.

= The day ___when___ they married was very cold.

2 The country is Korea. + We live in the country.

= The country _____ we live _____ is Korea .

= The country _____ _____ we live is Korea.

= The country _____ we live is Korea.

3 The way is simple. + The airplane flies in the way.

= The way _____ the airplane flies _____ is simple.

= The way _____ _____ the airplane flies is simple.

= The way _____ the airplane flies is simple.

4 The reason is not clear. + She called on me for the reason.

= The reason _____ she called on me _____ is not clear.

= The reason _____ _____ she called on me is not clear.

= The reason _____ she called on me is not clear.

simple 단순한   call on 방문하다

다음 ( ) 안에서 알맞은 관계부사를 골라 보자.

1 This is the hospital ((where), when) she is.

2 Today is the day (where, when) he left Tokyo.

3 Do you know the reason (when, why) she got angry?

4 I forgot the way (how, that) I should get to the shop.

5 Here is the library (why, where) I study.

6 The way (that, how) the ship is built is difficult.

7 The time (where, when) she goes to bed is 11;00 p.m.

8 Drinking water is the reason (how, why) Brian is healthy.

9 This is the day (why, when) I perform with my friends.

10 This grass is the place (where, why) children play soccer.

11 Is this the reason (why, where) we should take a picture?

12 He knows the way (how, that) he can see Jenny.

13 There is a spot on the mountain (where, when) I used to rest.

14 Is this the time (where, when) doctors feel bored?

15 Who knows the reason (when, why) she falls in love with him?

Tokyo 도쿄   difficult 어려운   perform 공연하다   grass 풀, 풀밭   spot 지점   fall in love 사랑에 빠지다

B 기본 TEST

정답 및 해설 p.15

다음 빈칸에 알맞은 관계부사를 써 넣어 보자.

1 The office   *where*   she works is not far from here.

2 I didn't remember the day   I last met him.

3 This is the reason   I am happy.

4 She doesn't know   she should withdraw cash from ATM.

5 This is the month   Paul was born.

6 Here is a restaurant   they cook fish well.

7 I don't know the reason   Kate looks sad.

8 That is the elementary school   we went.

9 Nobody knows   the baby climbed up the table.

10 I need a chair   I can sit.

---

withdraw 인출하다   cash 현금   ATM 현금자동인출기   elementary school 초등학교

다음 두 문장을 관계부사를 이용하여 한 문장으로 바꿔 보자.

1 I remember the year. + The dog died in the year.

= I remember *the year when the dog died*.

2 This is the park. + We play soccer in the park.

= This is _____.

3 He needs a sofa. + He will sit on a sofa.

= He needs _____.

4 They forgot the time. +They must leave at that time.

= They forgot _____.

5 Is hunger the reason? + The baby cried for the reason.

= Is hunger _____?

6 The pool isn't deep. + Children swim in the pool.

= _____ isn't deep.

7 Nobody knows the place. + He hides in the place.

= Nobody knows _____.

8 The way is simple. + He turns on the vacuum in the way.

= _____ is simple.

9 The reason is clear. + She is sick for the reason.

= _____ is clear.

10 Can you see the building? + He works in the building.

= Can you see _____?

---

hunger 배고픔   season 계절

01 빈칸에 알맞은 말을 고르시오.

> This is the hotel _____ Jenny stayed last year.

① at which
② with which
③ of which
④ at that
⑤ of that

02 다음 중 어법상 틀린 것을 고르시오.

① This is the city where Tom was born.
② This is the month when Jane was born.
③ This is the way how Susan studies English.
④ This is the reason why Bill called her.
⑤ This is the playground where we play baseball.

03 다음 밑줄 친 부분의 쓰임이 나머지와 다른 하나는?

① What you said is not true.
② Kate asked him what he was trying to do.
③ Mike doesn't know what your name is.
④ I'll not tell her what I am.
⑤ What do you want to be ?

04 빈칸에 공통으로 들어갈 말로 알맞은 것을 고르시오.

> _____ is important is to do your best.
> This is _____ he has been looking for.

① that
② which
③ whom
④ who
⑤ what

05 다음 우리말에 맞게 주어진 말을 배열하시오.

여기에 이 서류가 들어 있었던 서랍이 있어요.
(this, paper, in, was, which)

→ Here is the drawer _____

_____

06 밑줄 친 부분 중에서 어색한 것을 고르시오.

Do you know the man ① with ② who I share the room? That man is my roommate ③ whose name is Tom. Tom is very kind. Tom is a good cook. I think ④ that he is the best roommate. ⑤ 없음

07 다음 두 문장이 같은 뜻이 되도록 빈칸을 채우시오.

He bought a bike, and it had a small basket.
→ He bought a bike, _____ had a small basket.

[08–09] 다음 두 문장을 아래와 같이 바꿔 쓸 때, 관계대명사를 사용하여 빈칸을 채우시오.

Susan will enter the university. Her sister graduated from the university.

08 Susan will enter the university _____ her sister graduated from.

09 Susan will enter the university from _____ her sister graduated.

10 다음 밑줄 친 부분이 잘못 쓰인 것은?

① This is the classroom in which we had a class.
② She is the girl who likes a pink dress.
③ Tom keeps the cat which Susan gave to him.
④ He needs a friend with who he will travel.
⑤ Mary lives in the house which has two doors.

11 다음 문장에서 어법상 어색한 부분을 고치시오.

> This is the blue house in that they live.

_____ → _____

12 다음 중 어법상 어색한 것 둘을 고르시오.

① This is the town which I was born in.
② This is the town in which I was born.
③ This is the town where I was born.
④ This is the town where I was born in.
⑤ This is the town in that I was born.

13 다음 ✓로 표시된 곳의 생략된 말을 고르시오.

> Do you know the name of the actor ✓ acting the farmer?

① which is
② who is
③ whose is
④ what is
⑤ whom is

14 다음 밑줄 친 ⓐ~ⓔ 중 생략 가능한 것은?

> ⓐ Tony and Jason ⓑ live in ⓒ a green house ⓓ that was ⓔ built in the 1900s.

15 빈칸에 들어갈 알맞은 관계대명사를 고르시오.

> I couldn't believe _____ he said.

① that
② which
③ whom
④ who
⑤ what

16 다음 밑줄 친 부분 중 어법상 바른 것을 고르시오.

① My father drives the car which was made 20 years ago.
② The idea what is used in this plan is nice.
③ Kate has two sons, that are doctors.
④ This is the house which I live.
⑤ He is the boy which wants to see you.

[17–18] 다음 대화를 읽고 물음에 답하시오.

> *Nancy* : I'm full. I have potato chips,
>   __ⓐ__ are very delicious. Do
>   you want my potato chips?
> *Derek* : No thanks, I'm full, too.
> *Nancy* : Well, I'll just throw these out.
> *Derek* : Wait, ⓑ I know the boy and his
>   dog. They are walking together.
>   The boy loves potato chips.
>   You can give them to him.
> *Nancy* : Wait a moment while I offer my
>   chips to him.
> *Derek* : Okay.

17 밑줄 친 ⓐ에 들어갈 알맞은 관계대명사를 고르시오.

     ① what
     ② who
     ③ which
     ④ that
     ⑤ whose

18 밑줄 친 ⓑ를 한 문장으로 연결할 때 알맞은 관계대명사를 써 넣으시오.

     → I know the boy and his dog
        _____ are walking together.

[19–20] 다음 글을 읽고 물음에 답하시오.

> There is a school dance tonight. Linda is
> looking for a pretty dress to wear. There
> are many dresses at the mall to choose
> from.
> Linda's best friend, __ⓐ__ has very
> good style, is helping her choose. Linda
> wants to buy the dress which fits her
> best. She ends up buying a very cute,
> blue dress for the dance.

19 밑줄 친 ⓐ에 들어갈 관계대명사를 쓰시오.

     → _____

20 빈칸에 알맞은 관계대명사를 쓰시오.

> The blue dress _____ Linda
> bought is very cute.

01 다음 중 밑줄 친 that과 바꿔 쓸 수 있는 관계대명사를 고르시오.

> The Eiffel Tower <u>that</u> was built in 1889 is famous worldwide.

worldwide 세계적으로

① which
② who
③ whom
④ of which
⑤ 생략 가능

02 다음 밑줄 친 부분에 알맞은 관계대명사를 고르시오.

> Did you see a man and his dog _____ were running in the park?

① who
② which
③ that
④ whom
⑤ 생략 가능

03 밑줄 친 선행사 중 주로 that을 사용하는 선행사가 아닌 것은?

① She is <u>the only friend</u> that cares about me.
② He is <u>the very actor</u> that everyone loves.
③ This is <u>the longest bridge</u> that I have ever seen.
④ She is <u>a famous poet</u> that many people like.
⑤ He is <u>the last soldier</u> that survived from the war.

04 다음 밑줄 친 부분을 that으로 바꿔 쓸 수 없는 것을 모두 고르시오. (2개)

① He is the man <u>who</u> Jane likes.
② It is the cake <u>which</u> was baked this morning.
③ I have a sister <u>whom</u> wants to be a painter.
④ This is the house of <u>which</u> the walls are painted white.
⑤ He loves a girl <u>whose</u> eyes are round and pretty.

05 다음 문장을 우리말로 바르게 옮긴 것은?

> The woman playing the violin is Maria.

① Maria는 바이올린을 연주하고 있다.
② 바이올린을 연주하고 있는 여자는 Maria이다.
③ Maria는 바이올린을 즐겨 연주한다.
④ Maria는 다른 여성과 함께 바이올린을 연주하고 있다.
⑤ Maria는 바이올린을 연주하였다.

06 다음 중 생략할 수 있는 것을 고르시오.

> ① This ② is the camera ③ which
> ④ I ⑤ bought yesterday.

07 다음 문장에서 생략할 수 있는 부분에 -표 하시오.

> He can read a book which is written in French.

08 다음 두 문장의 뜻이 같도록 빈칸을 채우시오.

> He drank wine, which was made in Chile. = He drank wine, _____ was made in Chile.

09 다음 문맥에 맞는 것에 O표하시오.

> She has two dresses (which/ ,which) are red.
> 그녀는 빨간색인 드레스 2개를 가지고 있다.
> (그녀는 드레스가 2개 이상일 수 있다.)

[10~11] 다음 빈칸에 들어갈 말로 알맞은 것을 고르시오.

10
> I want a friend _____ I can talk.

① with
② with which
③ with that
④ with who
⑤ with whom

11

> This is the bakery _____ Hannah works.

① when
② why
③ which
④ where
⑤ how

12 다음 ( ) 안의 단어가 들어갈 알맞은 위치를 고르시오.

> She ① needs a boyfriend ② that ③ she feels ④ comfortable ⑤. (with)

comfortable 편안한

13 다음 두 문장의 뜻이 같도록 빈칸에 들어갈 알맞은 것을 고르시오.

> I bought the things that I wanted.
> = I bought _____ I wanted.

① them
② in which
③ which
④ what
⑤ that

[14–15] 다음 글을 읽고 물음에 답하시오.

> ⓐ I have a sister. She got into a college. She left home and went to the United States. The night before she left, I cried. She asked me ⓑ _____ I was crying. I told her that I was too sad to say goodbye to her. She promised me to come home on summer vacation.

14 밑줄 친 ⓐ를 관계대명사를 이용하여 한 문장으로 바꾸시오.

→ _____.

15 ⓑ에 들어갈 알맞은 관계부사를 고르시오.

① how
② when
③ where
④ why
⑤ that

16 다음 중 밑줄 친 that과 바꿔 쓸 수 있는 관계대명사를 고르시오.

> Wright Brothers <u>that</u> invented the first airplanes are very respectable.

respectable 존경할 만한

① which
② whom
③ whose
④ of whom
⑤ who

17 다음 두 문장의 뜻이 같도록 빈칸을 올바르게 채우시오.

> He has a wife, who is a famous lawyer. = He has a wife, _____ _____ is a famous lawyer.

18 문맥에 알맞는 관계부사에 O표 하시오.

> I remember the day (where / why / when) I first met him.

19 다음 두 문장의 뜻이 같도록 알맞은 것을 고르시오.

> He wishes to know the reason _____ she is angry.
> = He wishes to know the reason why she is angry.

① of which
② for which
③ at which
④ on which
⑤ in which

20 다음 중 어법상 틀린 것을 고르시오.

① This is the city where I met him first.
② This is the month when my sister was born.
③ This is the way how Susan studied Korean.
④ This is the reason why she called you.
⑤ This is the gym where we practice boxing.

Chapter 6

시제의 일치와 화법

UNIT 1

시제의 일치

시제의 일치란?
시제란 '때'를 나타내는 말이며, 주절과 종속절로 이루어진 문장에서 주절의 동사 시제에 따라 종속절의 동사 시제를 맞추는 것을 시제의 일치라고 한다.

1 주절과 종속절

한 문장이 두 개 이상의 절로 이루어져 있을 때, 중심이 되는 절을 주절, 그리고 거기에 딸린 절을 종속절이라고 한다.

ex. I think (that) he is honest. 나는 그가 정직하다고 생각한다
　　　주절　　　　종속절

2 시제의 일치

주절의 동사가 현재일 때 종속절의 동사 시제는 제한이 없다.

ex. I think that he is honest. 나는 그가 정직하다고 생각한다.
　　　현재　　　　　현재

　　　I think that he was honest. 나는 그가 정직했다고 생각한다.
　　　현재　　　　　　과거

　　　I think that he will be honest. 나는 그가 정직해질 것이라고 생각한다.
　　　현재　　　　　　미래

주절의 동사가 과거일 때 종속절의 동사 시제는 과거 또는 과거 완료가 된다.

ex. I thought that she was wise. 나는 그녀가 현명하다고 생각했다.
　　　과거　　　　　　　과거

　　　I thought that she had been wise. 나는 그녀가 현명했었다고 생각했다.
　　　과거　　　　　　　　과거완료

　　　~~I thought that she is wise.~~

3 시제의 일치의 예외

주절의 시제와 상관없이 종속절의 시제가 변하지 않는 경우를 말한다.

현재시제만 사용하는 경우

ⓐ 현재의 사실, 습관을 나타낼 때

〈현재사실〉 *ex.* She **said** that she **goes** to middle school. 그녀는 그녀가 중학교에 다닌다고 말했다.
　　　　　　　　　　　　　　　　 현재

〈현재습관〉 *ex.* He **said** that he **exercises** every day. 그는 그가 매일 운동을 한다고 말했다.
　　　　　　　　　　　　　 현재

ⓑ 불변의 진리를 나타낼 때

ex. He **says** that 2 plus 3 **is** 5. 그가 2 더하기 3은 5라고 말한다.
　　　　　　　　　　　 현재

He **said** that 2 plus 3 **is** 5. 그가 2 더하기 3은 5라고 말했다.
　　　　　　　　　　 현재

과거시제만 사용하는 경우

역사적 사실을 나타낼 때

ex. People **say** that Korean War **broke** out in 1950. 사람들은 한국 전쟁이 1950년에 일어났다고 말한다.
　　　　　　　　　　　　　　　　　 과거

시제일치

주절	종속절
현재	모든 시제 가능
과거	과거, 과거 완료

다음 중 알맞은 말을 골라 보자.

1 I didn't know that he (comes, came) to the party.

2 He said that 3 plus 5 (is, was) 8. (불변의 진리)

3 She told him that she (is, had been) in Paris since 2003.

4 It is said that July (comes, came) before August.

5 Jim told me that he (buys, bought) a cap yesterday.

6 I learned the moon (moves, moved) around the earth.

7 They said that it (is, was) cold last winter.

8 Daniel found that the oranges (tastes, tasted) sour.

9 She learned that China (is, was) larger than Japan.

10 He thought that it (will, would) be foggy the next morning.

11 I (wash, washed) my hands before meal these days. (현재 습관)

12 He said that he (will work, works) for a bank. (현재 사실)

13 We know that the sun (rose, rises) in the east.

14 He says that Picasso (dies, died) in 1973. (역사적 사실)

15 He realized that summer in Beijing (is, was) very hot. (현재 사실)

August 8월   die 죽다   realize 깨닫다   Beijing 베이징, 북경

주어진 동사를 우리말에 알맞게 바꿔서 빈칸에 써 넣어 보자.

1 She   *told*   that she   *had eaten*   breakfast at 8. (tell, eat)

그녀는 8시에 아침을 먹었다고 말했다.

2 Everyone _____ that he _____ the exam. (believe, pass)

모든 사람이 그가 그 시험을 통과할 것이라고 믿는다.

3 She _____ that 7 minus 3 _____ 4. (say, be)

그녀는 7 빼기 3은 4라고 말했다.

4 He _____ me yesterday that he _____ her 2 years before. (tell, love)

그는 어제 나에게 그가 2년 전에 그녀를 사랑했었다고 말했다.

5 I _____ that winter in N.Y. _____ very cold. (think, be)

나는 뉴욕의 겨울이 매우 춥다고 생각한다.

6 Anne _____ him after she _____ with him. (miss, break up)

Anne은 그녀가 그와 헤어진 후에 그를 그리워한다.

7 I _____ that you _____ late for school. (know, be)

나는 네가 학교에 늦지 않는다는 것을 안다.

8 Grandmom _____ that she _____ lunch at noon. (say, have)

할머니는 정오에 점심식사를 하신다고 말했다. (현재의 습관)

9 I _____ that the sun _____ in the west. (know, set)

나는 태양이 서쪽으로 진다는 것을 알고 있었다.

10 The teacher _____ that Columbus _____ America in 1492.
(say, discover)

선생님은 콜롬버스가 1492년에 미국을 발견했다고 말씀하셨다. (역사적 사실)

---

break up with ~와 헤어지다   **discover** 발견하다

UNIT 2 평서문의 화법

화법이란?
다른 사람의 말을 전달하는 방법을 말한다.

1 종류 : 직접화법과 간접화법이 있다.

직접화법과 간접화법

- **직접 화법** : 인용 부호 " "를 이용해서 말한 내용을 그대로 전달하는 것을 말한다.

  ex. He said, "I am happy." 그는 말했다. "나는 행복하다."라고.

  　　전달문　　　　피전달문

- **간접 화법** : 접속사를 이용해서 전달자의 입장에서 그 뜻을 전달하는 것을 말한다.

  ex. He said that he was happy. 그는 그가 행복했다고 말했다.

  　전달문　접속사　　피전달문

2 직접 화법을 간접 화법으로 바꾸는 법

평서문

아래 사항들을 바꿔 주어야 한다.

직접 화법	간접 화법
say, said	say, said
say to, said to	tell, told
(,)와 (" ")	that
주어, 동사, 목적어, 소유격, 부사(구)...	전달하는 사람의 입장에 맞게 바꾼다

ⓐ say / say to를 say / tell로 바꾸고, ,(comma)와 " "를 that으로 바꿔 준다.

ex. He **says**, "I am busy." → He **says that** he is busy.

ex. He **says to** me, "I am busy." → He **tells** me **that** he is busy.

ⓑ 주어, 동사를 내용에 맞추고, 그에 따른 목적어, 소유격 등도 맞춰 준다.

ex. He says to her, "**I know your** sister."

　　→ He tells her that **he knows her** sister.

ⓒ 동사의 시제를 맞춰 준다.

직접화법 → 간접화법	
전달문	피전달문
현재 → 현재	현재 → 현재
과거 → 과거	현재 → 과거
과거 → 과거	과거 → 과거 완료

ex. He always **says**, "I am busy."　　　→ He always **says** that he **is** busy.
　　　　　현재　　　현재　　　　　　　　　　　　　현재　　　　　　현재
　　그는　항상 "나는 바쁘다"고 말한다.　　　　그는　항상 그가 바쁘다고 말한다.

ex. He **said**, "I am busy."　　　　→ He **said** that he **was** busy.
　　　　과거　　　현재　　　　　　　　　　과거　　　　　　과거
　　그는 " 나는 바쁘다"고 말했다.　　　　그는 그가 바빴다고 말했다.

ex. He **said**, "I was busy."　　　→ He **said** that he **had been** busy.
　　　　과거　　　과거　　　　　　　　　과거　　　　　　과거완료
　　그는 " 나는 바빴다"고 말했다.　　　그는 그가 바빴었다고 말했다.

ⓓ 피전달문이 과거 또는 과거완료 로 바뀐 경우, 부사(구)를 바꿔 준다.

직접 화법	간접 화법	직접 화법	간접 화법
now	then	today	that day 그 날
here	there	tomorrow	the next day 그 다음 날
this	that	yesterday	the day before 그 전 날
~ago (~전에)	~before (~전에)	next week	the next week 그 다음 주

ex. She said, "I'm tired **now**." 그녀는 "지금 피곤하다'고 말했다.
　　　　　　　　　　　　현재

　　→ She said that she was tired **then**. 그녀는 그때 피곤했다고 말했다.
　　　　　　　　　　　　　　　과거

다음 두 문장의 뜻이 같도록 ( ) 안에서 알맞은 말을 골라 보자.

1 He says to me, "I am a mechanic."
   = He (tells, told) me that (she, he) (is, was) a mechanic.

2 She said, "I am going shopping."
   = She (says, said) that (she, I) (is, was) going shopping.

3 The coach says, "Jane can make a good shot."
   = The coach (says, said) that (he, Jane) (can, could) make a good shot.

4 The hostess said to Linda, "He is married to Kelly."
   = The hostess (told, said) Linda that he (was, is) married to Kelly.

5 Jane said, "I am very angry ."
   = Jane (said, told) that (she, I) (is, was) very angry.

6 His uncle said to us, "I will play tennis."
   = His uncle (told, said to) us that (I, he) (would, will) play tennis.

7 He says to me, "Your house is wonderful."
   = He (tells, says to) me that (my, your) house (is, was) wonderful.

8 He said to the actress, "You are very talented."
   = He (said to, told) the actress that (you, she) (is, was) very talented.

9 My brother said to mom, "I have a headache today."
   = My brother (tells, told) mom that (he, I) (has, had) a headache that day.

10 My sister said to me, "I am getting too fat."
    = My sister (said, told) me that (I, she) (was, is) getting too fat.

---

mechanic 정비사   coach 코치   shot 찌르기, 치기   hostess 여주인   marry 결혼하다
actress 여배우   talented 재능이 있는   headache 두통   get fat 뚱뚱해지다

다음 두 문장의 뜻이 같도록 빈칸에 알맞은 말을 써 보자.

1 Tom always says, "I am tired."

= Tom always ___*says*___ that ___*he is*___ tired.

2 Jack said to me, "You are smart."

= Jack _____ me that _____ smart.

3 He said, "My stomach hurts."

= He _____ that _____ .

4 Brian says to me, "You look great."

= Brian _____ me that _____ great.

5 She said to him, "I have homework to do."

= She _____ him that _____ homework to do.

6 I say to her, "I need a receipt."

= I _____ her that _____ a receipt.

7 The soccer player said, " He makes a foul."

= The soccer player _____ that _____ a foul.

8 He said, "I am running in the marathon."

= He _____ that _____ in the marathon.

9 Sarah says to Ricky, "I am not going to the dance."

= Sarah _____ Ricky that _____ to the dance.

10 Mom said to me, "I ironed the skirt."

= Mom _____ me that _____ the skirt.

---

receipt 영수증　　**soccer player** 축구 선수　　**foul** 반칙　　**marathon** 마라톤　　**iron** 다림질하다

다음 두 문장의 뜻이 같도록 ( ) 안에서 알맞은 말을 골라 보자.

1 He says to me, "She will need your help."
= He tells me that (I, she) will need (his, my) help.

2 She says to us, "I am your new teacher."
= She tells us that (I, she) is (her, our) new teacher.

3 Jake said to us, "I help her always."
= Jake told us that (he, I) helped (her, him) always.

4 I say to her, "You can see my dog at the park."
= I tell her that (she, you) can see (her, your, my) dog at the park.

5 She said to her boyfriend, "Your hair smells good."
= She told her boyfriend that (her, your, his) hair smelt good.

6 He said to me, "I want to go with you."
= He told me that (you, he) wanted to go with (him, me).

7 Tom says to her, "You have something in your hair."
= Tom tells her that (she, he) has something in (her, our) hair.

8 My neighbor said, "I am watering my lawn."
= My neighbor said that (I, he) was watering (his, my) lawn.

9 They say to his sister, "We will buy a doll for you."
= They tell his sister that (we, they) will buy a doll for (him, her).

10 He says to Linda, "I will grab your keys for you."
= He tells Linda that (he, she) will grab (my, her) keys for (her, me).

---

lawn 잔디   **neighbor** 이웃 사람   **grab** 움켜쥐다   **key** 열쇠

다음 두 문장의 뜻이 같도록 빈칸에 알맞은 말을 써 넣어 보자.

1 The boy said to her, "Your car is very nice."

= The boy told her that _her_ car was very nice.

2 She says to him, "You are my best friend."

= She tells him that _____ is _____ best friend.

3 My sister said to Jim, "I drove your car."

= My sister told Jim that _____ had driven _____ car.

4 My uncle says to him, "She can cut your hair."

= My uncle tells him that _____ can cut _____ hair.

5 The mailman says to me, "Your package is at the post office."

= The mailman tells me that _____ package is at the post office.

6 They say to her, "We will take care of your fish."

= They tell her that they will take care of _____ fish.

7 Dad said to the waitress, "I am not satisfied with your service."

= Dad told the waitress that _____ was not satisfied with _____ service.

8 Billy says to his mom, "School is very fun for me."

= Billy tells his mom that _____ is very fun for _____.

9 I say to the chef, "Your cooking is very delicious."

I tell the chef that _____ cooking is very delicious.

10 He said to the mother, "Your son is well-behaved."

= He told the mother that _____ son was well-behaved.

---

mailman 우체부　　**package** 소포　　**waitress** 웨이트리스(여종업원)　　**satisfy** 만족시키다
service 봉사, 서비스　　**well-behaved** 예의 바른

다음 두 문장의 뜻이 같도록 빈칸에 알맞은 말을 골라 보자.

1 He said to me, "I am busy now."

= He told me that he was busy (now, (then)).

2 She said to us, "Tom is coming here".

= She told us that Tom was coming (that, there).

3 I said to her, "I love this pen".

= I told her that I loved (that, there) pen.

4 Jane said to me, "Susan left for London 3 days ago".

= Jane told me that Susan had left for London 3 days (next, before).

5 Brian said to her, "You look nice today".

= Brian told her that she looked nice (this day, that day) .

6 Uncle said to me, "It snowed here yesterday".

= Uncle told me that It had snowed (then, there) (the day before, the before day).

7 She said to him, "I'll call you tomorrow".

= She told him that she would call him (the next day, the day next).

8 He says to us, "I am tired now".

= He tells us that he is tired (now, then).

9 Dad said to mom, "I had lunch 30 minutes ago".

= Dad told mom that he had had lunch 30 minutes (before, after).

10 He said to us, "I will be back next week".

= He told us that he would be back (the next week, the week next).

D 기본 TEST

정답 및 해설 **p.18**

다음 두 문장의 뜻이 같도록 빈칸에 알맞은 말을 써 넣어 보자.

1 She said to me, "You look tired today".

= She told me that I looked tired _____ *that day* _____.

2 He said to her, "I was busy yesterday".

= He told her that he had been busy _____.

3 Tom said to me, "I am at home now".

= Tom told me that he was at home _____.

4 Jane said to him, "Susan is with me here".

= Jane told him that Susan was with her _____.

5 He said to us, "She arrived in Seoul 2 hours ago".

= He told us that she had arrived in Seoul _____.

6 They said, "It will rain tomorrow".

= They said that It would rain _____.

7 The kid said, "I want this toy".

= The kid said that he wanted _____ toy.

8 I said to him, "She isn't here now".

= I told him that she wasn't _____ _____.

9 She says to us, "I am busy now".

= She tells us that she is busy _____.

10 He said to me, "I will return to Korea next month".

= He told me that he would return to Korea _____.

Chapter 6 157

다음 문장을 간접 화법으로 바꿔 써 보자.

1 She says, "I am interested in the video game."

= She ⟨*says that she is interested*⟩ in the video game.

2 He said, "I am tired."

= He _____ tired.

3 Sarah says, "Tom is very hard-working."

= Sarah _____ very hard-working.

4 They said to the teacher, "We want to have a class outside."

= They _____ to have a class outside.

5 Bill said to the cashier, "I need some change."

= Bill _____ some change.

6 He said, "She surprises me."

= He _____ him.

7 My mom says to my brother, "It is your new bicycle."

= My mom _____ new bicycle.

8 Jane said to Luke, "I am going on vacation."

= Jane _____ on vacation.

9 The little girl says to the fire-fighter, "You are my hero."

= The little girl _____ hero.

10 The mailman said to me, "I have no mail for you today."

= The mailman _____ .

---

hard-working 열심히 일하는   have a class outside 야외수업을 하다   cashier 계산원
surprise 놀라게 하다   go on vacation 휴가가다   hero 영웅

실력 TEST

정답 및 해설 **p.18**

다음 문장을 간접화법으로 바꾸어 써 보자.

1 Tim said to her, "You can swim very well."

= Tim *told her that she could swim* very well.

2 Nancy said to him, "You are very rude."

= Nancy ___ very rude.

3 Tom said to his mom, "I am at school."

= Tom ___ at school.

4 He said, "I can't smell anything because of my cold."

= He ___ because of his cold.

5 I said to my brother, "I am looking for your car in the parking lot."

= I ___ in the parking lot.

6 My sister says, "I will get a bonus from work."

= My sister ___ a bonus from work.

7 The coach says to him, "You need a little more practice."

= The coach ___ a little more practice.

8 My mom says to me, "You have to go to the academy."

= My mom ___ to the academy.

9 She said, "I visit my parents every Sunday."

= She ___ every Sunday.

10 My teacher said to us, " You have to study harder."

= My teacher ___ harder.

parking lot 주차장   academy 학원

Chapter 6 159

UNIT 3 의문문의 화법

1 의문사가 없는 의문문

아래 사항들을 바꿔 주어야 한다.

직접 화법	간접 화법
say, say to	ask
(,) 와 (" ")	whether/if~
어순	whether/if + 주어 + 동사
주어, 동사, 목적어, 소유격, 부사(구)...	전달하는 사람의 입장에 맞게 바꾼다.

ex. He said to me, "Are you free?" 그는 나에게 말했다. '너는 한가하니?' 라고.

   → He **asked** me **whether I was** free. 그는 나에게 내가 한가한지 아닌지 물었다.
                주어 + 동사

   = He **asked** me **if I was** free.
             주어 + 동사

2 의문사가 있는 의문문

아래 사항들을 바꿔 주어야 한다.

직접 화법	간접 화법
say, say to	ask
(,) 와 (" ")	없앤다
어순	의문사 (구) + 주어 + 동사
주어, 동사, 목적어, 소유격, 부사(구)...	전달하는 사람의 입장에 맞게 바꾼다.

ex. He said to me, "What do you want?"

   → He **asked** me <u>what</u> I wanted. 그는 나에게 내가 무엇을 원하는지 물었다.
           의문사 + 주어 + 동사

   She said to him, "How old are you?"

   → She **asked** him <u>how old</u> he was. 그녀는 그에게 몇 살인지를 물었다.
            의문사구 + 주어 + 동사

다음 두 문장의 뜻이 같도록 ( ) 안에서 알맞은 말을 골라 보자. (두 개 가능)

1 I said to him, "What do you need?"

= I (told, (asked)) him ((what), if, whether) ((he needed), needed he).

2 She said to him, "Are you hungry?"

= She (told, asked) him (whether, that, if) (he was, was he) hungry.

3 They said to me, "Why are you so nervous?"

= They (told, asked) me (if, why, whether) (I was, was I) so nervous.

4 He said to his teacher, "I will not be in class on Monday."

= He (asked, told) his teacher (if, that, whether) he (won't, wouldn't) be in class on Monday.

5 She said to me, "How do you go to school?"

= She (asked, told) me (if, how, that) (went I, I went) to school.

6 I said to him, "Do you like her?"

= I (told, asked) him (whether, if, why) (he likes, he liked) her.

7 He says to us, "Where do you live?"

= He (asked, asks) us (whether, where, if) (do we live, we live).

8 Jane said to me, "Can you help me?"

= Jane (said, asked) me (if, when, whether) (could I, I could) help her.

9 Paul says to him, "Are you my real friend?"

= Paul (tells, asks) him (that, who, if) (he is, is he) his real friend.

10 We said to the boss, "What is wrong with the plan?"

= We (asked, told) the boss (if, whether, what) (is wrong, was wrong) with the plan.

---

problem 문제   **nervous** 신경질적인   **wrong** 잘못된   **plan** 계획

A 기본 TEST

다음 두 문장의 뜻이 같도록 빈칸에 알맞은 말을 써 보자.

1 We said to Ann, "Where do you get sugar?"

= We _asked_ Ann _where she got_ sugar.

2 The man says to us, "Do you have enough money to pay for this?"

= The man _____ us _____ enough money to pay for this.

3 Frank said to Sally, "When are you free?"

= Frank _____ Sally _____ free.

4 They say to me, "Are you ill?"

= They _____ me _____ ill.

5 My dad said to her, "How much does the shirt cost?"

= My dad _____ her _____ .

6 She said to you, "What does he want for his birthday?"

= She _____ you _____ for his birthday.

7 Hannah said to the musician, "Your music is very touching."

= Hannah _____ the musician _____ very touching."

8 I said to him, "Do you like the scenery?"

= I _____ him _____ the scenery.

9 Rick said to him, "You didn't come to my lecture."

= Rick _____ him _____ to his lecture.

10 The teacher says to the student, "Do you understand this?"

= The teacher _____ the student _____ this.

---

lecture 강의   ill 병든   cost 비용이 든다   musician 음악가   touching 감동적인   scenery 풍경

다음 두 문장의 뜻이 같도록 빈칸에 알맞은 말을 써 보자.

1 They said to Linda, "What are you doing today?"

= They ___*asked Linda*___ ___*what she was doing that day*___ .

2 Tony said to Sarah, "Do you want a pen?"

= Tony ___ ___ .

3 I say to her, "When will he go to church?"

= I ___ ___ .

4 He said to my brother, "How long does it take to your school?"

= He ___ ___ .

5 Derek says to her, "Are you in trouble?"

= Derek ___ ___ .

6 I said to my mother, "Where are we going on a picnic?"

= I ___ ___ .

7 She said to me, "What will you wear for Halloween?"

= She ___ ___ .

8 They say to her, "What are you interested in?"

= They ___ ___ .

9 My music teacher said to me, "Why don't you practice?'

= My music teacher ___ ___ .

10 She said to the cab driver, "Can you drop me off here?"

= She ___ ___ .

---

cab driver 택시 기사   drop off 내려주다   trouble 문제   Halloween 핼러윈

UNIT 4 명령문의 화법

명령문

아래 사항들을 바꿔 주어야 한다.

직접 화법	간접 화법
say, say to	tell (order, ask, advise)
(,)와 (" ")	to
주어, 동사, 목적어, 소유격, 부사(구)...	전달하는 사람의 입장에 맞게 바꾼다.

ex. The king said to his helper, "Come close to me."

→ The king **told** (**ordered**) his helper **to** come close to **him**.

그 왕은 그의 신하에게 가까이 오라고 말했다 (명령했다).

My mother said to me, "Study hard."

→ My mother **told** (**advised**) me **to** study hard.

나의 어머니는 나에게 열심히 공부하라고 말했다 (충고했다).

부정 명령문은 to 앞에 **not**만 붙이면 된다.

ex. Tom said to me, "Don't go now."

→ Tom told me **not to** go then. Tom은 그 때 나에게 가지 말라고 말했다.

Tip! 명령문의 내용에 따라 say to는 tell 이외에 order, ask, advise 중에서 적절한 것으로 바꿀 수 있으며 2개 이상 가능할 수 있다.

Tip! **ask**의 2가지 해석

① 의문문의 간접화법 에서는 '묻다, 물어보다' 로 해석한다.

ex. He said to me, "Are you free?"

→ He **asked** me whether I was free (or not).   그는 나에게 내가 한가한지 아닌지 물었다.

② 명령문의 간접화법 에서는 '부탁하다, 요청하다' 로 해석한다.

ex. My sister said to me, "Help me."

→ My sister **asked** me to help her. 나의 여동생은 나에게 그녀를 도와달라고 부탁했다.

A 기초 TEST

정답 및 해설 **p.19**

다음 두 문장의 뜻이 같도록 (   ) 안에서 알맞은 말을 골라 보자. (두 개 가능)

1 My sister said to me, "Help me."

= My sister (asked, ordered) me to help her.

2 The general said to his soldiers, "Follow me."

= The general (ordered, advised) his soldiers (to follow, follow) (him, me).

3 He said to me, "Go to your room."

= He (told, ordered) me (that go, to go) to (my, your) room.

4 The king said to his helper, "Cut it in two."

= The king (ordered, advised) his helper (to cut, cut) it in two.

5 His mom said to his son, "Eat slowly."

= His mom (told, advised) him (eat, to eat) slowly.

6 My friend said to me, "Get some exercise."

= My friend (ordered, advised) me (to get, get) some exercise.

7 She said to him, "Make your bed."

= She (told, asked) him (that make, to make) (his, your) bed.

8 I said to him, "Wash my car."

= I (told, ordered) him (wash, to wash)(his, my) car.

9 He said to us, "Study harder."

= He (told, advised) us (that study, to study) harder.

10 Sam said to the clerk, "Show me another."

= Sam (told, asked) the clerk (to show, that show) (me, him) another.

---

general 장군   **helper** 신하, 조수   **clerk** 점원   **another** 또다른

다음 두 문장의 뜻이 같도록 문장을 완성해 보자.

1 My mom said to me, "Wake up."

= My mom *told me to wake up* .

2 I said to my brother, "Pick up the phone."

= I .

3 The teacher said to John, "Go back to your seat."

= The teacher .

4 My dad said to us, "Get in the car."

= My dad .

5 She said to me, "I have no money."

= She .

6 He said to me, "Cover me with the blanket."

= He .

7 The shopkeeper said to me, "You are a size 4."

= The shopkeeper .

8 I said to my sister, "Look under the bed."

= I .

9 He said to her, "Be diligent."

= He .

10 Tom said to her, "It is my birthday."

= Tom .

blanket 담요

B 기본 TEST

정답 및 해설 p.19, 20

주어진 단어를 알맞게 나열하여 문장을 완성해 보자.

1 He *told Linda not to keep* the banana in the refrigerator.
(not, Linda, to, keep, told)

2 I _____ her question.
(them, to, not, answer, advised)

3 Frank _____ the microwave oven.
(to, asked, not, me, turn off)

4 Eric _____ the door.
(close, not, to, told, me)

5 The teacher _____ a pen instead of a pencil.
(use, ordered, us, to, not)

우리말과 같은 뜻이 되도록 빈칸에 알맞은 말을 넣어 문장을 완성해 보자

1 My mom *told me not to buy* milk at this supermarket. (buy)
나의 엄마는 나에게 이 슈퍼마켓에서 우유를 사지 말라고 말씀하셨다.

2 She _____ the baby alone. (leave)
그녀는 우리에게 그 아기를 혼자 두지 말라고 충고했다.

3 My son _____ his sneakers. (clean)
나의 아들은 나에게 그의 운동화를 빨지 말라고 부탁했다.

4 He _____ late again. (be)
그는 그 여자에게 다시는 늦지 말라고 말했다.

5 My teacher _____ in the hallway. (run)
나의 선생님은 그들에게 복도에서 뛰지 말라고 말씀하셨다.

---

microwave oven 전자레인지   **instead of** ~대신에

A 실력 TEST

직접화법을 간접화법으로 바꾸어 보자.

1 She says, "I am lucky."

= She _____ *says that she is lucky* _____ .

2 He said to me, "Are you a cook?"

= He _____ .

3 Timothy said to me, "I need a ride to Hank's house."

= Timothy _____ .

4 The driver said to me, "Where do you want to go?"

= The driver _____ .

5 The teacher said to us, "Be honest."

= The teacher _____ .

6 The boss said to Karen, "Why do you want this job?"

= The boss _____ .

7 The teacher said to the naughty girl, "I will not tolerate this."

= The teacher _____ .

8 Mi-na said to us, "Can I take it?"

= Mi-na _____ .

9 The baker said to Jack, "What kind of cake do you want?"

= The baker _____ .

10 He said to her, "Don't go out at night."

= He _____ .

---

lucky 운이 좋은   job 일, 직업   ride 탈 것   naughty 버릇없는   tolerate 참다

B 실력 TEST

정답 및 해설 **p.20**

간접화법을 직접화법으로 바꾸어 보자.

1 My girlfriend tells Paul that she really enjoys this weather.

= My girlfriend says to Paul, *"I really enjoy this weather."*

2 Tammy asked her where his mom was.

= Tammy said to her,

3 They asked John when he would take a walk.

= They said to John,

4 She ordered Tom to keep an eye on his dog.

= She said to Tom,

5 I told the artist that his artwork was very pleasing to see.

= I said to the artist,

6 He asked me to open the window.

= He said to me,

7 I asked my brother what had made him trip and fall.

= I said to my brother,

8 The policeman ordered his dog to stay there.

= The policeman said to his dog,

9 I asked her whether she could ride a roller-coaster.

= I said to her,

10 The assistant advised her boss to put off the meeting.

= The assistant said to her boss,

---

keep an eye on ~을 지켜보다, 감시하다   **artwork** 예술 작품   **please** 기쁘게 하다   **trip** 걸려 넘어지다
fall 쓰러지다   **roller-coaster** 롤러코스터   **assistant** 조수   **put off** 연기하다

간접화법을 직접화법으로 바꾸어 보자.

1 He tells me that I look better.

= He says to me, *"You look better."*

2 Victor asked me if I could organize the event.

= Victor said to me,

3 They said that she was skinny then.

= They said,

4 Sam asked her to stay with him there.

= Sam said to her,

5 The dentist told Eric that he had to floss everyday.

= The dentist said to Eric,

6 Paul asked him whether he was a barber.

= Paul said to him,

7 He advised us to be patient with our family.

= He said to us,

8 He asked her what she wanted to eat for dinner.

= He said to her,

9 She told us not to worry too much.

= She said to us,

10 He advised me to be satisfied all the time.

= He said to me,

---

organize 기획하다　　floss 치실질하다　　barber 이발사　　patient 참을성 있는　　all the time 항상

01 빈칸에 알맞은 것을 고르시오.

> We know that the sun _____ in the east.

① rise
② rises
③ rose
④ has risen
⑤ is rising

02 우리말을 영어로 옮길 때 not이 들어갈 자리를 고르시오.

> 그 버스 운전기사는 그에게 뛰지 말라고 했다.
> The bus driver ① told ② him ③ to ④ run ⑤.

03 두 문장이 같은 뜻이 되도록, 빈칸에 알맞은 것을 고르시오.

> Dad said to me, "Do your homework."
> = Dad told me _____ .

① I do my homework
② to do your homework
③ I did his homework
④ to do my homework
⑤ to do his homework

04 다음 화법 전환에서 잘못된 것은?

① She said to me, "I will watch the movie tomorrow."
   → She told me that she would watch the movie the next day.
② He said, "I am reading this book."
   → He said that he was reading that book.
③ Mike said to me, "I want to visit my parents."
   → Mike told me that he wanted to visit his parents.
④ Jane said to me, "I know him well."
   → Jane told me that she knows him well.
⑤ John said to me, "I feel happy."
   → John told me that he felt happy.

05 다음 동사의 시제가 바르지 <u>않은</u> 것을 고르시오.

① She says that the war breaks out in 1889.
② He said that 1 plus 4 is 5.
③ Kate said that she always gets up early.
④ Tom said that the book was published last month.
⑤ I know that Jane will go there soon.

break out (전쟁이) 일어나다   publish 출판하다

06 다음을 간접화법으로 바르게 바꾼 것은?

> I said to him, "How tall are you?"

① I asked him how he is tall
② I asked him how you were tall.
③ I asked him how tall he was.
④ I asked him how tall are you
⑤ I asked him how he was tall.

07 다음 빈칸에 들어갈 말로 알맞은 것을 고르시오.

> He said that he _____ a good grade the next time.

① gain
② gains
③ gained
④ will gain
⑤ would gain

gain 얻다   next time 다음 번에

08 밑줄 친 부분 중 어색한 것을 고르시오.

> English class ① started. But our teacher ② didn't come to the classroom. We were ③ noisy. Then, other teacher came by classroom. She ④ told us ⑤ being quiet.

09 빈칸에 알맞은 것은?

> Linda told me that she wanted to go to the school with me the next day.
> →Linda said to me, "I want to go to the school with you _____."

① that day
② yesterday
③ tomorrow
④ today
⑤ this day

10 다음 문장의 화법을 바꿀 때 빈칸에 들어갈 말은?

Jenny said to me, "Is it raining?"
→ Jenny _____ me _____ raining.

① said to, if it was
② told, if it was
③ told, whether it is
④ asked, whether it was
⑤ asked, if it is

11 다음 중 화법 전환이 <u>잘못된</u> 것은?

① She said to me, "Help me."
→ She asked me to help her.
② He said to me, "Who is Tom?"
→ He asked me who Tom was.
③ She said to me, "Read the newspaper."
→ She told me to read the newspaper.
④ He said to me, "Where are you going?"
→ He asked me where I was going.
⑤ She said to us, "Don't touch it."
→ She ordered us to not touch it.

[12–13] 직접 화법을 간접 화법으로 바꿀 때 빈칸을 채우시오.

12

He said to me, "Close the door."
→ He asked me _____ the door.

13

Emily said to me, "Where do you live?"
→ Emily _____ me _____ I _____ .

14 밑줄 친 부분 중 <u>어색한</u> 것을 고르시오.

①The strange traveller ②asked me ③whether he ④can ⑤climb up the mountain.

15 다음 문장의 화법을 바꿀 때 <u>잘못</u> 쓰인 것은?

Nicole said to me, "I like science."
→ Nicole ①told me that ②she ③likes ④science. ⑤없음

[16–17] 다음 대화를 읽고 물음에 답하시오.

> *Mike* : Hey, Charles! (a) <u>Have you seen</u>
> <u>Eric?</u>
> *Charles* : No, why?
> *Mike* : (b) <u>He told me that he wanted to</u>
> <u>meet me in front of the library,</u>
> but he is not there.
> *Charles* : ⓐ <u>Maybe</u> he had to talk to his
> teacher after class. His teacher
> told Eric to ⓑ <u>met</u> her.
> *Mike* : I hoped that we ⓒ <u>could</u> study
> together before the library
> closed.
> *Charles* : Don't worry. If he said he
> ⓓ <u>would</u> meet you there, then
> he will.

16 ⓐ~ⓓ 중 어색한 것을 고르면?

① ⓐ

② ⓑ

③ ⓒ

④ ⓓ

⑤ 없음

17 밑줄 친 (a)를 간접 화법으로 바꿀 때 빈칸을 채우
시오.

→ Mike _____ Charles

_____ he had seen Eric.

18 밑줄 친 (b)를 직접 화법으로 바꾸면?

(b) <u>He told me that he wanted to meet</u>
<u>me in front of the library.</u>

→ He said to me, "_____

_____ in front of the library."

[19–20] 다음 글을 읽고 물음에 답하시오.

> I used to play in this park a long time
> ago. Back then, it was small and very
> old. Now, the playground looks brand
> new. My friend came here yesterday
> and __ ⓐ __ me that it had changed
> a lot. I am glad that the park has
> improved. ⓑ <u>My little brother told me</u>
> <u>to take him to the new playground.</u>

19 밑줄 친 ⓐ에 들어갈 알맞은 단어는?

① asked

② said

③ told

④ advised

⑤ ordered

20 밑줄 친 ⓑ를 직접 화법으로 고치시오.

→ My little brother said to me,

"_____

_____ "

[01-03] 다음을 간접화법으로 올바르게 바꾼 것을 고르시오.

01

> He said, "I am busy."
> → He said that _____ .

① I am busy
② I was busy
③ he is busy
④ he was busy
⑤ he am busy

02

> She said to me, "You look happy."
> → She told me that _____ .

① she looks happy
② I look happy
③ she looked happy
④ I looked happy
⑤ she had looked happy

03

> My mom told, "I stand right here."
> → My mom told that she _____ .

① stands right here
② stood right here
③ stood right there
④ had stood right here
⑤ had stood right there

04 다음 중 피전달문의 시제가 바뀔 때 부사구의 변화가 적절하게 짝지어지지 <u>않은</u> 것을 고르시오.

① now - then
② ago - before
③ this - that
④ yesterday - the before day
⑤ tomorrow - the next day

05 다음 문장의 틀린 부분을 찾아 바르게 고쳐보시오.

> He told us that 4 plus 3 was 7.
> 그는 우리에게 4 더하기 3은 7이라고 말했다.

_____ → _____

06 다음에서 밑줄 친 부분이 <u>어색한</u> 것을 고르시오.

① She told that she <u>will be</u> a college student.
② Copernicus found out that the Earth <u>moves</u> around the sun.
③ He says that he <u>swims</u> everyday.
④ I taught children that 1 plus 1 <u>is</u> 2.
⑤ People know that the World War II <u>broke</u> out in 1939.

07 다음 두 문장의 뜻이 같도록 빈칸을 알맞게 채워보시오.

> She said to me, "How tall are you?"
> → She asked me how tall _____
> _____ .

08 다음 빈칸에 들어갈 말이 바르게 짝지어진 것을 고르시오.

> He said to me, "Are you hungry?"
> → He _____ me _____
> I was angry.

① asked - if
② asked - that
③ asked - how
④ said - whether
⑤ said - which

09 다음 빈칸에 적절한 말을 고르시오.(답 2개)

> The king said to the prince, "Bring a sword."
> → The king _____ the prince to bring a sword.

beg 구걸하다

① begged
② told
③ ordered
④ advised
⑤ wanted

10 다음 괄호 안의 단어가 들어갈 알맞은 자리를 고르시오.

> (not)
> Sam ① asked ② me ③ to ④ leave ⑤ the company.
> Sam은 나에게 그 회사를 그만두지 말라고 부탁했다.

11 다음 빈칸에 알맞은 말을 쓰시오.

> My roommate said to me, "Did you turn off the light?"
> → My roommate asked me if I _____ off the light.

12 다음 빈칸에 들어갈 알맞은 것을 고르시오.

> Linda said to me, "I want to watch the movie today."
> = Linda told me that she wanted to watch the movie _____ .

① the day before tomorrow
② the next day
③ the day
④ that day
⑤ this day

13 다음 밑줄 친 단어와 바꿔 쓸 수 있는 단어를 고르시오.

> The lady asked me whether it was raining.

① that
② if
③ which
④ when
⑤ to

[14–15] 다음 대화를 읽고 물음에 답하시오.

> *Sonia* : Hi, Eric! ⓐ Do you know where the pharmacy is?
> *Eric* : Yes, I do. It is across the school gate.
> *Sonia* : Thanks.
> *Eric* : Why do you look for a pharmacy? Are you sick?
> *Sonia* : No, ⓑ my sister told me that she wanted to meet me there.

pharmacy 약국

14 밑줄 친 ⓐ를 간접 화법으로 바꿀 때 빈칸을 채우시오.

→ Sonia asked Eric _____ he knew where the pharmacy _____.

15 밑줄 친 ⓑ를 직접 화법으로 바꾸면?

→ My sister said to me,
"_____."

16 다음 두 문장의 뜻이 같도록 알맞은 것을 고르시오.

> He said to me, "What do you want?"
> → He asked me _____.

① what he wants
② what he wanted
③ what I want
④ what I wanted
⑤ what want I

17 빈칸에 알맞은 것은?

> I said to my parents, "I hope to
> spend time together tomorrow.
> = I told my parents that I hoped to
>   spend time together _____.

① yesterday
② today
③ tomorrow
④ next week
⑤ the next day

18 빈칸에 알맞은 것을 고르시오.

> People learned that the earth
> _____ round.

① is
② was
③ were
④ had been
⑤ being

19 두 문장이 같은 뜻이 되도록, 빈칸에 알맞은 것을 고르시오.

> Dad said to me, "Focus on your studying."
> = Dad told me _____.

① I focus on my studying
② to focus on your studying
③ I did focus on my studying
④ to focus on my studying
⑤ to focus on his studying

20 다음 빈칸에 들어갈 말로 알맞은 것을 고르시오.

> I promise that I _____ the test
> next time.

① have passed
② passes
③ passed
④ had passed
⑤ will pass

Chapter 7

가정법

UNIT 1 가정법 과거/가정법 과거완료

가정법이란?
사실과 다르거나, 반대되는 일을 가정, 소망하는 것을 말한다.

1 가정법 과거

🟦 **현재 사실과 반대되는 일을 나타낼 때 사용한다.**

If절의 동사는 과거형을 사용하지만 우리말 해석은 현재로 한다. 주절도 현재로 해석한다.

If	~	were 과거동사	, ~	would could should might	+	동사원형....,
		~라면,		~할텐데		

ex. **If I had money, I could buy the car.** (만일) 내가 돈이 있다면, 나는 그 차를 살 수 있을 텐데.

= **As I don't have money, I can't buy the car.** 내가 돈이 없기 때문에, 나는 그 차를 살수 없다.

Tip! if절의 be동사는 인칭에 상관없이 were를 쓴다.
ex. If he **were** diligent, he could finish the work today. 만일 그가 부지런하다면, 그는 오늘 그 일을 끝마칠 수 있을 텐데.

2 가정법 과거 완료

🟦 **과거 사실과 반대되는 일을 나타낼 때 사용한다.**

If절의 동사는 과거완료형을 사용하지만 우리말 해석은 과거로 한다. 주절도 과거로 해석한다.

If	~	had been had p.p	, ~	would could should might	+	have p.p...
		~이었다면,		~했을텐데		

ex. If I **had had** money, I **could have bought** the car.

(만일) 내가 돈이 있었더라면, 나는 그 차를 살 수 있었을 텐데.

= As I didn't have money, I couldn't buy the car.

내가 돈이 없었기 때문에, 나는 그 차를 살수 없었다.

* if절의 be동사는 had been을 사용한다.

ex. If he **had been** diligent, he could have finished the work. 만일 그가 부지런했다면, 그는 그 일을 끝마칠 수 있었을 텐데.

3 would, could, should, might의 사용

🔷 가정법과거와 가정법과거완료에서 모두 결과절(주절)의 would, could, should, might의 사용이 가능하며 그 의미는 조금 차이가 있다.

would	바램	~할 텐데
could	능력	~할 수 있을 텐데
should	확신	틀림없이 ~할 텐데
might	추측	~할지도 모를 텐데

ex. If she had money, she **would** buy the ring.

만일 그녀가 돈이 있다면, 그녀는 그 반지를 살 텐데.

ex. If she had money, she **could** buy the ring.

만일 그녀가 돈이 있다면, 그녀는 그 반지를 살 수 있을 텐데.

ex. If she had money, she **should** buy the ring.

만일 그녀가 돈이 있다면, 그녀는 그 반지를 틀림없이 살 텐데.

ex. If she had money, she **might** buy the ring.

만일 그녀가 돈이 있다면, 그녀는 그 반지를 살지도 모를 텐데.

	if절 (조건절)	결과절 (주절)
가정법 과거	were 과거동사	would / could / should / might + 동사원형
	~라면	~할 텐데/ ~할 수 있을 텐데/ 틀림없이 ~할 텐데/ ~할지도 모를 텐데
가정법 과거완료	had been had p.p	would / could / should / might + have p.p
	~이었다면	~했을 텐데/ ~할 수 있었을 텐데/ 틀림없이 ~했을 텐데/ ~했을지도 모를 텐데

기초 TEST

A 기초 TEST

주어진 가정법의 동사시제를 고르고 우리말을 골라 보자.

1 If ~ knew ~, ~.   (과거, 과거완료)   (알고 있다면, 알고 있었다면)
  If ~ had knew ~, ~.   (과거, 과거완료)   (알고 있다면 , 알고 있었다면)

2 If ~ were ~, ~.   (과거, 과거완료)   (이라면, 이었다면)
  If ~ had been ~, ~.   (과거, 과거완료)   (이라면, 이었다면)

3 If ~ had had ~, ~.   (과거, 과거완료)   (가지고 있다면, 가지고 있었다면)
  If ~ had ~, ~.   (과거, 과거완료)   (가지고 있다면, 가지고 있었다면)

주어진 가정법의 동사시제를 고르고 우리말을 골라 보자.

1 If ~, ~ could sleep ~.   (과거, 과거완료)   (잘 수 있을 텐데, 잘 수 있었을 텐데)
  If ~, ~ could have slept ~.   (과거, 과거완료)   (잘 수 있을 텐데, 잘 수 있었을 텐데)

2 If ~, ~ would have stayed~.   (과거, 과거완료)   (머무를 텐데, 머물렀을 텐데)
  If ~, ~ would stay ~.   (과거, 과거완료)   (머무를 텐데, 머물렀을 텐데)

3 If ~, ~ should tell ~.   (과거, 과거완료)   틀림없이 (말할 텐데, 말했을 텐데)
  If ~, ~ should have told ~.   (과거, 과거완료)   틀림없이 (말할 텐데, 말했을 텐데)

4 If ~, ~ might have been healthy ~. (과거, 과거완료) (건강할지도, 건강했을지도) 모를텐데
  If ~, ~ might be healthy ~.   (과거, 과거완료)   (건강할지도, 건강했을지도) 모를텐데

5 If ~, ~ would not meet ~   (과거, 과거완료)   (만나지 않을 텐데, 만나지 않았을 텐데)
  If ~, ~ would not have met~.   (과거, 과거완료)   (만나지 않을 텐데, 만나지 않았을 텐데)

기초 TEST

정답 및 해설 p.21

주어진 가정법의 동사시제에 맞는 우리말을 골라 보자.

1 If ~, ~might eat ~. (먹을 텐데, 먹을지도 모를 텐데)

If ~, ~could eat ~. (먹을 수 있을 텐데, 먹을지도 모를 텐데)

If ~, ~ should eat ~. (먹을 수 있을 텐데, 틀림없이 먹을 텐데)

If ~, ~would eat ~. (틀림없이 먹을 텐데, 먹을 텐데)

2 If ~, ~would be happy ~. (행복할 텐데, 행복할 수 있을 텐데)

If ~, ~should be happy ~. (행복할지도 모를 텐데, 틀림없이 행복할 텐데)

If ~, ~could be happy ~. (틀림없이 행복할 텐데, 행복할 수 있을 텐데)

If ~, ~might be happy ~. (행복할지도 모를 텐데, 행복할 수 있을 텐데)

주어진 가정법의 동사시제에 맞는 우리말을 골라 보자.

1 If ~, ~might have stayed ~ (머무를 지도 모를 텐데, 머물렀을지도 모를 텐데)

2 If ~, ~could work ~. (일할 수 있을 텐데, 일할 수 있었을 텐데)

3 If ~, ~ should be surprised (틀림없이 놀랄 텐데, 틀림없이 놀랐을 텐데)

4 If ~, ~ would be happy (행복 할 텐데, 행복했을 텐데)

5 If ~, ~ could have paid (지불할 수 있을 텐데, 지불할 수 있었을 텐데)

6 If ~, ~ might be clean (깨끗할지도 모를 텐데, 깨끗했을지도 모를 텐데)

7 If ~, ~should have gone ~. (틀림없이 갔을 텐데, 틀림없이 갈 텐데)

8 If ~, ~ would have gotten (얻을 텐데, 얻었을 텐데)

동사에 ○표 하고 보기에서 가정법의 종류를 고른 후 우리말로 옮겨 보자.

| 보기 |
1. 가정법 과거   2. 가정법 과거 완료

1 If the coat ⟨were⟩ thinner, she ⟨might get⟩ a cold.   *1*

만일 그 코트가   더 얇다면   , 그녀는 감기에   걸릴지도 모를텐데   .

If the coat had been thinner, she might have gotten a cold

만일 그 코트가   , 그녀는 감기에

2 If I had an eraser, I could lend it to him.

만일 내가 지우개를   , 나는 그것을 그에게

If I had had an eraser, I could have lent it to him.

만일 내가 지우개를   , 나는 그것을 그에게

3 If Jim were wise, he would accept it.

만일 Jim이   , 그는 그것을

If Jim had been wise, he would have accepted it.

만일 Jim이   , 그는 그것을

4 If she had known the answer, she should have raised her hand.

만일 그녀가 그 답을   , 그녀는 틀림없이 손을

If she knew the answer, she should raise her hand.

만일 그녀가 그 답을   , 그녀는 틀림없이 손을

---

thin 얇은   get a cold 감기에 걸리다   lend 빌려주다   quit 끊다   accept 받아들이다   raise 들다, 들어올리다

동사에 ○표 하고 보기에서 가정법의 종류를 고른 후 우리말로 옮겨 보자.

| 보기 |
1. 가정법 과거   2. 가정법 과거 완료

1 If I (were) not busy, I (would go) to the party.

만일 내가 　바쁘지 않다면　, 나는 그 파티에 　갈 텐데　.　　1

2 If the zoo had been open, I could have seen the animals.

만일 동물원이 　　　　, 나는 동물들을 　　　　.

3 If she had not been sick, she might have gotten a better grade.

만일 그녀가 　　　　, 그녀는 더 좋은 점수를 　　　　.

4 If Jason had broken the window, he should have run away.

만일 Jason이 창문을 　　　　, 그는 　　　　.

5 If he were diligent, they would hire him.

만일 그가 　　　　, 그들은 그를 　　　　.

6 If Jake had the key, he should start the car.

만일 Jake가 열쇠를 　　　　, 그는 틀림없이 차를 　　　　.

7 If dad had been there, he should have blamed me.

만일 아빠가 거기에 　　　　, 그는 나를 　　　　.

8 If the tiger had come out, people would have been in danger.

만일 호랑이가 밖으로 　　　　, 사람들은 위험에 　　　　.

---

run away 도망가다　　**hire** 고용하다　　**start the car** 차를 출발시키다　　**blame** 나무라다　　**be in danger** 위험에 처하다

A 기본 TEST

우리말에 알맞은 것을 골라 보자.

1 If Bob (came, had come) home early, he (might meet, might have met) his relatives.
만일 Bob이 일찍 집에 왔다면, 그는 그의 친척들을 만났을 지도 모를 텐데.

2 If I (caught, had caught) the bus, I wouldn't (run, have run) to the subway station.
만일 내가 그 버스를 탔더라면, 나는 지하철역으로 달려가지 않았을 텐데.

3 If I (were, had been) you, I would not (wait, have waited) for him.
만일 내가 너라면, 나는 그를 기다리지 않을 텐데.

4 If Linda (had, had had) more money, she should (go, have gone) shopping.
만일 Linda가 돈을 더 많이 가지고 있다면, 그녀는 틀림없이 쇼핑하러 갈 텐데.

5 If the shoes (were, had been) expensive, he might not (buy, have bought) them.
만일 그 신발이 비쌌다면, 그는 그것을 사지 않았을지도 모를 텐데.

6 If she (knew, had known) what to do, she would not (say, have said) so.
만일 그녀가 무엇을 해야 하는지 알고 있다면, 그녀는 그렇게 말하지 않을 텐데.

7 If she (stayed, had stayed) longer, I could (cook, have cooked) dinner for her.
만일 그녀가 더 오래 머물렀다면, 나는 그녀에게 저녁을 만들어줄 수 있었을 텐데.

8 If he (were not, had not been) tired, he could (play, have played) with his son.
만일 그가 피곤하지 않다면, 그는 그의 아들과 놀 수 있을 텐데.

9 If I (were, had been) free, I would (call, have called) you.
만일 내가 한가했다면, 나는 너에게 전화했을 텐데)

10 If Tom (were, had been) here, he should (help, have helped) us.
만일 Tom이 여기에 있다면, 그는 틀림없이 우리를 도울 텐데.

apologize 사과하다

우리말에 알맞은 것을 골라 보자.

1 If the rain (had come, came) more, my car would (be, have been) clean.

만일 비가 더 왔다면, 나의 차는 깨끗해졌을 텐데.

2 If the blanket (is, were) thicker, I (can, could) sleep better.

만일 담요가 조금 더 두껍다면, 나는 더 잘 잘 수 있을 텐데.

3 If the light (were, had been) brighter, he could (find, have found) his watch easily.

만일 불이 더 밝았다면, 그는 그의 시계를 쉽게 찾을 수 있었을 텐데.

4 If John (were, had been) athletic, he could (have joined, join) a sports team.

만일 John이 몸이 탄탄하다면, 그는 스포츠 팀에 가입할 수 있을 텐데.

5 If you (had decided, decided) to buy the shirt, I might (pay, have paid) for it.

만일 네가 그 셔츠를 사기로 결정했다면, 나는 그것을 지불했을 지도 모를 텐데.

6 If Gary (has, had) a car, he would (pick, picked) me up.

만일 Gary가 차를 가지고 있다면, 그는 나를 픽업할 텐데.

7 If I (left, had left) earlier, I would (boarded, have boarded) the airplane.

만일 내가 더 일찍 떠났다면, 나는 그 비행기에 탑승했을 텐데.

8 If the bag (is, were) ripped, all my notebooks (may fall, might fall) out.

만일 그 가방이 찢어져 있다면, 나의 모든 공책들이 밖으로 떨어질 지도 모를 텐데.

9 If Jenny (warned, had warned) me, I would (stay, have stayed) quiet.

만일 Jenny가 나에게 경고했다면, 나는 조용히 있었을 텐데.

10 If I (had, had had) a ruler, I could (lend, have lent) it to her.

만일 내가 자를 가지고 있었다면, 나는 그녀에게 그것을 빌려줄 수 있었을 텐데.

board (비행기, 배...)에 탑승하다   rip 찢다(찢어지다)

주어진 단어를 알맞은 형태로 바꾸어 빈칸에 써 넣어 보자.

1 If mom *had cooked* the meat more, it would not have been red inside. (cook)

2 If I _____ she, I would not meet him. (be)

3 If Bonny _____ the cat, it would not have been hungry. (feed)

4 If dad _____ me up, I would have been on time. (wake)

5 If my mom _____ a backache, I would give her a massage. (have)

주어진 단어를 알맞은 형태로 바꾸어 빈칸에 써 넣어 보자.

1 If the house alarm had rung, she *would have been* worried. (would, be)

2 If Rick had no money, he _____ unhappy. (would, be)

3 If the book had been boring, Rick _____ reading it. (should, stop)

4 If I knew how to ride a bike, I _____ the club. (could, join)

5 If you had worn that suit, you _____ the ladies. (might, impress)

inside 안에   backache 요통   massage 마사지   suit 정장   impress 감동시키다

D 기본 TEST

정답 및 해설 p.22

주어진 단어를 알맞은 형태로 바꾸어 빈칸에 써 넣어 보자.

1 If he _had caught_ a cold, he should have delayed the departure.(catch)

2 If it _____ last Saturday, we would have skied. (snow)

3 If she _____ everything, she would not be surprised. (know)

4 If the light _____ brighter, he could find his shoes easily. (be)

5 If he _____ to the library with her, he might have studied harder. (go)

주어진 단어를 알맞은 형태로 바꾸어 빈칸에 써 넣어 보자.

1 If I had drunk a lot of water, my skin _should have been_ moist. (should, be)

2 If you had looked at the map, you _____ earlier. (might, arrive)

3 If the game were interesting, Bill _____ playing it. (would, keep)

4 If she had gone to college, she _____ a better job (could, get)

5 If I were mom, I _____ at my children. (wouldn't, nag)

departure 출발   moist 촉촉한   nag at ~에게 잔소리하다

A 실력 TEST

다음 주어진 단어를 이용하여 우리말 뜻에 알맞게 빈칸을 채워 보자.

1 If he _were_ diligent, I _would hire_ him. (be, hire)
만일 그가 부지런하다면, 나는 그를 고용할 텐데.

2 If I _____ you. I _____ harder. (be, work)
만일 내가 너라면, 나는 더 열심히 일할지도 모를 텐데.

3 If he _____ poor, he _____ the house. (be, buy)
만일 그가 가난했었더라면, 그는 그 집을 살 수 없었을 텐데.

4 If I _____ the key, I _____ the car. (have, start)
만일 내가 열쇠가 있었다면, 나는 차를 출발시켰을 텐데.

5 If she _____ rich, she _____ the fur coat. (be, purchase)
만일 그녀가 부유하다면, 그녀는 그 모피코트를 구입할지도 모를 텐데.

6 If I _____ enough time, I _____ them. (have, help)
만일 내가 충분한 시간이 있다면, 나는 그들을 도와줄 텐데.

7 If I _____ you the story, you _____ shocked. (tell, be)
만일 내가 너에게 그 이야기를 말했었더라면, 너는 충격을 받았을 텐데.

8 If it _____ made out of cotton, it _____ very comfortable.
(be, feel)
만일 그것이 면으로 만들어졌다면, 그것은 매우 편한 느낌이 들었을지도 모를 텐데.

9 If the weather _____ nice, they _____ a walk. (be, take)
만일 날씨가 좋다면, 그들은 틀림없이 산책을 할 텐데.

10 If he _____ his seat belt, he _____ his life. (fasten, save)
만일 그가 그의 좌석 벨트를 매었더라면, 그는 그의 생명을 구할 수 있었을 텐데.

---

purchase 구입하다   make out of ~로 만들다   cotton 면   comfortable 편안한   save one's life 생명을 구하다

정답 및 해설 p.23

다음 주어진 단어를 이용하여 우리말 뜻에 알맞게 빈칸을 채워 보자.

1 If Peter _had been_ with you, you _would have been_ safe. (be, be)

Peter가 너와 함께 있었다면, 너는 무사했을 텐데.

2 If I _____ enough time, I _____ you. (have, help)

내가 충분한 시간이 있었다면, 나는 너를 도울 수 있었을 텐데.

3 If the tiger _____ hungry, it _____ the deer. (be, hunt)

만일 그 호랑이가 배가 고프다면, 틀림없이 그 사슴을 사냥할 텐데.

4 If it _____ in June, everybody _____ surprised. (snow, be)

6월에 눈이 왔다면, 모두 놀랐을 텐데.

5 If he _____ a soccer player, he _____ the ball farther.

(be, kick)

그가 축구선수였다면, 그는 공을 더 멀리 찰 수 있었을 텐데.

6 If I _____ you, I _____ in the house. (be, stay)

내가 너라면, 나는 그 집에 머물지 않을 텐데.

7 If I _____ you, I _____ him. (be, invite)

내가 너였다면, 나는 그를 초대했을지도 모를 텐데.

8 If Tom _____ an angel, he _____ me all the time.

(be, protect)

Tom이 천사라면, 틀림없이 나를 항상 보호해 줄 텐데.

9 If you _____ the truth, she _____ you. (tell, forgive)

네가 진실을 말했더라면, 그녀는 너를 용서해 주었을지도 모를텐데.

10 If she _____ your phone number, she _____ you. (know, call)

그녀가 너의 전화번호를 안다면, 그녀는 틀림없이 너에게 전화할 텐데.

---

farther 더 멀리   **kick** 차다   **protect** 보호하다   **truth** 진실   **forgive** 용서하다

UNIT 2

가정법의 직설법 전환

가정법과거와 가정법과거완료는 직설법으로 바꾸어 쓸 수 있다.

 가정법 과거 → 직설법 현재

- **If** 대신 **As**로 바꾸어 준다.
- **If**절의 동사는 '과거형'을 '현재형'으로, 긍정이면 부정으로, 부정이면 긍정으로 바꾸어 준다.
- 주절의 동사는 '**would (should, might)** 동사원형'을 '현재형'으로, 긍정이면 부정으로, 부정이면 긍정으로 바꾸어 준다.

  (단, 주절의 동사가 '**could** 동사원형'일 때는 '**can** 동사원형'으로 바꾸어 준다.)

  〈가정법〉 If she **had** money, she **would buy** the ring.
  만일 그녀가 돈이 있다면, 그녀는 그 반지를 살 텐데.

  〈직설법〉 = As she **doesn't have** money, she **doesn't buy** the ring.
  그녀는 돈이 없으므로, 그녀는 그 반지를 사지 못한다.

 가정법 과거완료 → 직설법 과거

- **If** 대신 **As**로 바꾸어 준다.
- **If**절의 동사는 '과거완료형'을 '과거형'으로, 긍정이면 부정으로, 부정이면 긍정으로 바꾸어 준다.
- 주절의 동사는 '**would (should, might) have P.P**'를 '과거형'으로, 긍정이면 부정으로, 부정이면 긍정으로 바꾸어 준다.

  (단, 주절의 동사가 '**could have P.P**'일 때는 '**could** 동사원형'으로 바꾸어 준다.)

  〈가정법〉 If she **had had** money, she **would have bought** the ring.
  만일 그녀가 돈이 있었다면, 그녀는 그 반지를 샀을 텐데.

  〈직설법〉 = As she **didn't have** money, she **didn't buy** the ring.
  그녀는 돈이 없었으므로, 그녀는 그 반지를 사지 못했다.

A 기초 TEST

정답 및 해설 **p.23**

가정법을 직설법으로 바꿀 때 알맞은 것을 골라 보자.

1 If he were smart, he would not say so.
→ As he (is, (isn't)) smart, he ((says), didn't say) so.

2 If she had been wise, she should have met him.
→ As she (was, wasn't) wise, she (met, didn't meet) him.

3 If I were free, I would go there.
→ As I (am not, wasn't) free, I (don't go, go) there.

4 If Joanna had cried, her eyes would have been red.
→ As Joanna (doesn't cry, didn't cry), her eyes (aren't, weren't) red.

5 If Jimmy were interested in video games, I would take him to the mall.
→ As Jimmy (isn't, wasn't) interested in video games, I (take, don't take) him to
    the mall.

6 If Kelly had put water in the pitcher, it might have been full.
→ As Kelly (doesn't put, didn't put) water in the pitcher, it (was, wasn't) full.

7 If he had enough money, he could buy the bike.
→ As he (doesn't have, didn't have) enough money, he (can't buy, can buy) the bike.

8 If you had practiced the violin for a longer time, you would have performed better.
→ As you (practiced, didn't practice) the violin for a longer time, you (don't, didn't)
    perform better.

9 If you had not opened the treasure chest, you could not have found jewels inside.
→ As you (opened, had opened) the treasure chest, you (could find, couldn't find) jewels
    inside.

10 If Daniel had sent the letter, I would have received it.
→ As Daniel (doesn't, didn't send) the letter, I (doesn't receive, didn't receive) it.

---

score a goal 골을 넣다   **red** 충혈된   **pitcher** 주전자   **full** 꽉 찬   **treasure chest** 보물 상자   **receive** 받다

가정법을 직설법으로 바꿔 써 보자.

1 If he were smart, he would not act like that.

→ As he _is not_ smart, he _acts_ like that.

If he had been smart, he would not have acted like that.

→ As he _was not_ smart, he _acted_ like that.

2 If I had money, I would buy it.

→ As I _____ money, I _____ it

If I had had money, I would have bought it

→ As I _____ money, I _____ it

3 If he were not here, she should be unhappy.

→ As he _____ here, she _____ unhappy.

If he had not been here, she should have been unhappy.

→ As he _____ here, she _____ unhappy.

4 If his eyes had been closed, he could not have seen the bug.

→ As his eyes _____ , he _____ the bug.

If his eyes were closed, he could not see the bug.

→ As his eyes _____ , he _____ the bug.

5 If she knew the fact, she would tell it to me.

→ As she _____ the fact, she _____ it to me.

If she had known the fact, she would have told it to me.

→ As she _____ the fact, she _____ it to me.

bug 벌레

가정법을 직설법으로 바꿀 때 빈칸에 알맞은 말을 써 넣어 보자.

1 If Alex had been good at soccer, he could have scored more.

→ As Alex _wasn't_ good at soccer, he _couldn't score_ more.

2 If Gary had a car, he would pick me up.

→ As Gary ＿＿＿＿＿ a car, he ＿＿＿＿＿ me up.

3 If I had been wise, I would not have accepted his offer.

→ As I ＿＿＿＿＿ wise, I ＿＿＿＿＿ his offer.

4 If I were tall, I would be happier.

→ As I ＿＿＿＿＿ tall, I ＿＿＿＿＿ happier.

5 If you were a child, mom would care you more.

→ As you ＿＿＿＿＿ a child, mom ＿＿＿＿＿ you more.

6 If the coat had been thicker, I would not have gotten a cold.

→ As the coat ＿＿＿＿＿ thicker, I ＿＿＿＿＿ a cold.

7 If she had offered him a cup of coffee, he would have drunken it.

→ As she ＿＿＿＿＿ him a cup of coffee, he ＿＿＿＿＿ it.

8 If he had enough time, he could help us.

→ As he ＿＿＿＿＿ enough time, he ＿＿＿＿＿ us.

9 If I knew the way to get there, I would guide you.

→ As I ＿＿＿＿＿ the way to get there, I ＿＿＿＿＿ you.

10 If the cough had not gotten worse, I would have gone to school.

→ As the cough ＿＿＿＿＿ worse, I ＿＿＿＿＿ to school.

---

score 득점하다　　accept 받아들이다　　offer 제안　　cough 기침　　get worse 나빠지다

UNIT 3

다른 형태의 가정법
I wish ~, ... as if ~

1 I wish + 가정법

I wish	주어 + be동사 (were) 주어 + 일반동사 (과거형)	~라면 좋을 텐데
I wish	주어 + had P.P	~이었더라면 좋을 텐데

ex. I wish I **were** a violinist. 내가 바이올린 연주자라면 좋을 텐데.

I wish I **had been** a violinist. 내가 바이올린 연주자였더라면 좋을 텐데.

직설법으로 바꿀 때는 I wish~를 I am sorry~로 바꾸어 주고 나머지는 앞에서 공부한대로 동일하게 적용한다.

ex. I wish I **were** a violinist.

= I **am sorry** I **am not** a violinist. 내가 바이올린 연주자가 아니라서 유감이다.

ex. I wish I **had been** a violinist.

= I **am sorry** I **was not** a violinist. 내가 바이올린 연주자가 아니었던 게 유감이다.

Tip! I am sorry는 '미안하다'가 아니라 '~라서 유감이다'로 해석한다.

2 동사의 현재형 + as if (= as though) + 가정법

과거	as if 주어 + were 동사의 과거	마치 ~인 것처럼
과거완료	as if 주어 + had P.P	마치 ~이었던 것처럼

ex. He talks **as if** he **were** a teacher. 그는 마치 그가 선생님인 것처럼 말한다.

He talks **as if** he **had been** a teacher. 그는 마치 그가 선생님이었던 것처럼 말한다.

직설법으로 바꿀 때는 ...as if~를 In fact~로 바꾸어 주고 나머지는 앞에서 공부한대로 동일하게 적용한다.

ex. He talks **as if** he **were** a teacher.

→ **In fact**, he **is** not a teacher. 사실, 그는 선생님이 아니다.

ex. He talks **as if** he **had been** a teacher.

→ **In fact**, he **was** not a teacher. 사실, 그는 선생님이 아니었다.

다음 영어 문장을 우리말로 옮겨 보자.

1 I wish I were taller.

내가   *키가 더 크다면*   좋을 텐데.

I wish I had been taller.

내가   좋을 텐데.

2 I wish she had been wise.

그녀가   좋을 텐데.

I wish she were wise.

그녀가   좋을 텐데.

3 I wish I had a foreign friend.

나는 외국인 친구가 한 명   좋을 텐데.

I wish I had had a foreign friend.

나는 외국인 친구가 한 명   좋을 텐데.

다음 영어 문장을 우리말로 옮겨 보자.

1 He walks as if he were a headmaster.

그는   *마치 (그가) 교장선생님인 것처럼*   걷는다.

He walks as if he had been a headmaster.

그는   걷는다.

2 Joe speaks as if he had known everything.

Joe는   말한다.

Joe speaks as if he knew everything.

Joe는   말한다.

3 His voice sounds as if he had had a very bad cold.

그의 목소리는   들린다.

His voice sounds as if he had a very bad cold.

그의 목소리는   들린다.

다음 중 우리말에 알맞은 것을 골라 보자.

1 I wish I (took, had taken) a look into the man's luggage.

내가 그 남자의 수하물을 조사했다면 좋을 텐데.

2 I wish I (could buy, could have bought) a curved television.

내가 곡면 TV를 살 수 있으면 좋을 텐데.

3 That bag looks as if it (were, had been) very luxury.

그 가방은 마치 매우 고급스러운 것처럼 보인다.

4 Sam treats me as if I (were, had been) a child.

Sam은 내가 마치 어린아이인 것처럼 대한다.

5 I wish we (got off, had got off) work earlier.

우리가 좀 더 일찍 퇴근했다면 좋을 텐데.

6 Her dog barks at Laura as if she (were, had been) a stranger.

그녀의 개는 마치 그녀가 낯선 사람인것처럼 Laura에게 짖는다.

7 I wish the rugs (were, had been) clean.

그 깔판들이 깨끗하다면 좋을 텐데.

8 I wish I (were, had been) five years older than she.

내가 그녀보다 5살 더 많았다면 좋을 텐데.

9 She acts as though she (knew, had known) what to do.

그녀는 마치 무엇을 할지 아는 것처럼 행동한다.

10 Joe explains as though he (saw, had seen) the scene.

Joe는 마치 그 장면을 보았던 것처럼 설명한다.

---

take a look into ~을 조사하다   curved television 곡면 TV   luxury 호화로운   get off work 퇴근하다

주어진 말을 이용하여 우리말에 알맞게 빈칸을 채워 보자.

1 I wish Jane _had seen_ that movie. (see)

Jane이 그 영화를 보았다면 좋을 텐데.

2 Bill talks as if he _____ it. (experience)

Bill은 마치 그것을 경험했던 것처럼 말한다.

3 I wish I _____ faster than Chris. (be)

내가 Chris보다 더 빠르면 좋을 텐데.

4 I wish dad _____ the wedding day. (miss)

아빠가 결혼기념일을 놓치지 (잊어버리지) 않았으면 좋을 텐데.

5 Chris shops as though he _____ a million bucks. (have)

Chris는 마치 백만 달러가 있는 것처럼 쇼핑한다.

6 Brandon plays as if he _____ free of worries. (be)

Brandon은 마치 걱정없는 것처럼 논다.

7 I wish she _____ better at mathematics. (be)

그녀가 수학을 더 잘하면 좋을 텐데.

8 He talks as though he _____ at the tennis match himself. (be)

그는 마치 그 자신이 테니스 시합을 했던 것처럼 말한다.

---

wedding day 결혼기념일　　**experience** 경험하다　　**a million bucks** 백만 달러　　**free of worries** 걱정이 없는

A 기본 TEST

1 I wish I were prettier.

= I am sorry I (am not, was not) prettier.

2 I wish I had been healthy.

= I am sorry I (am not, was not) healthy.

3 I wish he had not made a mistake.

= I am sorry he (makes, made) a mistake.

4 I wish my house were in good shape.

= I am sorry my house (wasn't, isn't) in good shape.

5 I wish I had felt much warmer at night.

= I am sorry I (don't feel, didn't feel) much warmer at night.

다음 중 알맞은 것을 골라 보자.

1 She walks as if she were a teacher.

→ In fact, she (is not, was not) a teacher.

2 He talks as if he had been a genius.

→ In fact, he (is not, was not) a genius.

3 It sounds as though it were not true.

→ In fact, it (is, was) true.

4 She talks as if the weather had improved.

→ In fact, the weather (didn't improve, had not improved).

5 She laughs as if she had heard the joke.

→ In fact, she (doesn't hear, didn't hear) the joke.

shape 모양, 형태   **genius** 천재   **joke** 농담   **improve** 나아지다

가정법을 직설법으로 바꿔 써 보자.

1 I wish I had not made that error.

→ *I'm sorry I made that error* .

2 They greet as though they liked each other.

→ .

3 I wish he were tall.

→ .

4 Sally speaks as if she had known the actress.

→ .

5 I wish he had not forgotten to put gas in the car.

→ .

6 I wish I had heard what they were saying.

→ .

7 The reporter talks as if Mr. Brown had been hurt.

→ .

8 They walk as though they were soldiers.

→ .

---

error 실수　**great** 인사하다　**reporter** 기자　**hurt** 다치게 하다

( ) 안의 말을 사용하여 우리말에 알맞게 빈칸을 채워 보자.

1 I wish *I had treated* Ben better. (treat)

내가 Ben에게 더 잘 대했더라면 좋을 텐데.

2 He talks _____ his dad. (be)

그는 마치 그가 그의 아빠인 것처럼 말한다.

3 I wish _____ rich enough to travel. (be)

우리가 여행할 만큼 충분히 부자라면 좋을 텐데.

4 I wish _____ a good dog. (keep)

그들이 착한 개를 길렀더라면 좋을 텐데.

5 Tom eats _____ hungry. (be)

Tom은 마치 그가 배고팠던 것처럼 먹는다.

6 Jane talks _____ it. (see)

Jane은 마치 그것을 본 것처럼 말한다.

7 I wish _____ a king. (be)

내가 왕이라면 좋을 텐데.

8 She acts _____ a teacher. (be)

그녀는 마치 그녀가 선생님인 것처럼 행동한다.

9 I wish _____ more popular. (be)

내가 좀 더 인기가 있었다면 좋을 텐데.

10 The mailman behaves _____ me say hello. (hear)

그 우체부는 마치 내가 안부 전하는 것을 못 들은 것처럼 행동한다.

---

treat 대하다   popular 인기 있는   say hello (to) 안부를 전하다

[01~03] 다음 빈칸에 알맞은 것을 고르시오.

01

> If I _____ in his company,
> I would work hard.

① am
② is
③ be
④ were
⑤ have been

02

> If I _____ wings, I would fly
> to England.

① will have
② had had
③ had
④ have
⑤ have been

03

> Tom speaks _____ he had
> never seen her.

① as though
② even if
③ But for
④ if
⑤ unless

04 다음 대화의 빈칸에 알맞은 것을 고르시오.

> *Jane* : I need a bike.
> *Penny* : Me too. _____ ,
>   I would buy such a bike.

① As I were rich
② Though I have much money
③ If I have much money
④ If I had lots of money
⑤ If I will have lots of money

05 다음 문장에서 어색한 부분을 고르시오.

> ① If I ② had sold the car then,
> I ③ would ④ lose a lot of money.
> ⑤ 없음

then 그 때

06 다음 우리말을 영어로 옮긴 것 중 가장 알맞은 것을 고르시오.

> 점심을 먹었으면 좋을 텐데

① I wish I have lunch.
② I wish I had lunch.
③ I wish I had had lunch.
④ I wish I would have lunch.
⑤ I wish I will have lunch.

07 다음 빈칸에 알맞은 말을 고르시오.

> If Joseph _____ on our team,
> we could have won the game.

① has played
② would play
③ will play
④ had played
⑤ have played

08 다음 밑줄 친 부분 중 어법상 어색한 것을 고르시오.

① Mary talks as if she <u>had been</u> there.
② I wish I <u>were</u> rich.
③ He looks as if he <u>knew</u> it.
④ If it <u>rained</u> yesterday, I would have stayed there.
⑤ John would have gotten upset if I <u>had told</u> him the truth.

09 다음 문장과 뜻이 같은 것을 고르시오.

> I am sorry I can't speak English.

① I am pleased to speak English.
② I wish I can speak English.
③ I wish I could speak English.
④ I wish I could have spoken English.
⑤ I wish I could had spoken English.

10 다음 빈칸에 가장 적절한 것을 고르시오.

> If he had a laptop, he _____
> anywhere.

① will work
② could work
③ could have worked
④ worked
⑤ can work

11 다음 중 어법상 바른 문장을 고르시오.

① She looks as if she <u>is</u> sick then.
② If I <u>had</u> a car, I would drive to you.
③ I wish I <u>swim</u> well last year.
④ If it <u>were fine</u> yesterday, we would have gone on a hike.
⑤ If you <u>studied</u> harder, you could have succeeded.

12 다음 문장 중 잘못된 부분을 고르시오.

> ① If James had been ② <u>stupid</u>
> ③ <u>then</u>, he ④ <u>would</u> ⑤ <u>fail</u>.

13 다음 빈칸에 들어갈 알맞은 말로 연결된 것을 고르시오.

> Frances looks as if she had been sick.
> → _____ , Frances _____ sick.

① But for - is
② But for - isn't
③ In fact - was
④ In fact - wasn't
⑤ In fact - had been

14 우리말과 같은 뜻이 되도록 빈칸에 알맞은 말로 바르게 짝지어진 것을 고르시오.

> 만일 크리스티가 학생이었다면, 그녀는 학교에 갔었을 텐데.
> → If Christie _____ a student, she _____ to the school.

① was - would go
② were - would go
③ were - would have gone
④ had been - would have gone
⑤ had been - would go

15 다음 빈칸에 알맞은 것을 고르시오.

> If Daniell had been taller, he _____ a good player.

① will be
② would be
③ would have been
④ would had been
⑤ would not been

16 우리말과 일치하도록 빈칸에 알맞은 말을 고르시오.

> 제리는 그가 그 영화관의 모든 영화를 보았던 것처럼 말한다.
> → Jerry talks as if he _____ all the movies in the theater.

① watch
② have watched
③ had watched
④ would watch
⑤ watched

[17–18] 다음 대화를 읽고 물음에 답하시오.

> *Nancy* : Hey Billy!
>
> *Billy* : Hey Nancy. I didn't see you at school today. Where were you?
>
> *Nancy* : ⓐ In fact, I was sick.
>
> *Billy* : Oh no, are you feeling better?
>
> *Nancy* : Yes, much better. Did I miss anything important at school?
>
> *Billy* : Mrs. Lee said, "If it _____ⓑ_____ last week, we would have gone on the trip."
>
> *Nancy* : I see. Thanks for telling me.
>
> *Billy* : No problem!

in fact 사실은　feel 느끼다　sick 아픈　miss 그리워하다
important 중요한　trip 여행　snow 눈이 내리다

17 밑줄 친 ⓐ와 같은 뜻이 되도록 빈칸에 알맞은 말을 고르시오.

> Nancy speaks _____ she had not been sick.

① as if
② but for
③ that
④ unless
⑤ if

18 밑줄 친 ⓑ에 들어갈 말로 알맞은 것을 고르시오.

① didn't snow
② hasn't snowed
③ snowed
④ has snowed
⑤ had not snowed

[19–20] 다음 글을 읽고 물음에 답하시오.

> Karen goes shopping every weekend. If I _____ⓐ_____ she, I would get tired of going to the mall all the time. However, she loves shopping. She says it relieves her stress and makes her happy. Therefore, she shops as though she _____ⓑ_____ a rich person. If she were actually rich, she ⓒ (buy) more things.

19 밑줄 친 ⓐ와 ⓑ에 공통으로 들어갈 말로 알맞은 것을 고르시오.

① am
② is
③ were
④ isn't
⑤ have been

20 ( ) 안의 동사를 사용하여 밑줄 친 ⓒ에 들어갈 알맞은 말을 완성하시오.

→ should _____

[01–04] 다음 빈칸에 차례대로 알맞은 것을 고르시오.

01

> If I _____ you, I _____ it to him.
> 만일 내가 너라면, 나는 그것을 그에게 말할텐데.

① am – should tell
② am – would tell
③ were – would tell
④ were – will tell
⑤ had been – would tell

02

> If he _____ the fact, he _____ there. 만일 그가 그 사실을 알고 있다면, 그는 거기에 가지 않을 텐데.

① knows – will not go
② knows – would not go
③ knew – will not go
④ knew – would not go
⑤ had known – would not go

03

> If I _____ he, I _____ her.
> 만일 내가 그였더라면, 나는 그녀를 만났을 텐데.

① were – would met
② were – would have met
③ had been – would met
④ was – would have met
⑤ had been – would have met

04

> If she _____ money, she _____ the bag. 만일 그녀가 돈을 가지고 있었다면, 그녀는 틀림없이 그 가방을 샀을 텐데.

① had – should buy
② had – should bought
③ had – should have bought
④ had had – should have bought
⑤ had had – would have bought

[05–06] 다음 문장을 직설법으로 바르게 고친 것을 고르시오.

05

> If I were not busy, I could watch the movie.

① As I am busy, I cannot watch the movie.
② As I am not busy, I can watch the movie.
③ As I am busy, I didn't watch the movie.
④ As I am not busy, I watched the movie.
⑤ As I am busy, I can watch the movie.

06

> If he had had a car, he would have picked me up.

① As he had a car, he picked me up.
② As he had a car, he didn't picked me up.
③ As he doesn't have a car, he didn't pick me up.
④ As he didn't have a car, he didn't pick me up.
⑤ As he didn't have a car, he picked me up.

07 다음 문장을 가정법으로 바르게 고친 것은?

> As I don't have time, I can't go to the party.

① If I do have time, I can go to the party.
② If I had time, I can go to the party.
③ If I had time, I could go to the party.
④ If I have time, I can go to the party.
⑤ If I don't have time, I can go to the party.

08 다음 문장을 바르게 해석한 것을 고르시오.

> If I had money, I could buy the house.

① 만일 내가 돈이 있다면, 그 집을 살 수 있었을 텐데.
② 만일 내가 돈이 있었다면, 그 집을 살 수 있었을 텐데.
③ 만일 내가 돈이 있었다면, 그 집을 살 수 있을 텐데.
④ 만일 내가 돈이 있다면, 그 집을 살 수 있을 텐데.
⑤ 만일 내가 돈이 생긴다면, 그 집을 살 수 있을 텐데.

09 다음 괄호 안의 단어가 들어갈 알맞은 자리를 고르시오.

> (had)
> If ① I ② had time, I ③ would ④ have ⑤ visited my grandparents.

10 다음 괄호 안의 단어를 문맥에 맞게 알맞은 형태로 변형하여 빈칸에 쓰시오.

> If I had been good at cooking,
> I _____ for you.
> (can, cook)
> 만약 내가 요리를 잘했더라면, 너를 위해 요리할 수 있었을 텐데.

11 다음 빈칸에 들어갈 말이 알맞게 짝지어진 것을 고르시오.

> As I didn't have money, I didn't eat lunch. = If I _____ money, I would _____ lunch.

① had - ate
② had - eat
③ had - have eaten
④ had had - eat
⑤ had had - have eaten

12 다음 두 문장의 뜻이 같도록 빈칸을 바르게 채워 보시오.

> I wish I were 20 years old. = I am sorry I _____ 20 years old.

13 다음 빈칸에 차례대로 알맞은 말로 연결된 것을 고르시오.

> He speaks as if he had watched the movie.
> → _____, he _____ the movie.

① In fact - watched
② In fact - will watch
③ In fact - didn't watch
④ Instead - watched
⑤ Instead - will watch

[14–15] 다음 글을 읽고 물음에 답하시오.

> James, my brother, studies mathematics. But, he wants to be a comedian. Sometimes, ⓐ <u>he acts as if he were a comedian.</u> He always makes me laugh.

14 다음 글의 내용과 일치하지 <u>않는</u> 것을 고르시오. .

① James는 수학을 공부한다.
② James는 코미디언이 되고 싶어 한다.
③ James는 날 항상 웃긴다.
④ James는 유명한 코미디언들과 친하다.
⑤ James는 가끔 코미디언처럼 행동한다.

15 ⓐ를 직설법으로 바꾸어 쓸 때 빈칸을 알맞은 말로 채워보시오.

> → In fact, he _____ a comedian.

[16–17] 다음 두 문장의 뜻이 같도록 알맞은 것을 고르시오.

16

> I wish I were a child.
> = I am sorry I _____ a child.

① am
② am not
③ was
④ was not
⑤ had been

17

> I wish I had passed the test.
> = I am sorry I _____ the test.

① have passed
② passed
③ did not pass
④ was not passed
⑤ do not pass

18 다음 우리말을 영어로 옮긴 것 중 가장 알맞은 것을 고르시오.

> 그 샌드위치를 먹지 않았더라면 좋을 텐데.
> (그 샌드위치를 먹었음)

① I wish I don't eat the sandwich.

② I wish I will not eat the sandwich.

③ I wish I didn't eat the sandwich.

④ I wish I have not eaten the sandwich.

⑤ I wish I had not eaten the sandwich.

19 다음 우리말을 영어로 옮긴 것 중 가장 알맞은 것을 고르시오.

> He talks as if he were my brother.
> = _____ , he is not my brother.

① I wish

② Although

③ Though

④ In fact

⑤ To be honest

20 다음은 가정법을 직설법으로 바꾼 것이다. 밑줄 친 문장에서 **틀린** 부분을 찾아 바르게 고치시오.

> She walks as if she had been a fashion model.
> → In fact, she were not a fashion model.

_____ → _____

종합문제

[01-02] 빈칸에 알맞은 말을 고르시오.

01

> I know a boy _____ dad is Mayor.

① who
② whose
③ which
④ that
⑤ what

Mayor 시장

02

> _____ Tom is saying is true.

① Who
② Whose
③ Which
④ That
⑤ What

true 사실인

03 다음 빈칸에 차례대로 알맞은 것을 고르시오.

> This is the house _____ I was born in.
> = This is the house _____ I was born.
> 이곳이 내가 태어난 집이다.

① which - what
② whose - which
③ which - where
④ that - which
⑤ which - what

04 다음 두 문장이 같은 뜻이 되도록 할 때 빈칸에 알맞은 것을 고르시오.

> This is the tallest building in Korea.
> = This is taller than _____ building in Korea.

① any other
② any others
③ all
④ no other
⑤ no others

05 다음 밑줄친 부분 중 생략할 수 **없는** 것을 고르시오.

① Do you know the town in <u>which</u> I live?

② Look at the girls <u>who are</u> playing the violin.

③ She is the woman <u>whom</u> I hate.

④ He is the doctor <u>whom</u> Jane likes.

⑤ This is the book <u>that</u> I wrote.

06 다음 중 옳은 문장을 고르시오.

① Do you know the time which I met you?

② Here is Vancouver which is the most peaceful city in the world.

③ This is the place in that we play.

④ Please show me the thing what you are eating.

⑤ Kate is the first woman which graduated from the school.

graduate 졸업하다

07 다음 문장을 간접 화법으로 바꿀 때 빈칸에 알맞은 말을 고르시오.

> Dad said to me, "Clean your room."
> → Dad told me _____ .

① that I clean your room

② to clean your room

③ to clean my room

④ whether I clean his room

⑤ whether I cleaned your room

08 빈칸에 알맞은 것을 고르시오.

> If Mary had been fatter, she _____ in the car.

① wouldn't have gotten

② wouldn't had gotten

③ wouldn't gotten

④ wouldn't has gotten

⑤ won't get

09 빈칸에 알맞은 말을 고르시오.

> I don't know _____ she will come here.

① whether
② and
③ since
④ before
⑤ what

10 빈칸에 공통으로 알맞은 말을 고르시오.

> · This is the city _____ is famous for art.
> · This is the hospital in _____ the kids are born.

① who
② whose
③ which
④ that
⑤ what

11 다음 두 문장이 같은 뜻이 되도록 할 때 빈칸에 알맞은 것을 고르시오.

> Jane is the wisest girl in the class.
> = _____ in the class is wiser than Jane.

① Any other girl
② Any girl
③ All girls
④ No other girl
⑤ No other girls

12 빈칸에 알맞은 말을 고르시오.

> 내 할아버지는 시간은 화살처럼 날아간다고 말씀하셨다.
> My grandfather said that time _____ like an arrow.

① fly
② flew
③ to fly
④ flies
⑤ flying

like ~처럼   arrow 화살

13 다음 두 문장의 뜻이 같도록 빈칸에 들어갈 알맞은 말을 고르시오.

> The Niagara is the largest waterfall in America.
> = No other waterfall in America is _____ the Niagara.

① the largest of
② as large as
③ as the large
④ the large as
⑤ larger as

waterfall 폭포

14 다음 중 올바른 문장을 고르시오.

① He is the man whose I saw yesterday.
② He likes fish, what he eats everyday.
③ That is the bicycle who I bought two years ago.
④ He is the only friend that I have.
⑤ I know the boy who name is Mike.

15 다음 밑줄 친 부분 대신에 쓸 수 있는 것을 고르시오.

> The hill is the place where I and Jake used to meet.

① of which
② when
③ for which
④ in which
⑤ why

used to ~하곤 했다

16 우리말과 같은 뜻이 되도록 빈칸에 알맞은 말을 쓰시오.

> 나는 피아노를 칠 수 있으면 좋을 텐데.
> I wish I _____ _____ the piano. (play)

[17–20] 빈칸에 가장 알맞은 말을 보기에서 골라 번호를 쓰시오.

| 보기 |
① as soon as   ② every time   ③ so
④ Even though

17 _____ I stay at my uncle's house, I read many books.

18 _____ Mary is poor, she is always happy.

19 He was very busy, _____ he didn't come there.

20 Frances began her work _____ she finished having her lunch.

21 다음 문장에서 밑줄 친 곳의 뜻이 다른 하나를 고르시오.

① As he did his best, he felt great.
② Because he did his best, he felt great.
③ He felt great, because he did his best.
④ He felt great, for he did his best.
⑤ He did his best for 5 years.

[22–23] 다음 대화를 읽고 물음에 답하시오.

Julie : ⓐ Can you come to my house today? My parents went to Busan to see my grandparents.
Sally : I'd like to, but I am busy helping mom with cooking now. If I ⓑ_____ free, I would go to play with you.
(만일 내가 한가하다면, 가서 너와 함께 놀 텐데.)
Julie : I see. You are a good daughter.
Sally : Thanks. I will call you later.

22 밑줄 친 ⓐ를 간접화법으로 바꿀 때 알맞은 말을 빈칸에 채우시오.

Julie asked Sally_____ she could come to Julie's house that day.

23 밑줄 친 ⓑ에 알맞은 것을 고르시오.

① am
② is
③ were
④ are
⑤ can be

[24-25] 다음 글을 읽고 물음에 답하시오.

There is a reason ___ⓐ___ I can't go in swimming pool. I am afraid of water. ___ⓑ___ I don't like swimming. Instead I like to go hiking. When I climb a mountain, I provide fresh air to my body and mind. It makes me active. Therefore, I want to climb a mountain during summer vacation.

be afraid of ~을 두려워하다   instead 그 대신에
provide 제공하다   active 활동적인

24 밑줄 친 ⓐ에 들어갈 알맞은 말을 고르시오.

① why
② who
③ which
④ how
⑤ what

25 밑줄 친 ⓑ에 들어갈 알맞은 말을 고르시오.

① Because
② Why
③ What
④ Therefore
⑤ Though

[01–02] 다음 빈칸에 알맞은 말을 고르시오.

01

> This is <u>one of</u> _____
> in the world.
> 이곳이 세상에서 <u>가장 큰 댐 중에 하나</u>이다.

① the bigest dam
② the bigest dams
③ the biggest dam
④ the biggest dams
⑤ the big dams

dam 댐

03 다음 문장의 화법을 바꿀 때 빈칸에 들어갈 말로 알맞은 것을 고르시오.

> I said to her, "Where are you going?"
> →I _____ her _____ .

① asked, where she was going
② asked, where you are going
③ told, where she goes
④ told, where are you going
⑤ said to, are you going where

02

> If you don't run faster, you will miss the bus.
> = _____ you run faster, you will miss the bus.

① Though
② While
③ Whether
④ Unless
⑤ Because

04 다음 밑줄 친 부분을 생략할 수 있는 것을 고르시오.

① This is the doll <u>that</u> I bought yesterday.
② I knew a girl <u>who</u> sings very well.
③ There is much <u>that</u> can be taught.
④ The dog <u>which</u> is running fast is mine.
⑤ We saw a house <u>whose</u> roof is blue.

05 다음 밑줄 친 부분에 들어갈 알맞은 말을 고르시오.

> Wednesday is the day _____
> I am busy.

① who
② when
③ where
④ why
⑤ what

06 다음 중 바르게 쓰인 문장을 고르시오.

① There is some truth in that he says.
② This is the dictionary about that I
   told you.
③ That's the way how we did it.
④ He went to N.Y, which is one of the
   biggest cities in the world.
⑤ I don't know the reason how you
   bought it.

07 다음을 직설법으로 바꿀 때 빈칸에 알맞은 말을 쓰시오.

> If I had money, I could buy it.
> → As I _____ money,
>   I can't buy it.

08 다음 밑줄 친 말 대신에 쓸 수 있는 것을 고르시오.

> Jane wonders if he will go to
> school today.

① since
② whether
③ but
④ that
⑤ and

09 빈칸에 알맞은 말을 고르시오.

> Do you know _____ ?
> 너는 이 나무가 얼마나 오래되었는지 아니?

① how old is this tree
② how is this tree old
③ how this tree is old
④ how old this tree is
⑤ how this old tree is

10 빈칸에 들어갈 말로 알맞은 것을 고르시오.

> It is the most interesting story
> _____ .
> 그것은 내가 이제까지 들어 본 중에서 가장 재미있는 이야기이다.

① ever that I have heard
② I have that ever heard
③ ever heard that I have
④ that I have ever heard
⑤ that ever heard I have

11 밑줄 친 부분을 생략할 수 <u>없는</u> 것을 고르시오.

① This is the book <u>which</u> my friend bought for me.
② She is the woman <u>whom</u> I love.
③ Do you know the girl <u>who is</u> eating candy?
④ That is the office in <u>which</u> I work.
⑤ He is wearing a red hat <u>which was</u> made in Canada.

12 다음 우리말을 영어로 옮길 때 알맞은 것을 모두 고르시오.

> 나는 영화를 보았는데 나는 그것이 아주 재미있다는 것을 알았다.

① I watched a movie, which I found interesting.
② I watched a movie, which I found it interesting.
③ I watched a movie, that I found interesting.
④ I watched a movie, and I found it interesting.
⑤ I watched a movie, who I found interesting.

13 다음 두 문장을 바르게 연결한 것을 고르시오.

> ・Do you know?
> ・What did she eat?

① Do you know what did she eat?
② Do you know what did eat she?
③ Do you know what she ate?
④ What do you know she ate?
⑤ What do you know did she eat?

14 빈칸에 들어갈 말로 알맞은 것을 고르시오.

> I don't know _____ it is true
> or not.

① who
② whether
③ that
④ which
⑤ what

[15–16] 다음 문장의 밑줄 친 것과 바꾸어 쓸 수 있는 것을 고르시오.

15

> <u>Though</u> he is tall, he is still a child.

① Although
② Because
③ As soon as
④ While
⑤ Whether

still 여전히, 아직도

16

> The night was cold, and <u>moreover</u>
> it was windy.

① above all
② in addition
③ for herself
④ for instance
⑤ however

17 다음 두 문장의 뜻이 같도록 빈칸에 알맞은 말을 쓰시오.

> I wish I had been smart.
> = I am sorry I _____ smart.

[18–19] 밑줄 친 곳에 알맞은 말을 |보기|에서 골라 쓰시오.

| 보기 |
① who ② whose ③ which ④ what

18 The office in _____ my father works is just across the street.

19 Show me _____ you have in your hand.

20 빈칸에 알맞은 말을 모두 고르시오.

This is _____ I solved the problem.

① who
② which
③ the way
④ how
⑤ the way that

21 다음 밑줄 친 곳을 바꾸어 쓸 때 빈칸에 알맞은 단어를 쓰시오.

As soon as the dog saw a stranger, he started to bark.
= _____ seeing a stranger, the dog started to bark.

stranger 낯선사람 bark 짖다

[22–23] 다음 대화를 읽고 물음에 답하시오.

Mom : ⓐ_____ are you going to the store?
Mary : Well. ⓑ_____ I finish my homework, I will go.
I don't know ⓒ_____ I can finish it today or not.
Mom : Really? I have to make a cheesecake by 5 o'clock.
I can go to the store now. Do you need anything?
Mary : No, mom. Thanks.

22 밑줄 친 ⓐ와 ⓑ에 공통으로 들어갈 말로 알맞은 것을 고르시오.

① who
② which
③ when
④ where
⑤ what

23 밑줄 친 ⓒ에 들어갈 말로 알맞은 것을 모두 고르시오.

① who
② if
③ when
④ that
⑤ whether

[24-25] 다음 글을 읽고 물음에 답하시오.

Mike left England ⓐ_____ he spent his childhood and came back to Korea ⓑ_____ he was born. He met his family. Because he was too young, he couldn't remember the day ⓒ_____ they first met. But he always missed his family. Mike will finish studying in Korea and he will get a job there. He doesn't want to leave and to travel anymore.

miss 놓치다, 그리워하다   travel 여행하다   anymore 더 이상

24 밑줄 친 ⓐ와 ⓑ에 공통으로 들어갈 말로 알맞은 것을 고르시오.

① who
② whom
③ which
④ when
⑤ where

25 밑줄 친 ⓒ에 들어갈 알맞은 관계부사를 쓰시오.

→ _____

GRAMMAR JOY
중등영문법

2b

정답 및 해설

Grammar Joy
중등 영문법

2b

정답과 해설

POLY BOOKS

Chapter 1
비교

 A

1 어떤 다른 소녀보다 더 현명하다, 어떤 다른 소녀도 Jane보다 더 현명하지 않다, 어떤 다른 소녀도 Jane만큼 현명하지 않다

2 가장 위대한 발명가 중에 한 명

3 내가 이제까지 건너본 것 중에서 가장 긴 다리

4 어떤 다른 나무도 이것보다 더 오래되지 않았다, 어떤 다른 나무도 이것만큼 오래되지 않았다, 어떤 다른 나무보다 더 오래되었다
  ▶비교급과 원급을 이용한 최상급 표현

5 그녀가 이제까지 본 것 중에서 가장 멋진 가방
  ▶the 최상급+명사(that)주어+have ever P.P

6 가장 인기 있는 배우 중에 한 명
  ▶most popular: popular의 최상급 표현

B

1 smarter than any other girl / No other girl, smarter than / No other girl, as smart as
  ▶반에서 Susan이 가장 똑똑하다.

2 No other river, longer than / No other river, as long as / longer than any other river
  ▶비교급 다음에는 any other을 씁니다.

3 No other animal, larger than / larger than any other animal / No other animal, as large as

---

 ## 기본 TEST
p.16~17

A

1 one of the most diligent workers
  ▶one of the 최상급+복수명사: 가장 ~한 것 중의 하나

2 one of the tallest buildings

3 one of the most beautiful flowers
  ▶most beautiful: beautiful의 최상급

4 one of the best ideas ▶best: good의 최상급

1 the most delicious pizza that I have ever eaten
  ▶the 최상급+명사(that)주어+have ever P.P: 이제까지 ~한 것 중에서 가장 ~한

2 the cleverest dog that we have ever kept
  ▶keep a dog: 개를 기르다

3 the most interesting movie that she has ever watched ▶most interesting: interesting의 최상급

4 the longest tunnel that he has ever passed through ▶he+has

B

1 bigger than any other city / No (other) city, bigger than / No (other) city, as big as
  ▶뉴욕은 미국에서 가장 큰 도시이다.

2 No (other) barber, as old as / No (other) barber, older than / older than any other barber

3 more expensive than any other cap, No (other) cap, as expensive as, No (other) cap, more expensive than
  ▶expensive-more expensive-most expensive

4 No (other) swimmer, as fast as / faster than any other swimmer / No (other) swimmer, faster than ▶Peter는 그 나라에서 가장 빠른 수영선수이다.

실력 TEST p.18

A

1 one of the most famous painters
▶ one of the 최상급+복수명사: 가장 ~한 것 중의 하나

2 the biggest watermelon that I have ever seen
▶ the 최상급+명사+(that)주어+have ever P.P

3 one of the coldest places ▶ coldest: cold의 최상급

4 the sweetest music that he has ever listened to

5 the most honest person that I have ever met
▶ most honest: honest의 최상급

6 one of the most well-known singers
▶ known 알려진, well-known 잘 알려진

7 one of the strictest teachers
▶ strictest: strict의 최상급

8 one of the funniest animals
▶ funniest: funny의 최상급

9 the wisest person that we have ever known

10 the most special experience that I have ever had ▶ most special: special의 최상급

내신대비1 p.19~22

01 ② 02 ③ 03 scientist → scientists
04 the most beautiful flower that I have ever
seen 05 longer than that 06 ③ 07 ④ 08
as tall as/as high as 09 the most expensive
jewel in the world 10 ever 11 thicker than
any other book 12 No (other) book, thicker
than 13 No (other) book, as thick as 14 ②
15 ② 16 ① 17 ② 18 the biggest duckling
in the lake 19 storybook → storybooks 20
the sweetest strawberries that I have ever
eaten

01 최상급을 비교급으로 나타낼 때 than 뒤에는 any other+단수명사
가 와야 합니다.

02 최상급을 비교급으로 나타낼 때 문장 앞에는 No (other)+단수명사
가 와야 합니다.

03 one of the 최상급+복수명사 가 와야 합니다.

04 the 최상급+명사+(that)+주어+have ever P.P

05 longer: long의 비교급

06 ③ any → any other, any other에서 other은 생략하지 않습니다.

07 ④ are → is, one 하나를 가리키는 것이므로 단수 동사가 와야 합니다.

08 No other ~ is as~as

09 해석: 다이아몬드는 세계에서 가장 비싼 보석이다.

10 ever 여태까지, 이제까지

11 비교급 than any other 명사

12 No other 명사 is 비교급 than

13 No other 명사 is as 원급 as

14 no other에서 other은 생략이 가능합니다.

15 ② temple → temples, one of 최상급+복수 명사

16 ① are → is, one of+ 복수명사는 단수 동사를 사용합니다.

17 해석: 너는 호수에서 가장 못생긴 오리새끼이다. ②번은 호수의 다
른 오리 새끼들이 너보다 못생겼다 는 뜻입니다.

18 big-bigger(비교급)-biggest(최상급)

19 one of+최상급+복수 명사

20 the 최상급+명사+(that)+주어+have ever P.P

내신대비2 p.23~26

01 ② 02 ① 03 ④ 04 ④ 05 cars/is 06 I
have ever eaten 07 one of the oldest churches
in Korea 08 as long as 09 the richest man
10 taller than 11 ① 12 one of 13 ①
14 ③,④ 15 most famous models 16 ③
17 scientist → scientists 18 the most beautiful
castle I have ever visited 19 ② 20 ④

01 any other + 단수명사

02 '~만큼 ~한'은 원급비교이므로 'as ~ as'를 사용합니다.

03 'No other +단수명사'에서 other는 생략 가능합니다.

04 one of the +최상급 복수명사

05 'one of the +최상급 복수명사' 그 전체는 단수취급합니다.

08 '~만큼 ~한'은 원급비교이므로 'as ~ as'를 사용합니다.

09 최상급 사용; the richest man

13 비교급 강조 (훨씬 더)로 사용되는 부사(구)는 much/even/far/
still/a lot입니다.

14 'No other +단수명사'에서 other는 생략 가능합니다.

15 one of the +최상급 복수명사

19 ② tree → trees

20 ④ are → is

Chapter 2
명사절

기초 TEST
p.30~35

1 whether Jane likes meat or not, Jane이 고기를 좋아하
는지 아닌지, 목적어

2 Whether she loves him or not, 그녀가 그를 사랑하는지
아닌지, 주어 ▶whether or not ~인지 아닌지

3 if she will come here, 그녀가 여기에 올지 안 올지, 목적어
▶이 문장에서 if는 whether와 바꿔 쓸 수 있습니다.

4 whether we may drink this water or not, 우리가 이
물을 마셔도 될지 아닐지, 보어

5 if it will be fine tomorrow, 내일 날이 화창할지 아닐지, 목
적어

1 if there is a monster under her bed, 그녀의 침대 아래
괴물이 있는지 없는지, 명사절

2 if the weather is good, (만일) 날씨가 좋다면, 부사절
▶부사절은 의미가 미래라도 현재로 나타냅니다.

3 if she should wear the blue dress or the red
one, 그녀가 파란색 드레스를 입어야 할지, 빨간색 드레스를 입어야
할지, 명사절 ▶should ~해야 한다

4 if he is a miser, (만일) 그가 구두쇠라면, 부사절
▶부사절은 의미가 미래라도 현재로 나타냅니다.

5 if she will be helpful for him or not, 그녀가 그에게 도
움이 될지 아닐지를, 명사절
▶명사절은 의미가 미래이면 미래로 나타냅니다.

B **1** will look ▶명사절 **2** is ▶부사절 **3** will meet
▶명사절 **4** survives ▶부사절 **5** will be **6** start **7** is
▶부사절 **8** finished **9** will work **10** will answer

 1 is ▶if ~ or not은 가능한 표현입니다. **2** turn on
3 is **4** rains ▶ 의미는 미래이지만 부사절이기에 현재 시제로 나타
냅니다. **5** are **6** will succeed ▶명사절 **7** will come
▶명사절 **8** want **9** will like **10** need ▶부사절

D

1 if, whether **2** whether, if
3 Whether **4** if, whether
5 Whether ▶if절은 문장의 맨 앞에서 주어 역할을 하지 못합니다.
6 whether ▶if 뒤에는 to부정사를 사용하지 않습니다.
7 whether ▶if or not은 사용하지 않습니다.
8 whether **9** Whether
10 whether, if ▶if와 or not 사이에 문장이 올 때는 사용 가능합니다.
11 whether ▶if or not은 사용하지 않습니다.
12 whether, if ▶그는 직장에 차로 갈지 걸어갈지 결정하지 못했다.
13 whether
14 Whether ▶문장의 앞에서 주어로 사용
15 whether ▶whether or not

E

1 whether, if ▶내가 DVD를 볼지, 책을 읽을지
2 whether, if **3** whether ▶whether to
4 whether ▶whether or not은 가능하고, if or not은 사용하지 않
습니다.
5 Whether ▶문장의 앞에서 주어로 사용
6 whether, if **7** Whether
8 Whether **9** whether ▶그들은 공부할지, 놀
지를 토론하고 있다. whether 뒤에는 to부정사가 올 수 있습니다.
10 whether, if

1 whether
2 whether, if ▶whether(if) ~ or not
3 whether ▶whether to **4** whether ▶whether or not
5 whether, if ▶ask whether/if ~인지 아닌지를 묻다
6 Whether **7** whether
8 whether **9** whether, if
10 whether, if ▶Joe, my friend: 나의 친구인 Joe로 해석합니다.

A

1 Whether(or not) he is honest or not
▶whether은 or not과 바로 붙여 써도 되고 중간에 문장이 와도 됩니다.

2 whether she is Tom's auntie

3 Whether Susan likes a dog
▶Whether 주어 동사: ~가 ~인지 아닌지

4 if she would buy the backpack

5 if I finished homework ▶ask if ~인지 아닌지를 물어보다

6 Whether(or not) Paul will call me or not
▶Whether ~ is concern. ~인지 아닌지가 관심거리이다.

7 If my younger sister turned off the gas or not

8 Whether(or not) he is poor or not

B

1 Whether(or not) Tom wears a suit(or not)

2 whether (or not) the dog is hungry(or not)
/ if the dog is hungry (or not)

3 Whether(or not) the mail will be delivered (or not) ▶whether 절이 주어로 쓰였습니다.

4 whether(or not) you like her present (or not)
/ if you like her present(or not) ▶목적어

5 Whether(or not) my friend texted me (or not)
▶주어

6 whether(or not) it is fine in New York(or not)
/ if it is fine in New York(or not)

7 whether(or not) grandfather is sick(or not)
/ if grandfather is sick(or not)

8 Whether(or not) they will end the meeting (or not)

9 whether(or not) dinner is ready (or not)
/ if dinner is ready(or not) ▶ask if ~인지 아닌지를 묻다

10 whether to go to the party (or not)
▶whether to ~: ~할지 안할지

A

1 The dream / that she sees her son again, 그녀가 그녀의 아들을 다시 만난다는 꿈은
▶the 추상명사+that+명사절: ~라는 추상명사

2 the news / that he won a gold medal, 그가 금메달을 땄다는 소식을 ▶the news: 소식

3 The fact / that the teacher is strict, 그 선생님이 엄격하다는 사실은 ▶the fact that: ~라는 사실

4 the idea / that new bridge should be built over the river, 새 다리가 그 강에 지어져야 한다는 생각
▶the idea: 생각

5 The report / that we were at war in the west sea, 우리가 서해에서 교전 중이라는 보고 ▶the report: 보고

1 knows the fact that

2 have the hope that ▶the hope that: ~라는 희망

3 surprised at the news that ▶be surprised at ~에 놀라다

4 announced the report that ▶the report that: ~라는 보고

5 The idea that ▶the 추상명사+명사절이 주어의 역할을 합니다.

A

1 what he wanted to be, 그가 무엇이 되기를 원하는지. 목적어
▶목적어: 그가 아들에게 묻는 대상이다.

2 why he is here, 그가 왜 여기 있는지. 목적어
▶목적어: 그녀가 궁금해 하는 대상이다.

3 What he is making, 그가 무엇을 만들고 있는지. 주어
▶주어: 확실하지 않은 대상이다.

4 how old this cathedral is, 이 성당이 얼마나 오래되었는지. 보어

5 where I lost my umbrella, 내가 어디서 우산을 잃어버렸는지. 목적어 ▶목적어: 내가 기억하지 못하는 대상이다.

1 how much it costs
2 where Tom is playing now
3 what he is working for
4 when the carnival began
5 how you got it

기본 TEST
p.42~43

A

1 It is not sure who broke the base
  ▶누가 꽃병을 깼는지는 확실하지 않다.
2 How deep the cave is isn't known
  ▶이 동굴이 얼마나 깊은지는 알려지지 않았다.
3 Where he comes from is doubtful
  ▶그가 어디 출신인지 의심스럽다.
4 It is very important when I take this medicine
  ▶내가 이 약을 언제 먹는지는 매우 중요하다.
5 What she will ask for me at Christmas is clear
  ▶그녀가 내게 크리스마스에 무엇을 요구할 것인지는 분명하다.

1 why she moved to Chicago ▶move to~ :~로 이사 가다
2 what my son wants ▶sure은 certain과 바꿔 쓸 수 있습니다.
3 how you made it ▶how 어떻게
4 how far his company is ▶how for 얼마나 먼(멀리)

B

1 what Susan likes, Susan이 무엇을 좋아하는지
2 how well Nancy skates, Nancy가 얼마나 스케이트를 잘 타
  는지 ▶how well ~: 얼마나 ~를 잘 하는지
3 when David left for Africa, David가 언제 아프리카로 떠났
  는지 ▶leave for~: ~로 떠나다
4 what the cake was made of, 그 케이크가 무엇으로 만들어
  졌는지 ▶be made of ~로 만들어지다
5 What Bill is planning, 빌이 무엇을 계획하고 있는지
6 how many people will attend the meeting, 오늘
  얼마나 많은 사람이 그 모임에 참석할지 ▶attend 참석하다
7 when the movie will end, 이 영화가 언제 끝날지
8 what Sam is drawing, Sam이 땅 위에 무엇을 그리고 있는지
  ▶wonder 궁금해 하다

실력 TEST
p.44

A

1 where I put my ring, 내가 나의 반지를 어디에 두었는지
  ▶put 놓다, 두다
2 how he made the pasta, 그가 어떻게 파스타를 만들었는지
3 why he laughed at her, 그가 왜 그녀를 보고 웃는지를
  ▶laugh at: ~에 웃다
4 when the meeting will begin. 그 회의가 언제 시작할지는
5 what his wife said, 그의 아내가 무엇이라고 말했는지
6 how the semifinal was, 준결승전이 어땠는지
7 where the earthquake started, 그 지진이 어디서 시작되
  었는지
8 who the chairman is, 회장이 누구인지
9 how much my parents love me, 나의 부모님이 나를 얼마
  나 많이 사랑하시는지 ▶how much 얼마나 많이
10 how the spaceship was built, 그 우주선이 어떻게 만들
  어졌는지 ▶how: 방법

내신대비1
p.45~48

01 ④   02 ①   03 if → whether   04 ③
05 It is not certain what he wants to say   06 ③
07 ④   08 ②   09 ③   10 ③   11 ⑤   12 ②
13 Did you forget where you parked your car?
14 그의 아빠가 돌아가셨다는 소식에   15 ④   16 how
old this bridge was   17 Do you know who
the boy is?   18 ②   19 ⑤ will see → see
20 Do you know how long he will live there?

01 if he will come: 그가 올지 안 올지
02 whether은 문장 앞에서 주어 역할을 하며, 목적어, 보어 역할도 모
  두 가능합니다.
03 if or not이라는 표현은 쓸 수 없습니다. whether or not이 올바른
  표현입니다.
04 해석: 나는 그가 어디에 살았는지 모른다.
05 의문사 what으로 시작되는 명사절은 가주어 it으로 바꾸어 쓸 수 있
  습니다.
06 해석: 너는 그녀가 언제(when) 그 곳에 갈지 아니? 아마 내일이야.
07 whether ~ or not
08 ② if → whether, if는 문장의 맨 앞에서 주어 역할을 할 수 없습니다.
09 who 명사절보다 do you know가 먼저 와야 합니다.
10 whether ~or not: ~인지 아닌지

11 ⑤ finishes → will finish 나는 그녀가 언제 그녀의 일을 끝낼지(미래) 모릅니다.

12 Do you know+'의문사+주어+동사'

13 Where did you park(직접의문문) → where you parked(간접의문문: 명사절)

14 be shocked at the news that: ~라는 소식에 충격을 받다

15 ④ If → Whether

16 간접의문문 의문사구 (how+형용사)+주어+동사

17 who 의문문보다 do you know가 먼저 와야 합니다.

18 whether or not = if : ~인지 아닌지

19 if 부사절일 때 의미는 미래라도 현재 시제로 나타냅니다.
해석: 그를 다시 만나면 나는 기쁠 것이다.

20 Do you know+직접의문문 → Do you know+간접의문문(명사절)

내신대비2
p.49~52

01 ④ 02 ① 03 whether 04 ⑤ 05 if she likes me or not 06 if → whether 07 ③ 08 ②
09 ⑤ 10 Where he is from 11 how old he is
12 ② 13 It, who 14 whether(if) 15 doesn't come 16 ⑤ 17 if they are married or not 18 ②
19 ② 20 ⑤

01 부사절을 이끄는 if 는 시제가 미래라도 현재형을 사용합니다.
④ will come → comes

02 문장의 주어역할을 하는 명사절에는 if를 사용하지 않습니다.

03 명사절을 이끄는 if 바로 뒤에 'or not'을 사용하지 않습니다.

04 명사절의 맨 뒤에 'or not'이 오는 경우 whether 와 if 둘 다 사용 가능합니다.

07 'to 부정사'가 바로 뒤에 오는 경우와 'ot not'이 바로 뒤에 오는 경우는 if 를 사용하지 않고 whether을 사용합니다.

08 사실; the fact

09 소식; the news

10 의문사가 이끄는 명사절의 어순은 '의문사(where)+주어+동사....' 입니다.

11 의문사구가 이끄는 명사절의 어순은 '의문사구(how old)+주어+동사....' 입니다.

12 명사절을 이끄는 의문사(who)가 절의 주어로 사용되었을 때는 별도의 주어(you)가 필요하지 않습니다.

13 의문사가 이끄는 명사절이 문장의 주어로 사용되었을 때는, 대개 가주어(it)를 사용하고 '의문사가 이끄는 절(who he is)'은 문장의 맨 뒤로 옵니다.

14 'or not'이 문장의 맨 뒤에 있으므로 whether 와 if 둘 다 사용가능합니다.

15 if 가 부사절을 이끌고 있으므로 미래라도 현재형을 사용합니다.
(will not come → doesn't come)

16 동격을 나타내는 절이 문장의 주어로 사용되었습니다.

20 that 이 이끄는 명사절이 문장의 목적어로 사용되었을 때는 접속사 that을 생략할 수 있습니다.

Chapter 3
부사절 및 접속부사

 1 기초 TEST
p.58~59

Ⓐ

1 그녀는 집에 오자마자 ▶as soon as ~하자마자

2 내가 그에게 전화를 걸 때마다 ▶every time ~할 때마다

3 그래서 그는 일하러 가지 않았다 ▶bad cold 심한 감기

4 왜냐하면 나는 너무 많이 걸었기 때문이다
▶for~ 왜냐하면 ~하기 때문이다

5 (비록) 그들은 부자가 아닐지라도 ▶though 비록

6 (만일) 비가 오지 않는다면

7 Jane이 셔츠를 입길 원했기 때문에 ▶Because ~ 때문에, ~이므로

8 Bill은 숙제를 끝내자마자

9 (비록) 그녀는 어릴지라도

10 Sam은 거짓말을 할 때마다 ▶tell a lie 거짓말을 하다

Ⓑ **1** E-f **2** C-j ▶every time = each time **3** F-b-d-e
▶because = since =, for~ = as ~ 때문에, ~이므로 **4** A **5** B-g
▶if~not = unless 만일 ~ 하지 않으면 **6** D-a-c-h ▶though = although = even if = even though 비록 ~일지라도

기본 TEST
p.60~63

Ⓐ **1** so **2** As soon as ▶그녀는 얘기를 듣자마자, 웃음을 터뜨렸다. **3** for **4** Because ▶원인, 이유 **5** If ▶If: 가정의 의미를 나타냅니다. **6** Every time **7** As soon as
8 Though **9** so **10** Because

Ⓑ **1** as **2** Unless ▶미팅이 취소되지 않으면, 나는 집에 일찍 갈 수 없다. **3** since ▶원인, 이유 **4** On arriving ▶On~ing: ~하자마자 **5** so **6** Although ▶비록, ~에도 불구하고
7 Unless ▶그가 Jane을 믿지 않는다면, 그는 그녀에게 그의 통장을 맡기지 않을 것이다. **8** Each time **9** Even though (Even if)
10 so

C

1 for, As, Since, so ▶이유, 원인

2 Unless ▶If you don't mind = Unless you mind

3 Each time

4 Because, Since, for, As ▶원인, 이유

5 Although, Even though, Even if

6 If

D

1 Unless you are patient
  ▶If you are not patient = Unless you are patient

2 Every time I looked at him ▶내가 그를 볼 때마다

3 If you don't eat breakfast ▶당신이 아침을 먹지 않으면

4 so he didn't ride a bike, for(because) he was too short, Because/As the child was too short
  ▶사용하는 접속부사에 따라 문장의 구조는 바뀌지만 의미는 유사합니다.

5 Though/Although/Even if he doesn't watch TV
  ▶유사한 뜻을 가지는 접속 부사입니다.

2 기초 TEST
p.66~67

A **1** ~이므로 ▶돈이 없으므로

2 ~하는 동안 ▶그가 길을 따라 걷는 동안

3 ~부터 ▶내가 7살일 때부터

4 만일 ~라면 ▶만일 그가 자신감이 있다면

5 ~부터 ▶내가 영어를 배우기 시작한 때부터

6 ~인지 아닌지 ▶내가 그것을 만들 수 있는지 아닌지

7 ~하면서

8 ~이므로 ▶눈이 왔으므로

9 ~인지 아닌지 ▶이야기가 사실인지 아닌지

10 ~하는 동안

B **1** ~하면서 ▶엄마는 운전을 하면서

2 ~이므로 ▶Jane은 감기에 걸렸으므로

3 ~하는 동안 ▶Tom이 말을 타는 동안

4 만일 ~라면

5 ~이므로

6 ~하는 동안

7 ~이므로 ▶그는 미국에 살았으므로

8 ~하는 동안

9 ~인지 아닌지 ▶Bill이 시험을 위해 공부를 했는지 안 했는지

10 ~부터 ▶그녀가 고등학교를 졸업했을 때부터

기본 TEST
p.68~69

A **1** Because, Since ▶drop by ~에 들리다

2 whether ▶이번 주말에 날씨가 좋을지 아닐지 **3** so, for
(because, since, as) **4** As ▶Jack은 밥을 먹는 동안

5 whether **6** As, Since ▶James가 부주의했기 때문에

7 As

B **1** As (While) ▶동시동작 **2** If ▶가정, 만약에 **3** As
(Because, Since) ▶이유, 원인 **4** since ▶~때부터

5 As (Because, Since) **6** whether (if) ▶~일지 아닐지

7 While (As) **8** As(Because, Since)

3 기초 TEST
p.71

A **1** nevertheless ▶He is old, nevertheless he is very
healthy. 그는 늙었다, 그럼에도 불구하고 그는 매우 건강하다.

2 besides ▶besides = moreover **3** therefore ▶therefore =
so **4** in fact ▶In fact, I am tired. 사실 나는 피곤하다.

5 instead ▶I didn't go home. Instead, I studied at the library.
  나는 집에 가지 않았다. 대신, 도서관에서 공부를 했다.

6 however **7** by the way **8** otherwise ▶Wake up
now. Otherwise, you will be late. 지금 일어나. 그렇지 않으면, 너 늦
을 거야. **9** in addition **10** moreover ▶She is kind,
moreover, she is pretty. 그녀는 친절한데, 게다가 예쁘다.

기본 TEST
p.72~73

A **1** In addition ▶그는 강하다. 게다가 똑똑하다.

2 Therefore ▶그곳에 가는 데까지 30분이 걸린다. 그러므로 우리는
지금 출발해야 한다. **3** However ▶몇 년 동안 영어를 공부했다.
그러나 나는 영어를 잘 못 말한다. **4** In fact ▶사실은

5 Moreover ▶게다가 **6** Otherwise ▶그렇지 않으면

7 Besides ▶게다가 **8** Instead ▶그 대신에 **9** By the
way ▶그런데 / 주제나 이야기 거리의 전환 **10** Nevertheless
▶그럼에도 불구하고

B **1** Nevertheless ▶그 영화는 잘 알려져있지 않다. 그럼에
도 불구하고 그 영화는 나를 감동시켰다. **2** However

3 Otherwise ▶조용히 하지 않으면 **4** Besides ▶피곤한데.
게다가 일도 많다. **5** In fact **6** Therefore ▶앞의 내용에 대
한 결과 **7** Instead **8** In addition ▶게다가 **9** By the
way ▶그런데, 그는 누구이니? **10** moreover

실력 TEST p.74

A

1 Besides, Moreover, In addition ▶Jane은 엄마가 빨래하는 것을 도와야 한다. 게다가 해야 할 숙제도 많다.

2 However ▶그는 그녀에게 청혼했다. 그러나 그녀는 거절했다.

3 Besides, Moreover, In addition
▶게다가 나는 그의 사진도 찍었다.

4 In fact ▶사실, 실제로

5 Therefore
▶어둡고 추워지고 있었다. 그래서 그들은 밤에 묵을 곳이 필요했다.

6 Nevertheless

7 By the way ▶그런데, 그나저나 아트센터는 어디 있나요?

8 Otherwise
▶저녁 먹기 전에 숙제를 해라. 그렇지 않으면, 밥을 굶을 것이다.

내신대비1 p.75~78

01 ④ **02** ① **03** ①, ② **04** ③ **05** Unless
06 whether **07** ④ **08** ④,⑤ **09** ④
10 Otherwise **11** By the way **12** Moreover
13 I took a taxi, for I got up too late. **14** They were brave, so they won the battle. **15** We went to the beach, for it was hot. **16** arriving
17 you have enough money, I'll lend you some. **18** ③ **19** ④ **20** ①

01 As soon as = On ~ing ~하자마자

02 Every time = Each time ~할 때마다

03 Since = Because, As ~해서, ~이므로

04 안개가 껴서, 우리는 아무것도 볼 수 없다.

05 Unless = If ~not

06 if = whether 그가 옳은지 틀린지

07 As = While ~하면서(동시동작)

08 Though = Although, Even though, Even if

09 Brown씨 부인은 약합니다. 그럼에도 불구하고(Nevertheless) 그녀는 많은 집안일을 합니다.

10 너는 열심히 공부해야 한다, 그렇지 않으면(Otherwise) 낙제 할 것이다

11 너는 건강해 보인다. 그런데(By the way), 여름 방학은 언제 시작하니?

12 여기는 비가 많이 오고 있다. 게다가(Moreover), 바람도 분다.

13 . for~ : 왜냐하면 ~하기 때문이다.

14 그들은 용감했다. 그래서 전투에서 승리했다.

15 날씨가 더워서 우리는 해변으로 갔다.

16 As soon as = On ~ing 그녀는 도착하자마자, 울기 시작했다.

17 If you don't have enough money = Unless you have enough money

18 해석: 로봇은 나에게 너무 비싸므로, 나는 곰인형을 살 것이다. / ③번 해석: 나는 곰인형을 살 것이기 때문에 로봇은 나에게 너무 비싸다. (문장의 뜻이 명확하지 않음)

19 나는 약간의 고기를 먹고 싶다. 그래서(therefore), 나는 베이컨과 햄을 주문할 것이다.

20 그것들은 건강에 좋지 않다. 대신에(Insead), 우리는 채소 새싹이 있는 참치 샌드위치를 먹을 것이다.

내신대비2 p.79~82

01 ② **02** ⑤ **03** ③ **04** so **05** ④ **06** ②
07 ① **08** ⑤ **09** ⑤ **10** ③ **11** ④ **12** ①
13 ③ **14** instead **15** ② **16** ① **17** ③
18 I was embarrassed, for I made a mistake
19 ⑤ **20** ②

01 as soon as ~ = on ~ing

02 every time = each time

03 because = as

04 결과(그래서)를 나타내는 접속사는 so입니다.

06 If .... not = Unless ....

07 Though ~ = Even if ~

09 ⑤ '~이래로' 는 since 를 사용합니다.

10 '~하는 동안에'를 나타내는 접속사는 while 또는 as를 사용하며, '~동안을' 나타내는 전치사는 for 또는 during을 사용합니다.

11 그러므로, 따라서 ; therefore

12 그렇지 않으면 ; otherwise

13 그럼에도 불구하고 ; nevertheless

14 그 대신에 ; instead

16 since 의 2가지 사용 ; 1)~이래로 2)~이므로(=because)

17 ③ so → because

18 for ~ ; 왜냐하면 ~이기 때문이다

20 그 대신에 ; instead, ~하는 동안에 ; while ~

 A

1 my sister = She, my sister, who ▶수줍은 나의 여동생
2 The sky = it, The sky, which
　　▶The sky which Jinny is drawing: Jinny가 그리고 있는 하늘
3 a basket = it, a basket, which
　　▶우리가 피크닉에 사용할 수 있는 바구니
4 a girl = She, a girl, who ▶느리게 걷고 있는 소녀
5 a ring = It, a ring, which ▶매우 비싼 반지
6 The soup = it, The soup, which ▶그가 요리한 수프
7 the boy = His, the boy, whose ▶나는 소년을 안다. 소
년의 아버지는 의사이다. → 나는 아버지가 의사인 소년을 안다.
8 a sister = Her, a sister, whose
　　▶Jenny는 (그녀의) 꿈이 자동차 디자이너가 되는 것인 여동생이 있다.

 B

1 who works here, 여기서 일하는. 주격
2 whose arms are very long, (그의) 팔이 매우 긴. 소유격
　　▶소년의 팔
3 which they are selling, 그들이 팔고 있는. 목적격
4 whose shirts were red, (그들의) 셔츠가 붉은 색인. 소유격
　　▶한국인들의 셔츠
5 which is called Central Park, 센트럴파크라고 불리는. 주격
　　▶센트럴파크라고 불리는 공원
6 who Tom married three months ago, Tom이 세 달 전
에 결혼한. 목적격 ▶Tom이 세 달 전에 결혼한 여자
7 which he made during vacation 그가 방학 동안 만든.
목적격 ▶during+명사
8 whose cell-phone looked nice, (그의) 핸드폰이 멋져 보
이는. 소유격 ▶친구의 핸드폰
9 which she passed, 그녀가 통과한(합격한). 목적격
　　▶그녀가 합격한 시험
10 which is near the post office, 우체국과 가까이 있는. 주
격 ▶우체국과 가까이 있는 학교

 C

1 the salt which are on the table, 식탁 위에 있는 소금을.
주격 ▶pass 건네다
2 the book which he read yesterday, 그가 어제 읽은 책.
목적격 ▶선행사 the book
3 a book whose cover was really old, (그것의) 겉표지가
정말 오래된 책을. 소유격 ▶책의 표지
4 a painting which was drawn by my mom, 나의 엄
마에 의해 그려진 그림. 주격 ▶선행사 a painting
5 one of my friends who are interested in music,
음악에 관심이 있는 나의 친구들중의 하나. 주격 ▶선행사 friends
6 the woman whose interest is beauty, (그녀의) 관심이
아름다움에 있는 여자. 소유격 ▶여자의 관심
7 a son who is older than you, 너보다 더 나이 든 아들을.
주격 ▶선행사 a son
8 the kite which was flying in the sky, 하늘에서 날고 있
는 연을. 주격 ▶선행사 the kite
9 a nephew whose job is too hard, (그의) 일이 너무 힘든
조카가. 소유격 ▶조카의 일
10 a house whose garden was beautiful, 정원이 아름
다운 집을. 소유격 ▶집의 정원

 D

1 the cook, who ▶선행사 the man 사람 -who
2 The pigs, which ▶선행사 the pigs 동물-which
3 The girl, who
4 the old lady, whose ▶나이 든 여인의 모자
5 a musician, who, whom ▶선행사 a musician 사람-who
6 the cup, which ▶선행사 the cup 사물-which
7 a rich man, whose ▶부유한 남자의 삶
8 the chair, whose ▶의자의 다리
9 My brother, who
10 The movie, which ▶선행사 the movie 사물-which
11 the baby, whose ▶아기의 엄마
12 The dishes, which
13 a fish, whose ▶물고기의 이빨
14 my friend, whose ▶내 친구의 지갑
15 the person, who, whom ▶선행사 the person 사람-who

기본 TEST
p.90~93

A 1 who 2 who 3 which 4 who, whom
▶목적격이므로 who와 whom을 둘 다 쓸 수 있습니다. 5 whose
▶교회의 종 6 which ▶선행사: the puppy 7 which
8 who ▶선행사: the baby 9 which 10 who, whom
▶내가 좋아하는 배우(목적격) 11 which 12 who, whom
▶그가 찾고 있는 조수(목적격) 13 whose ▶팔찌의 가격
14 whose ▶늙은 남자의 아들 15 which

B 1 who 2 whose ▶남자의 이름 3 whose
▶소년의 바람 4 which ▶선행사: the recipe 5 which
6 which 7 whose ▶집의 천장 8 which 9 who,
whom ▶소설에서 언급했던 여성(목적격) 10 who
11 whose ▶소녀의 재능 12 which 13 which
▶a sneakers: 운동화 한 켤레 14 whose ▶우산의 손잡이
15 whose ▶딸의 몸무게

C 1 whose ▶여동생의 친구 2 who 3 which
4 whose ▶늑대의 눈(소유격) 5 which 6 who, whom
▶선행사가 사람이자 목적어이다. 7 whose ▶대통령의 연설
8 who, whom ▶많은 손님들이 좋아하는 이발사(목적격)
9 which 10 which

D 1 which 2 whose ▶원숭이의 코(소유격) 3 who,
whom ▶그녀가 방금 전에 전화한 학생(목적격) 4 who, whom
▶그가 어제 집에 데려간 남자는(목적격) 5 which 6 which
7 which ▶선행사: the sport 8 who, whom ▶우리가 절대
잊지 못하는 9 whose ▶TV 세트의 사이즈 10 which

실력 TEST
p.94~95

A 1 who, whom ▶그가 지난 밤 파티에서 만난 소녀
2 whose ▶책의 제목 3 which 4 whose ▶남자의 꿈
5 who ▶선행사: my best friend 6 who, whom ▶내가 돌봐
야 하는 아기 7 which ▶선행사: the dog 8 whose ▶친구의
취미 9 which 10 who, whom ▶사람들이 존경하는 영웅

B
1 of which the backyard, the backyard of which
2 of which the legs, the legs of which
▶of which the 명사, the 명사 of which 둘 다 가능한 표현입니다.
3 whose bell, the bell of which ▶교회의 종
4 whose beak, of which the beak ▶새의 부리
5 of which the material, the material of which
▶코트의 소재

기초 TEST
p.98~99

A 1 the letter, comes ▶"D"는 "C" 다음에 오는 글자입니다.
2 two watermelons, were
▶선행사가 복수이므로 복수 동사가 옵니다.
3 the boy, is ▶우유를 마시고 있는 소년
4 someone, understands ▶someone은 단수 선행사입니다.
5 some candies, likes
▶목적격 관계대명사이므로 선행사와 관계가 없습니다. 형용사절 안의
주어(Jane)에 동사의 수를 맞추어 줍니다.
6 the work, makes ▶the work는 단수 선행사입니다.
7 The cars, go, are
▶선행사(the cars)가 문장의 주어역할도 하므로, 복수동사(are)가 옵니다.

1 some bears, eat
2 a house, has ▶a house: 단수 선행사
3 two daughters, are ▶음악을 잘하는 두 명의 딸들
4 The season, comes, is ▶봄 전에 오는 계절은 겨울입니다.
선행사(the season)가 문장의 주어역할도 하므로, 단수동사(is)가 옵니다.
5 the cathedral, are ▶소유격 관계대명사이므로 형용사절 안의
주어(whose windows)에 동사의 수를 맞추어 줍니다.

B
1 a runner = He, who, a runner who ▶선행사: a runner
2 the place = it, which, the place which
▶선행사: the place
3 an old book = its, whose, an old book whose
▶책의 표지
4 a lawyer = His, whose, a lawyer whose
▶변호사의 사무실
5 The building = It, which, The building which
▶선행사: the building

A

1 the woman = She, the woman, who, the woman
who ▶Tom과 얘기하고 있는 여자

2 a pet pig = Its, a pet pig, whose, a pet pig
whose ▶애완용 돼지의 코

3 An old man = He, An old man, who, An old man
who ▶선행사: an old man

4 the plane = it, the plane, which, the plane
which ▶내가 최초로 조종했던 비행기

5 two boys = They, two boys, who, two boys who
▶선행사: two boys

B

1 The clerk = She, who is standing at the lobby,
The clerk who is standing at the lobby ▶로비에 서
있는 직원은 친절합니다.

2 This kitten = it, which Mary brought, This kitten
which Mary brought
▶Mary가 가져온 아기고양이는 매우 귀엽다.

3 The boy = His, whose cheeks turned red, The
boy whose cheeks turned red ▶소년의 뺨

4 The woman = She, who is picking peaches, The
woman who is picking peaches ▶복숭아를 따고 있는
여성은

5 The cell-phone = it, which my dad bought for
me, The cell-phone which my dad bought for
me ▶아빠가 내게 사준 핸드폰

C

1 who sings well ▶노래를 잘 부르는 소년

2 whose dad is a dentist lives here
▶아버지가 치과의사인 학생은 이 곳에 삽니다.

3 which I don't like ▶내가 좋아하지 않는 헤어핀

4 who(m) Andy takes care of
▶이 아이들은 Andy가 돌보는 고아들입니다.

5 whose daughter works at this library
▶늙은 여인의 딸

6 which live in Alaska ▶알래스카에 사는 곰들

7 which was made in Japan ▶일본에서 만들어진 자

8 whose wheels are very big
▶나의 삼촌은 바퀴가 매우 큰 트럭을 운전하십니다.

9 which the soldiers carry

10 who(m) Jim has seen before
▶Jim이 예전에 만난 은행가

D

1 who is quarreling with Sam
▶Sam과 말다툼하고 있는 소년

2 who goes to the elementary school
▶초등학교에 다니는 남동생

3 whose tail is short ▶꼬리가 짧은 강아지

4 who studied in Germany

5 whose face is small ▶얼굴이 작은 소녀

6 whose feathers were wonderful
▶그들의 깃털이 멋진 공작들

7 which he wrote in English ▶그가 영어로 쓴 편지

8 whose size is 90 ▶그것의 사이즈가 90인 셔츠

9 which the chef cooked ▶요리사가 요리한 음식들

10 which Jenny wanted so badly
▶Jenny가 간절히 원한 장난감들

 1 which he likes ▶선행사: the coke

2 who is wearing ▶선행사: the boy

3 which I have watched ▶once 한 번

4 who lives ▶선행사: the child

5 which she carries ▶선행사: the bag

6 which was sleeping ▶선행사: a cat

7 which he should study ▶선행사: the subject

8 whose father drives ▶소녀의 아버지(소유격)

9 which was built

10 whose eyes are ▶토끼의 눈(소유격)

B

1 which we planted
2 which Karen sent ▶선행사: an e-mail
3 who(m) he worked
  ▶선행사: the girl 사람-who/whom
4 whose wings were ▶새의 날개
5 which she is making ▶선행사: the wedding dress
6 which Marry drew
7 who is popular ▶선행사: a singer 사람
8 whose fur was ▶고양이의 털
9 who goes
10 which she wore

C

1 who is studious ▶선행사: a brother- who
2 which frightened me yesterday
  ▶선행사: the dog-which
3 whose job is a vet ▶남자의 직업(소유격)
4 who(m) young people love ▶목적격 who, whom
5 who(m) I wanted to see ▶내가 만나기를 원했던(목적격)
6 who plays soccer well ▶선행사: the boy
7 which comes before August ▶선행사: the month
8 whose dad is a fire-fighter ▶소녀의 아버지(소유격)
9 which I know
10 whose eyes are big ▶인형의 눈(소유격)

 내신대비1 p.107~110

---

01 whose 02 who 03 which 04 who,
whom 05 whose mother tongue is not
English 06 ③ 07 ② 08 ④ 09 ③ 10 ⑤
11 ⑤ 12 ④ 13 ④ 14 ③ 15 ② 16 ⑤
17 ① 18 I love the pen which means a lot to
me. 19 ⑤ 20 whose

---

01 소녀의 오빠(소유격)
02 선행사 The kid-관계대명사 who
03 선행사 a company-관계대명사 which
04 내가 얘기한 여성(목적격)-who, whom
05 부모들의 모국어(소유격)
06 선행사 The bag-관계대명사 which
07 해석: 그의 친구가 상을 탄 소녀는 흥분해 있다. 주어: the boy – 단수동사 is
08 선행사 the cake, the house-관계대명사 which
09 선행사(writer) 바로 뒤에 관계대명사(who)가 옵니다.
10 주어가 The boys 이므로 단수 동사 is가 아닌 복수 동사 are이 와야 합니다.

11 ①②③④번의 who는 선행사 뒤에 관계대명사로 쓰였습니다. ⑤번의 who는 가리키는 선행사가 나타나 있지 않습니다. 명사절을 이끄는 의문사(who: 누가)입니다.
12 선행사 the garden 사물-which, 단수 명사이므로 단수 동사 was를 써야 합니다.
13 ④ whom → who, whom은 목적격에만 사용할 수 있습니다.
14 선행사 a dog은 사람이 아니므로 ③ who → which로 바꿔야 합니다.
15 선행사 a bag 사물-관계대명사 which
16 ①②③④의 which는 가리키는 선행사가 문장에 나타나 있지만, ⑤번의 which는 선행사가 없습니다. 의문사(which: 어느 것)로 쓰였습니다.
17 선행사 a friend 사람-주격 관계대명사 who
18 the pen = It 이므로 the pen-사물을 선행사로 갖는 관계대명사 which를 사용해야 합니다.
19 someone 사람-who, 강아지의 이름-whose(소유격)
20 남자의 딸(소유격)

 내신대비2 p.111~114

---

01 ② 02 ①,④ 03 ③ 04 ⑤ 05 ⑤ 06 ③
07 ① 08 is, is 09 is, are 10 ④ 11 ④
12 ⑤ 13 ① 14 ② 15 which my girlfriend
gave to me 16 ③ 17 ⑤ 18 whose English
abilities are good 19 ④ 20 ③

---

01 선행사(the subject)가 사물이므로 which 를 사용합니다.
02 선행사(the girl)가 사람이며 목적격이므로 whom 또는 who를 사용합니다.
03 소유격이므로 선행사에 관계없이 whose를 사용합니다.
04 ⑤ whose는 소유격관계대명사이므로 her을 생략해야 합니다.
05 선행사(the girl)가 사람이며 주격이므로 who를 사용하며, 관계대명사가 이끄는 절이 선행사(the girl) 바로 뒤에 와야 합니다.
06 who가 주격으로 사용 되었으므로 주어(he)를 없애야 합니다.
07 선행사가 사람이며 목적격으로 사용되었을 때 who 대신 whom으로 바꾸어 쓸 수 있습니다.
08 선행사(the boy)가 단수이므로, 절 안의 동사도 단수(is)이며, 문장의 동사(is)도 단수입니다.
09 절 안에 주어(Kate)가 있으므로 절 안의 동사는 주어에 일치(is)하며, 문장의 동사는 선행사(the rings)가 복수이므로 복수동사(are)를 사용합니다.
10 소유격관계대명사 whose = of which the
11 ④ 선행사(a friend)가 사람일 때는 whose를 of which the 로 바꾸어 쓰지 않습니다.
15 the ring = it 이므로 관계대명사 which를 사용합니다.
16 the necklace = it
17 ⑤ is → are
19 선행사가 사물이므로 which를 사용합니다.
20 ③ the famous actor 가 선행사입니다.

Chapter 5
관계대명사B, 관계부사

 기초 TEST p.117~119

A 1 the only daughter, that
2 the same pen, that
▶선행사에 the same이 포함될 경우 that을 사용합니다.

3 The pen, which, that
4 All trees, that ▶선행사에 all이 포함될 경우 that을 사용합니다.
5 The boy, who, whom, that
6 No food, that ▶선행사에 no가 포함될 경우 that을 사용합니다.
7 the very dress, that
▶선행사에 the very가 포함, that을 사용합니다.

8 The book, whose ▶책의 표지
9 the boy and wolf, that
▶선행사가 사람+사물인 경우 that을 사용합니다.

10 The largest animal, that ▶최상급, that을 사용합니다.
11 the map, which, that
12 the last tiger, that ▶최상급, that
13 my boyfriend, whose ▶내 남자친구의 삼촌
14 the man and his monkey, that
▶선행사가 사람+사물인 경우 that을 사용합니다.

15 a sleeping bag, which, that

B 1 that   2 which, that   3 which, that ▶선행사:
a hair cut   4 that   5 that   6 whose ▶소녀의 어머니(소유격)

7 that   8 whose ▶운전사의 눈(소유격)   9 who(m), that
▶내가 존경하는 매니저(목적격)   10 that ▶선행사: 사람+동물

C 1 which ▶목적격 관계대명사 which는 생략할 수 있습니다.
2 that was ▶주격 관계대명사+be동사는 함께 생략할 수 있습니다.
3 ×   4 that   5 who is ▶주격 관계대명사+be동사는 함께 생략
할 수 있습니다.   6 who is   7 ×   8 that ▶목적격 관계대명사
that은 생략할 수 있습니다.   9 ×   10 ×   11 who is ▶who
is holding 주격 관계대명사+be동사+분사구의 경우 who is가 생략 가능
합니다.   12 which   13 ×   14 that   15 which ▶목적
격 관계대명사 which는 생략할 수 있습니다.

 기초 TEST p.122~125

A

1 아름답고 친절한, 그런데 그들은 아름답고 친절했다.
2 중국에서 만든, 그런데 그것들은 중국산이다.
3 그런데 그들은 멀리 떨어져 산다. 멀리 떨어져 사는
4 그녀에게 관심이 없는 그 소년을 좋아한다. / 그 소년을 좋아한다. 그런
데 그는 그녀에게 관심이 없다.
5 캐나다에서 온 두 명의 선생님이 있다. /두 분이 선생님이 계시는데, 그
들은 캐나다에서 왔다.

B

1 1개 이상일 수 있음 ▶제한적 용법: (,)가 없는 경우
2 3명 이상일 수 있음
3 3자루뿐임 ▶계속적 용법: (,)가 있는 경우
4 3명 이상일 수 있음
5 50마리뿐임
▶계속적 용법, 암소가 50마리밖에 없다는 의미를 갖습니다.
6 7명 이상 일 수 있음
▶제한적 용법, 학생이 7명 이상일 수 있다는 의미를 갖습니다.
7 2명 이상일 수 있음 ▶그가 함께 사는 삼촌(목적격)
8 5개뿐임
9 3명뿐임
10 5권 이상 수 있음 ▶sell well 잘 팔리다

C 1 but he ▶. who는 and 또는 but 대명사로 바꿔 쓸 수 있습
니다.   2 and he   3 but, them ▶. whom = but 대명사
4 but, it ▶a video tape → it   5 and, her   6 but, he
7 and, he(she) ▶. who = and 대명사   8 but, it ▶a black
cap → it

D 1 whom ▶전치사+whom   2 which ▶전치사+which
3 which ▶선행사: the bed   4 which ▶선행사: the place   5
which ▶전치사+which   6 whom ▶to whom   7 which
8 which   9 who, whom   10 whom ▶with whom

기본 TEST   p.126~129

Ⓐ

1 who he plays soccer with, that he plays soccer with, with whom he plays soccer
▶who~with = that~with = with whom

2 that we played on, on which we played
▶which~on = that~on = on which

3 that I told you about, who I told you about, about whom I told you
▶that ~ about = who ~ about = about whom

4 which she paid 20 dollars for, for which she paid 20 dollars ▶which ~ for = for which

Ⓑ

1 내가 어제 산 것 ▶what ~하는 것
2 그가 원하는 것들 ▶the things that ~하는 것들
3 그녀가 좋아하는 것(들)을 ▶what = the thing(s) that
4 우체부가 배달한 편지는 ▶that을 which와 바꿔 쓸 수 있습니다.
5 내가 필요한 것은
6 그들이 보았던 것(들)을
7 중요한 것은 ▶What is important 중요한 것
8 그녀가 만든 종이배는
9 네가 네 가방 안에 가지고 있는 것(들)을
10 엄마가 찾고 있는 목걸이

Ⓒ
1 that, what **2** what, that ▶what = the thing(s) that **3** what, that ▶what = the thing **4** that, What **5** what, that **6** that, what ▶모두가 그가 거짓말쟁이라는 것을 안다. / 아무도 그가 무엇인지(그의 직업이 무엇인지) 모른다. **7** That, What ▶그가 파리로 떠났다는 것은 사실이다. / 그가 버스에 놓고 내린 것은 그의 서류이다. **8** that, What ▶Jane이 입고 있는 것은 구명조끼이다.

Ⓓ
1 that **2** What ▶David가 읽는 것은 만화책들입니다. **3** that ▶which도 가능합니다. **4** that ▶which도 가능합니다. **5** what ▶이 장난감은 아이들이 가지고 놀고 싶어 하는 것입니다. **6** That ▶접속사 that이 이끄는 명사절입니다. **7** what **8** What **9** that ▶건조기에서 오그라든 내 스웨터를 보세요. **10** what

---

기초 TEST p.132~133

Ⓐ

1 the hotel / which, at, at which, where
▶at which = where

2 the year / which, in, in which, when
▶in which = when

3 the reason / which, for, for which, why
▶for which = why

4 the way / which, in, in which, that, the way, how
▶방법을 나타낼 때 the way how는 사용하지 않으며, the way that 또는 the way나 how를 사용합니다.

Ⓑ

1 the day / which, on, on which, when
▶on which = when

2 the country / which, in, in which, where
▶in which = where

3 the way / which, in, in which, that
▶비행기가 나는 방법은 간단합니다.

4 the reason / which, for, for which, why
▶그녀가 날 찾아온 이유는 확실하지 않다.

기본 TEST p.134~135

Ⓐ
1 where ▶the hospital 장소 **2** when ▶the day 시간 **3** why ▶the reason 이유 **4** that ▶the way that = how 방법 **5** where **6** that **7** when ▶the time 시간 **8** why **9** when **10** where ▶the place 장소 **11** why **12** that **13** where ▶a spot 장소 **14** when **15** why
▶누가 그녀가 그와 사랑에 빠지는 이유를 알겠는가?

Ⓑ
1 where ▶그녀가 일하는 사무실 **2** when ▶내가 그를 마지막에 만난 날 **3** why **4** how ▶현금자동인출기에서 현금을 인출하는 방법 **5** when ▶Paul이 태어난 달 **6** where ▶생선을 잘 요리하는 식당 **7** why **8** where **9** how ▶아기가 탁자에 올라간 방법 **10** where ▶내가 앉을 수 있는 의자

실력 TEST

p.136

1 the year when the dog died ▶개가 죽었던 해(시간)

2 the park where we play soccer ▶축구를 하는 공원(장소)

3 a sofa where he will sit ▶그가 앉을 소파(장소)

4 the time when they must leave
▶그들이 떠나야 하는 시간(시간)

5 the reason why the baby cried ▶아기가 운 이유(이유)

6 The pool where children swim

7 the place where he hides ▶the place 장소–where

8 The way that he turns on the vacuum, The
way(How) he turns on the vacuum
▶the way that= how, 방법

9 The reason why she is sick ▶the reason 이유–why

10 the building where he works
▶the building 장소–where

내신대비1

p.137~140

01 ① 02 ③ 03 ① 04 ⑤ 05 which this
paper was in, in which this paper was 06 ②
07 which 08 which(that) 09 which 10 ④
11 that → which 12 ④, ⑤ 13 ② 14 ⓓ
15 ⑤ 16 ① 17 ③ 18 that 19 who
20 which(that)

01 Jenny가 작년에 묵었던 호텔이므로 장소를 나타내는 at which가 와야 합니다.

02 the way와 how는 같이 쓸 수 없습니다. the way that 또는 how나 the way 단독으로 사용해야 합니다.

03 ①번은 관계대명사(~하는 것), ②③④⑤번은 의문사(무엇)

04 what: ~하는 것. 해석: 중요한 것은 최선을 다하는 것이다. / 이것은 그가 찾던 것이다.

05 in which도 가능하고 which ~ in도 가능합니다.

06 전치사+whom 형태로 바뀌어야 합니다. with who → with whom

07 ,and it = which

08 뒤에 전치사 from이 있으므로 관계대명사 which 또는 that을 사용할 수 있습니다.

09 전치사 from이 있으므로 which만 가능합니다.

10 전치사 with가 있으므로 ④ who → whom이 옳은 표현입니다.

11 전치사 in이 있으므로 in which가 옳은 표현입니다.

12 ④ where → which, where와 전치사 in은 함께 쓰이지 않습니다.
⑤ that → which, that과 전치사 in은 함께 쓰이지 않습니다.

13 선행사가 the actor 배우–사람(주격)이므로 who가 와야 합니다.

14 a green house built in the 1900s: 1900년대에 지어진 초록색 집

15 나는 그가 말한 것을 믿을 수가 없었다.

16 ② what → which/that ③ that → who ④ which → in which/
where ⑤ which → who 로 각각 바꿔야 합니다.

17 ,which로 앞의 선행사 potato chips를 부연 설명하고 있습니다.

18 선행사가 사람+동물이므로 관계대명사 that만 사용이 가능합니다.

19 선행사가 Linda의 가장 친한 친구, 사람이며 주격이므로 who를 씁니다.

20 Linda가 구입한 파란색 드레스는 매우 귀엽습니다. 선행사가 사물이므로 which 또는 that을 사용합니다.

내신대비2

p.141~144

01 ① 02 ③ 03 ④ 04 ④,⑤ 05 ② 06 ③
07 which is 08 and it 09 which 10 ⑤
11 ④ 12 ⑤ 13 ④ 14 I have a sister who got
into a college 15 ④ 16 ⑤ 17 and she
18 when 19 ② 20 ③

01 선행사(The Eiffel Tower)가 사물이므로 that 대신 which 사용가능합니다.

02 선행사(a man and his dog)가 '사람+사물'이므로 that 만 사용가능합니다.

04 소유격 whose 또는 'of which the'의 which는 that으로 바꾸어 쓸 수 없습니다.

05 '관계대명사+be동사'(who is)가 생략 된 문장입니다.

06 목적격 관계대명사는 생략가능 합니다.

07 '관계대명사+be동사'(which is)는 생략가능 합니다.

08 ',which'는 ',and(또는 but) +대명사'로 바꾸어 쓸 수 있습니다.

09 드레스가 2 개이상 일 수 있으므로, 관계대명사(which)앞에 comma(,)를 붙이지 않습니다.

10 전치사 + whom, 전치사 + which 만 사용합니다.

11 선행사(the bakery)가 장소를 나타내므로, 관계부사로 where를 사용합니다.

12 관계대명사로 that이 사용되었으므로 전치사는 절의 맨 뒤에 와야합니다.

13 the thing(s) that = what ; ~하는 것(들)

15 이유를 나타내는 관계부사 why를 사용 합니다.

17 , who = , and(또는 but) + 대명사

18 선행사 (the day)가 시간을 나타내므로 관계부사 when 을 사용합니다.

19 why = for which

20 ③ the way how → the way that (=the way 또는 how만 사용)

Chapter 6
시제의 일치와 화법

 기초 TEST p.148~149

A **1 came** ▶주절과 종속절의 시제가 과거로 일치합니다.
2 is ▶3+5=8인 것은 불변의 진리입니다. **3 had been** ▶2003년부터 파리에 있었다. **4 comes** ▶7월이 8월 전에 오는 것은 불변의 진리입니다. **5 bought 6 moves** ▶자연 현상-불변의 진리 **7 was 8 tasted 9 is** ▶현재 사실 **10 would 11 wash** ▶손을 씻는 습관 **12 works 13 rises 14 died** ▶역사적 사실 **15 is**

B

1 told, had eaten
  ▶그녀가 8시에 아침을 먼저 먹은 것을(과거 완료) 말했다(과거).
2 believes, will pass ▶시험에 통과하는 것은 미래의 일입니다.
3 said, is ▶불변의 진리(현재)
4 told, had loved ▶과거, 과거 완료
5 think, is
6 misses, broke up
  ▶그와 헤어진 후(과거) 지금 그를 그리워하는 것입니다.(현재)
7 know, are not
8 said, has ▶현재 습관(현재)
9 knew, sets ▶불변의 진리(과거)
10 said, discovered ▶역사적 사실(과거)

 기초 TEST p.152~153

A **1 tells, he, is** ▶say to = tell
2 said, she, was ▶동사의 시제 일치
3 says, Jane, can
4 told, was ▶시제 일치

5 said, she, was ▶I am → she was
6 told, he, would ▶will-would
7 tells, my, is ▶나의 집이 멋지다는 것
8 told, she, was ▶여배우가 재능이 있다는 것
9 told, he, had
10 told, she, was ▶그녀 자신이 살이 쪘다는 것을 의미합니다.

B **1 says, he is** ▶직접화법 → 간접화법 **2 told, I was** ▶나에게 똑똑하다고 말한 것 **3 said, his stomach hurt** ▶그의 배가 아픈 것 **4 tells, I look 5 told, she had 6 tell, I need 7 said, he made** ▶자신이 아닌 다른 선수를 의미합니다. **8 said, he was running 9 tells, she is not going** ▶그녀 자신이 댄스파티에 가지 않겠다는 것 **10 told, she had ironed** ▶엄마가 셔츠를 다림질했다고 내게 말했습니다.

기본 TEST p.154~157

A **1 she, my 2 she, our** ▶그녀는 우리에게 그녀가 우리의 새로운 선생님이라고 말합니다. **3 he, her** ▶그가 그녀를 항상 도왔다. **4 she, my 5 his** ▶그의 머리에서 좋은 냄새가 난다는 것 **6 he, me** ▶그는 나랑 같이 가고 싶어 했다. **7 she, her** ▶그녀는 그녀의 머리에 무언가 있다. **8 he, his** ▶그가 그의 잔디에 물을 주고 있었다. **9 they, her** ▶그들은 그의 여동생에게 그들이 인형을 사줄 것이라고 말한다. **10 he, her, her**

B **1 her 2 he, her** ▶그녀가 그에게 그는 그녀의 제일 좋은 친구라고 말한다. **3 she, his 4 she, his 5 my** ▶내 소포가 우체국에 있는 것 **6 her** ▶그들이 그녀에게 그녀의 물고기를 잘 돌봐주겠다고 말한다. **7 he, her** ▶그는 그녀의 서비스에 만족하지 못했다. **8 school, him** ▶Billy가 그의 어머니에게 학교가 그에게 굉장히 재밌다고 말한다. **9 his** ▶요리사의 요리 **10 her**

C **1** then ▸now → then **2** there ▸here → there
3 that ▸this → that **4** before **5** that day ▸today → that day **6** there, the day before ▸yesterday → the day before **7** the next day ▸tomorrow → the next day
8 now ▸시제가 바뀌지 않으면, 부사(구)도 바뀌지 않습니다.
9 before **10** the next week ▸직접 화법에서 간접 화법으로 바뀔 때 부사(구)에도 여러 변화가 생깁니다.

D **1** that day **2** the day before **3** then
4 there **5** 2 hours before ▸ago → before **6** the next day **7** that ▸this → that **8** there, then ▸here now → there then **9** now ▸시제가 바뀌지 않으면, 부사(구)도 바뀌지 않습니다. **10** the next month ▸the를 추가해야 합니다.

실력 TEST
p.158~159

A **1** says that she is interested
2 said that he was ▸그는 그가 피곤하다고 말했다.
3 says that Tom is
▸Sarah는 Tom이 매우 열심히 일한다고 말한다.
4 told the teacher that they wanted
5 told the cashier that he needed ▸said to = told
6 said that she surprised
▸그는 그녀가 그를 놀라게 했다고 말했다.
7 tells my brother that it is his
▸나의 어머니가 나의 남동생에게 이것은 그의 새로운 자전거라고 말한다.
8 told Luke that she was going
9 tells the fire-fighter that he is her
10 told me that he had no mail for me that day
▸우편부가 내게 오늘은 나를 위한 우편물이 없다고 말했다.

B **1** told her that she could swim
2 told him that he was
▸Nancy는 그에게 그가 매우 무례했다고 말했다.
3 told his mom that he was
4 said that he couldn't smell anything
▸그는 감기 때문에 아무 냄새도 맡을 수 없다고 말했다.
5 told my brother that I was looking for his car
▸나는 그에게 내가 그의 차를 주차장에서 찾고 있었다고 말했다.
6 says that she will get
▸내 여자 형제는 그녀가 직장에서 보너스를 받을 것이라고 말한다.
7 tells him that he needs
▸코치는 그에게 그가 좀 더 연습이 필요하다고 말한다.
8 tells me that I have to go
▸엄마는 내게 내가 학원에 가야 한다고 말한다.
9 said that she visited her parents
▸그녀는 그녀가 매주 일요일마다 그녀의 부모님을 방문했다고 말했다.
10 told us that we had to study
▸선생님은 우리에게 우리가 공부를 더 열심히 해야 한다고 말했다.

3 기초 TEST
p.161

A **1** asked, what, he needed ▸의문사+주어+동사
2 asked, whether/if, he was ▸그가 배가 고팠는지 아닌지
3 asked, why, I was ▸내가 왜 신경질적이었는지
4 told, that, wouldn't ▸will not→would not
5 asked, how, I went ▸내가 어떻게 학교에 갔는지
6 asked, whether/if, he liked
▸그가 그녀를 좋아하는지 아닌지
7 asks, where, we live
▸그는 우리에게 우리가 어디 사는지 묻는다.
8 asked, if/whether, I could
▸내가 그녀를 도울 수 있는지 아닌지
9 asks, if, he is ▸그가 그의 진짜 친구인지 아닌지
10 asked, what, was wrong ▸계획에 뭐가 잘못되었는지

기본 TEST
p.162~163

A
1 asked, where she got

2 asks, whether(if) we have

3 asked, when she was ▶그녀가 언제 한가한지

4 ask, whether(if) I am
▶그들은 내가 아픈지 아닌지를 묻는다.

5 asked, how much the shirt cost
▶cost-cost-cost 값이 들다, 값이다

6 asked, what he wanted ▶생일에 무엇을 원하는지

7 told, that his(her) music was
▶그의(그녀의) 음악이 매우 감동적이었다고

8 asked, whether(if) he liked
▶나는 그에게 그가 풍경을 좋아하는지 아닌지 물었다.

9 told, that he hadn't come ▶시제 과거, 과거완료

10 asks, whether(if) he(she) understands
▶학생이 그것을 이해하는지 아닌지

B
1 asked Linda / what she was doing that day
▶what+주어+동사

2 asked Sarah / whether(if) she wanted a pen

3 ask her / when he will go to church.
▶when+주어+동사

4 asked my brother / how long it took to his school ▶그의 학교까지 가는 데 얼마나 오래 걸렸는지

5 asks her / whether(if) she is in trouble
▶그녀가 곤경에 처해 있는지 아닌지

6 asked my mother / where we were going on a picnic

7 asked me / what I would wear for Halloween
▶할로윈에 무엇을 입을지

8 ask her / what she is interested in
▶그녀가 무엇에 흥미가 있는지

9 asked me / why I didn't practice
▶내가 왜 연습을 안 했는지

10 asked the cab driver / whether(if) he(she) could drop her off there ▶그녀는 택시기사에게 그녀를 거기서 내려줄 수 있는지 아닌지를 물었다.

④ 기초 TEST
p.165

A
1 asked ▶도와 달라고 부탁했다

2 ordered, to follow, him
▶장군은 그의 병사들에게 그를 따를 것을 명령했다.

3 told/ordered, to go, my ▶내 방에 가라고 말했다/명령했다

4 ordered, to cut

5 told/advised, to eat
▶그의 어머니는 그에게 천천히 먹으라고 말했다/조언(충고)했다.

6 advised, to get
▶나의 친구는 나에게 약간의 운동을 하라고 조언했다

7 told, to make, his
▶그녀는 그에게 그의 침구를 정리하라고 말했다.

8 told, to wash, my ▶내 차를 닦으라고 말했다.

9 told/advised, to study

10 told/asked, to show, him
▶Sam은 점원에게 그에게 다른 것을 보여달라고 말했다/부탁했다.

기본 TEST
p.166~167

A
1 told me to wake up

2 told(asked) my brother to pick up the phone

3 told(ordered) John to go back to his seat

4 told us to get in the car

5 told me that she had no money

6 told(asked) me to cover him with the blanket

7 told me that I was a size 4

8 told my sister to look under the bed

9 told(advised) her to be diligent

10 told her that it was his birthday

B
1 told Linda not to keep
▶부정 명령문은 to 앞에 not만 붙이면 됩니다.

2 advised them not to answer
▶나는 그들에게 그녀의 질문에 답하지 말 것을 조언했다.

3 asked me not to turn off

4 told me not to close
▶Eric은 내게 문을 닫지 말라고 말했다.

5 ordered us not to use

1 told me not to buy ▶not to buy 사지 말라고
2 advised us not to leave
3 asked me not to clean ▶ask 부탁하다, 요청하다
4 told the woman not to be ▶not to be late 늦지 말라고
5 told them not to run ▶hallway 복도

실력 TEST

p.168~170

A

1 says that she is lucky ▶그녀는 그녀가 운이 좋다고 말한다.
2 asked me whether(if) I was a cook
▶내가 요리사인지 아닌지
3 told me that he needed a ride to Hank's house
▶Hank의 집에 갈 탈 것이 필요하다
4 asked me where I wanted to go
▶내가 어디에 가고 싶은지
5 told(advised) us to be honest
▶정직하라고 말했다/조언했다.
6 asked Karen why she wanted that job
▶왜 그녀가 그 직업을 원하는지
7 told the naughty girl that he(she) would not
tolerate that ▶will → would, this → that
8 asked us whether(if) she could take it
9 asked Jack what kind of cake he wanted
▶어떤 종류의 케이크를 그가 원하는지
10 told(ordered/advised) her not to go out at
night ▶밤에 나가지 말라고 말했다/명령했다/조언했다

B

1 "I really enjoy this weather."
2 "Where is my mom?"
3 "When will you take a walk?"
4 "Keep an eye on your dog."
5 "Your artwork is very pleasing to see."
6 "Open the window."
7 "What made you trip and fall?"
8 "Stay here."
9 "Can you ride a roller-coaster?"
10 "Put off the meeting(, please.)."

C

1 "You look better."
2 "Can you organize the event?"
3 "She is skinny now."
4 "Stay with me here."
5 "You have to floss everyday."
6 "Are you a barber?"
7 "Be patient with your family."
8 "What do you want to eat for dinner?"
9 "Don't worry too much."
10 "Be satisfied all the time."

내신대비1

p.171~174

01 ②　02 ③　03 ④　04 ④　05 ①　06 ③
07 ⑤　08 ⑤　09 ③　10 ④　11 ⑤　12 to
close　13 asked, where, lived　14 ④　15 ③
16 ②　17 asked, whether(if)　18 I want to
meet you　19 ③　20 Take me to the new
playground.

01 자연현상은 불변의 진리이므로 항상 현재 시제를 사용합니다.
02 to부정사의 부정은 to 앞에 바로 위치합니다.
03 아버지가 내게 나의 숙제를 하라고 말씀하셨다.
04 ④ knows → knew 로 시제 일치를 해야 합니다.
05 전쟁이 일어난 것은 과거의 역사적 사실이므로 ① breaks → broke
로 바꿔야 합니다.
06 said to = asked, 직접의문문에서 간접의문문으로 바뀔 때 의문사
(구)+주어+동사로 어순도 함께 변화합니다.
07 시제 일치를 해주기 위해 would gain을 써야 합니다.
08 ⑤ being → to be 로 바뀌어야 합니다.
09 간접 화법에서 the next day는 직접 화법에서 tomorrow를 의미합
니다.
10 said to → asked, 해석: Jenny는 내게 비가 오는지 안 오는지를 물
었습니다.
11 to not → not to
12 그는 내게 문을 닫을 것을 부탁했다.
13 Emily는 내게 내가 어디 사는지 물었다.
14 ④ can → could, 시제 일치를 위해 변화합니다.
15 ③ likes → liked, 시제 일치를 위해 변화합니다.
16 to부정사 다음에는 동사 원형이 와야 합니다. ⓑ met → meet
17 해석: Mike는 Charles에게 그가 Eric을 보았는지 물었다.

18 해석: 그는 내게 그가 나를 도서관 앞에서 만나고 싶다고 말했다.

19 내게 말했다 → told me

20 해석: 나의 남동생은 내게 새로운 놀이터에 데려가 달라고 말했다.

 내신대비2 p.175~178

```
01 ④   02 ④   03 ③   04 ④   05 was → is
06 ①   07 I was   08 ①   09 ②,③   10 ③
11 had turned   12 ④   13 ②   14 whether(=if),
was   15 I want to meet you here   16 ④   17 ⑤
18 ①   19 ④   20 ⑤
```

01 I 는 he 로, 피전달문의 동사(said)가 과거이므로 am 이 was 로 바 뀝니다.

03 피전달문의 동사(said)가 과거이므로, stand 가 stood 로, here 가 there 로 바뀝니다.

04 ④ the before day → the day before

05 불변의 진리 ; 현재시제 만 사용합니다.

06 ① 주절의 시제가 과거 일 때는 종속절의 시제로 미래를 사용하지 않습니다.

07 간접화법의 어순 ; 의문사(구) + 주어 + 동사 …

08 의문문의 간접화법 ; said to→asked, 접속사로 whether 또는 if 사용

10 부정사의 부정 ; not + to ~

11 피전달문의 동사(said)가 과거이므로, 전달문의 동사는 과거에서 과거완료(had turned)로 바뀝니다.

12 ④ today → that day

14 의문문 이므로 whether 또는 if 사용합니다.

15 과거시제이므로 wanted → want 로, there → here 로 되돌아 옵니다.

16 간접화법의 어순 ; 의문사(구) + 주어 + 동사 …

17 tomorrow → the next day

18 불변의 진리 ; 현재시제 만 사용합니다

19 명령문의 간접화법 ; to ~

20 next time(다음 번에) 이 있으므로 미래시제를 사용합니다.

 Chapter 7

가정법

 기초 TEST p.182~185

A

1 과거, 알고 있다면 / 과거완료, 알고 있었다면

2 과거, 이라면 / 과거완료, 이었다면

3 과거완료, 가지고 있었다면 / 과거, 가지고 있다면

1 과거, 잘 수 있을 텐데 / 과거완료, 잘 수 있었을 텐데
  ▶sleep-slept-slept

2 과거완료, 머물렀을 텐데 / 과거, 머무를 텐데 ▶stay-stayed-stayed

3 과거, 말할 텐데 / 과거완료, 말했을 텐데
  ▶should have p.p 틀림없이 ~했을 텐데

4 과거완료, 건강했을지도 / 과거, 건강할지도
  ▶might have p.p ~했을지도 모를 텐데

5 과거, 만나지 않을 텐데 / 과거완료, 만나지 않았을 텐데
  ▶would ~할 텐데(바람)

B

1 먹을지도 모를 텐데, 먹을 수 있을 텐데, 틀림없이 먹을 텐데, 먹을 텐데
  ▶would 바람 could 능력 should 확신 might 추측

2 행복할 텐데, 틀림없이 행복할 텐데, 행복할 수 있을 텐데, 행복할지도
  모를 텐데

1 머물렀을지도 모를 텐데 ▶might have p.p

2 일할 수 있을 텐데

3 틀림없이 놀랄 텐데

4 행복 할 텐데 ▶가정법과거

5 지불할 수 있었을 텐데 ▶pay-paid-paid

6 깨끗할지도 모를 텐데

7 틀림없이 갔을 텐데 ▶should have p.p

8 얻었을 텐데 ▶get-got-gotten

C

1 were, might get **1**, 더 얇다면, 걸릴지도 모를 텐데 / had been, might have gotten **2**, 더 얇았다면, 걸렸을지도 모를 텐데 ▶take-took-taken

2 had, could lend **1**, 가지고 있다면, 빌려줄 수 있을 텐데 / had had, could have lent **2**, 가지고 있었다면, 빌려줄 수 있었을 텐데

3 were, would accept **1**, 현명하다면, 받아들일 텐데 / had been, would have accepted **2**, 현명했다면, 받아들였을 텐데 ▶were-had been

4 had known, should have raised **2**, 알고 있었다면, 들었을 텐데 / knew, should raise **1**, 알고 있다면, 들 텐데 ▶keep-kept-kept

D

1 were, would go **1**, 바쁘지 않다면, 갈 텐데
▶주어에 상관없이 가정법 과거의 be동사는 were입니다.

2 had been, could have seen **2**, 열려 있었다면, 볼 수 있었을 텐데 ▶see-saw-seen

3 had not been, might have gotten **2**, 아프지 않았다면, 받았을지도 모를 텐데
▶과거완료의 부정은 have 동사와 일반 동사 사이에 위치합니다.

4 had broken, should have run **2**, 깨뜨렸다면, 틀림없이 도망쳤을 텐데 ▶break-broke-broken

5 were, would hire **1**, 부지런하다면, 고용할 텐데

6 had, should start **1**, 가지고 있다면, 출발시킬 텐데

7 had been, should have blamed **2**, 있었다면, 틀림없이 나무랐을 텐데 ▶blame 나무라다, 비난하다

8 had come, would have been **2**, 나왔다면, 처했을 텐데
▶come out 밖으로 나오다

기본 TEST   p.186~189

A **1** had come, might have met ▶가정법 과거 완료
2 had caught, have run ▶catch-caught-caught
3 were, wait ▶가정법 과거
4 had, go ▶가정법 과거

5 had been, have bought ▶가정법 과거 완료
6 knew, say ▶가정법 과거
7 had stayed, have cooked ▶stay longer 더 오래 머무르다
8 were not, play ▶주어에 상관없이 be동사는 were을 사용합니다.
9 had been, have called
10 were, help ▶가정법 과거

B

1 had come, have been
▶would have p.p ~했을 텐데/바람, 소망
2 were, could ▶비교급 thicker, better
3 had been, have found ▶가정법 과거 완료
4 were, join
5 had decided, have paid
6 had, pick ▶가정법 과거
7 had left, have boarded ▶leave-left-left
8 were, might fall ▶might ~할지도 모를 텐데
9 had warned, have stayed
10 had had, have lent ▶have-had-had

C **1** had cooked ▶가정법 과거 완료 **2** were
3 had fed ▶feed-fed-fed **4** had woken ▶wake-woke-woken **5** had

1 would have been ▶만약 집 경보가 울렸다면, 그녀는 걱정되었을 텐데 **2** would be **3** should have stopped
4 could join ▶가정법 과거 **5** might have impressed
▶네가 만약 그 양복을 입었다면, 여자들을 감동시켰을 지도 모를 텐데

D **1** had caught **2** had snowed ▶만약 토요일에 눈이 왔다면 **3** knew **4** were **5** had gone ▶그가 그녀와 함께 도서관에 갔다면

1 should have been
2 might have arrived ▶너는 더 일찍 도착했을지도 모를 텐데
3 would keep
4 could have got ▶그녀는 더 좋은 직업을 구할 수 있었을 텐데
5 wouldn't nag
▶내가 엄마라면, 나는 아이들에게 잔소리하지 않을 텐데

Ⓐ **1** were, would hire

2 were, might work

3 had been, couldn't have bought

▶could have bought의 부정은 could not have bought입니다.

4 had had, would have started

▶had had 있었다면, 가졌다면

5 were, might purchase

6 had, would help

7 had told, would have been

8 had been, might have felt ▶가정법 과거 완료

9 were, should take ▶가정법 과거

10 had fastened, could have saved ▶가정법 과거 완료

Ⓑ

1 had been, would have been ▶be with ~와 함께 있다

2 had had, could have helped

▶enough+명사 충분한 ~ 것

3 were, should hunt ▶가정법 과거

4 had snowed, would have been

5 had been, could have kicked ▶had been ~였다면

6 were, wouldn't stay ▶가정법 과거

7 had been, might have invited

8 were, should protect ▶all the time 항상

9 had told, might have forgiven

▶forgive-forgave-forgiven

10 knew, should call

Ⓐ **1** isn't, says ▶그는 똑똑하지 않으므로 그렇게 말한다.

2 wasn't, didn't meet ▶직설법 과거

3 am not, don't go ▶직설법 현재

4 didn't cry, weren't ▶직설법 과거

5 isn't, don't take ▶take A to: A를 ~에 데려가다

6 didn't put, wasn't

▶Kelly가 주전자에 물을 넣지 않아서 그것은 꽉 차지 않았다.

7 doesn't have, can't buy

8 didn't practice, didn't

▶for a longer time 더 오랜 시간 동안

9 opened, could fine

10 didn't send, didn't receive

▶Daniel이 편지를 보내지 않았으므로 나는 그것을 받지 못했다.

Ⓐ **1** is not, acts / was not, acted

2 don't have, don't buy / didn't have, didn't buy

3 is, is not / was, was not

4 weren't closed, could see / aren't closed, can see

5 doesn't know, doesn't tell / didn't know, didn't tell

Ⓑ **1** wasn't, couldn't score ▶score 득점하다

2 doesn't have, doesn't pick

▶Gary는 차가 없으므로, 나를 데리러 오지 못한다.

3 wasn't, accepted

▶나는 현명하지 않았으므로, 그의 제안을 받아들였다.

4 am not, am not

5 aren't, doesn't care

▶네가 아이가 아니므로, 엄마는 너에게 더 이상 신경을 쓰지 않는다.

6 wasn't, got ▶코트가 더 두껍지 않아서 나는 감기에 걸렸다.

7 didn't offer, didn't drink

8 doesn't have, can't help

9 don't know, don't guide

10 got, didn't go

▶기침이 심해졌으므로, 나는 학교에 가지 않았다.

③ 기초 TEST

p.197~199

A

1 키가 더 크다면, 키가 더 컸더라면
  ▶be동사는 were을 사용합니다.

2 현명했더라면, 현명하다면
  ▶had been ~이었다면, ~했더라면

3 있다면, 있었다면

1 마치 (그가) 교장선생님인 것처럼, 마치 (그가) 교장선생님이었던 것처럼
2 마치 (그가) 모든 것을 알았던 것처럼, 마치 (그가) 모든 것을 아는 것처럼
  ▶as if 주어 + 동사의 과거형
3 마치 (그가) 매우 심한 감기에 걸렸던 것처럼, 마치 (그가) 매우 심한 감기에 걸린 것처럼 ▶as if 주어 + had p.p

B

1 had taken ▶had p.p **2** could buy **3** were
4 were **5** had got off **6** were **7** were **8** had been **9** knew ▶as though(= as if) 마치 ~인 것처럼
10 had seen ▶had p.p

C

1 had seen ▶영화를 봤다면 **2** had experienced
▶경험했던 것처럼 **3** were **4** had not missed ▶had+부정+p.p **5** had ▶had p.p 가 아닌 동사 have의 단순과거형입니다.
6 were **7** were **8** had been ▶테니스 시합에 있었던 것처럼

기본 TEST

p.200~201

A

1 am not ▶내가 더 예쁘지 않아서 유감이다. **2** was not ▶나는 내가 건강하지 않았기 때문에 유감이다. **3** made
4 isn't ▶in good shape 좋은 모습의 **5** didn't feel

1 is not **2** was not **3** is ▶그것은 사실이 아닌 것처럼 들린다. 사실, 그것은 사실이다. **4** didn't improve ▶사실, 날씨는 좋아지지 않았다. **5** didn't hear ▶사실, 그녀는 농담을 듣지 못했다.

B

1 I'm sorry I made that error ▶내가 그 실수를 해서 유감이다.
2 In fact, they don't like each other.
  ▶사실, 그들은 서로를 좋아하지 않는다.
3 I am sorry he is not tall.
  ▶그가 키가 크지 않아서 유감이다.
4 In fact, Sally didn't know the actress.
  ▶had p.p → 과거형
5 I am sorry he forgot to put gas in the car.
  ▶had p.p → 과거형
6 I am sorry I didn't hear what they were saying.
  ▶나는 그들이 무엇을 얘기하고 있었는지 듣지 못해서 유감이다.
7 In fact, Mr. Brown was not hurt. ▶had p.p → 과거형
8 In fact, they are not soldiers.
  ▶사실, 그들은 군인이 아니다.

실력 TEST

p.202

A

1 I had treated ▶treat A better: A를 더 잘 대하다
2 as if (as though) he were
  ▶as if(= as though) 마치 ~인 것처럼
3 we were
4 they had kept ▶had p.p
5 as if (as though) he had been
6 as if (as though) she had seen ▶그것을 봤던 것처럼
7 I were
8 as if (as though) she were
9 I had been
10 as if (as though) he had not heard ▶had 부정 p.p

내신대비1

01 ④ 02 ③ 03 ① 04 ④ 05 ④ 06 ③
07 ④ 08 ④ 09 ③ 10 ② 11 ② 12 ⑤
13 ④ 14 ④ 15 ③ 16 ③ 17 ① 18 ⑤
19 ③ 20 buy

01 가정법 과거에서 주어에 상관없이 be동사는 were을 사용합니다.

02 had는 동사 have의 과거형입니다.

03 해석: Tom은 마치 그녀를 전혀 본 적이 없었던 것처럼 말한다.

04 해석: 내가 돈이 많다면, 그런 자전거를 살 텐데.

05 ④ lose → have lost, 가정법 과거 완료 문장입니다.

06 가정법 과거 완료 문장입니다. I wish I had p.p

07 해석: 만약 Joseph이 우리 팀에서 경기를 했다면, 우리는 시합을 이길 수 있었을 텐데

08 ④ rained → had rained / 가정법 과거 완료 문장입니다.

09 해석: 나는 내가 영어를 말할 수 있으면 좋겠다. = 나는 내가 영어를 말하지 못해 유감이다.

10 가정법 과거 문장입니다.

11 ① is → had been ③ swim → had swum ④ were fine → had been fine ⑤ studied → had studied로 각각 고쳐야 합니다.

12 ⑤ fail → have failed / 가정법 과거 완료 문장입니다.

13 해석: Frances는 그녀가 아팠던 것처럼 보입니다. 사실, Frances는 아프지 않았습니다.

14 가정법 과거 완료 문장입니다.

15 had been, would have been / 가정법 과거 완료 문장입니다.

16 영화를 봤던 것처럼– 가정법 과거 완료 문장입니다.

17 해석: Nancy는 그녀가 아프지 않았던 것처럼 말합니다.

18 had not snowed, would have gone, 가정법 과거 완료 문장입니다.

19 가정법 과거에서 주어에 상관없이 be동사는 were을 사용합니다.

20 해석: 그녀가 정말 부자라면, 그녀는 틀림없이 더 많은 것들을 살 텐데

내신대비2

01 ③ 02 ④ 03 ⑤ 04 ④ 05 ① 06 ④
07 ③ 08 ④ 09 ② 10 could have cooked
11 ⑤ 12 am not 13 ③ 14 ④ 15 is not
16 ② 17 ③ 18 ⑤ 19 ④ 20 were → was

01 가정법 과거 ; 현재사실의 반대

03 가정법 과거완료 ; 과거사실의 반대

05 과거는 현재로, 긍정이면 부정으로 부정이면 긍정으로 바꾸어 줍니다.

06 과거완료는 과거로, 긍정이면 부정으로 부정이면 긍정으로 바꾸어 줍니다.

07 현재는 과거로, 긍정이면 부정으로 부정이면 긍정으로 바꾸어 줍니다.

10 가정법 과거완료 ; if절은 had +p.p, 주절은 could(would,…) + have p.p 입니다.

11 과거는 과거완료로, 긍정이면 부정으로 부정이면 긍정으로 바꾸어 줍니다.

12 과거는 현재로, 긍정이면 부정으로 부정이면 긍정으로 바꾸어 줍니다.

13 ~ as if …… → In fact, ….,로, 과거완료는 과거로, 긍정이면 부정으로 부정이면 긍정으로 바꾸어 줍니다.

15 ~ as if …… → In fact, ….,로, 과거는 현재로, 긍정이면 부정으로 부정이면 긍정으로 바꾸어 줍니다.

16 I wish ~ 가정법 = I am sorry ~직설법 ; 과거는 현재로, 긍정이면 부정으로 부정이면 긍정으로 바꾸어 줍니다.

17 주어 wish 가정법 ; 과거완료는 과거로, 긍정이면 부정으로 부정이면 긍정으로 바꾸어 줍니다.

18 I wish ~ 가정법 과거완료

20 In fact, ~ 는 직설법이므로 주어가 3인칭 단수일 때는 were을 사용하지 않고 was를 사용합니다.

01 ②   02 ⑤   03 ③   04 ①   05 ①   06 ②

07 ③   08 ①   09 ①   10 ③   11 ④   12 ④

13 ②   14 ④   15 ④   16 could play   17 ②

18 ④   19 ③   20 ①   21 ⑤   22 whether(if)

23 ③   24 ①   25 ④

01 소년의 아버지(소유격)

02 Tom이 말하는 것은 사실이다.

05 '전치사+관계대명사'의 형태에서는 관계대명사를 생략하지 않습니다.

06 ① which → when ③ in that → in which ④ what → that
⑤ which → that 또는 who 로 각각 고쳐야 합니다.

07 명령문은 to부정사를 사용해 간접 화법으로 바꿉니다.

08 had been-wouldn't have gotten, 가정법 과거 완료 문장입니다.

09 나는 그녀가 여기에 올지 안 올지 모르겠다.

10 전치사 다음에는 whom이나 which를 사용합니다.

11 Jane은 교실에서 가장 똑똑한 소녀이다. No other 단수명사~ 비교
급 than: 누구도 ~보다 ~하지 않습니다.

12 불변의 진리이기에 현재 시제를 사용합니다.

14 ① whose → who ② what → which ③ who → which
⑤ who → whose 로 각각 고쳐야 합니다.

15 where은 in which와 같은 표현입니다.

16 가정법 과거 문장입니다. I wish I 과거

17 every time ~할 때마다

19 so 그래서,

20 as soon as ~하자마자

21 ①②③④의 as, because, for 는 원인, 이유를 가리키는 접속사입니다.
⑤번의 for는 ~동안, 기간을 가리키는 전치사입니다.

22 ask whether/if: ~인지 아닌지 묻다

23 가정법 과거에서 주어에 상관없이 be동사는 were을 사용합니다.

24 a reason why ~하는 이유

01 ④   02 ④   03 ①   04 ①   05 ②   06 ④

07 don't have   08 ②   09 ④   10 ④   11 ④

12 ①, ④   13 ③   14 ②   15 ①   16 ②

17 wasn't   18 ③   19 ④   20 ③, ④, ⑤

21 On   22 ③   23 ②, ⑤   24 ⑤   25 when

01 one of the 최상급+복수명사

02 If ~ not = Unless와 같은 표현입니다.

03 said to = asked, 시제와 주어에 유의하여 직접 화법을 간접 화법으
로 바꿉니다.

05 시간+when을 씁니다.

06 ① in that → in what ② about that → the about which ③ the
way how → the way that ⑤ how → why 로 각각 고쳐야 합니다.

07 나는 돈이 없으므로, 그것을 살 수 없다.

08 ~인지 아닌지의 의미를 가질 때 if는 whether와 바꿔 쓸 수 있습니다.

09 의문사(구)+주어+동사 어순입니다.

11 전치사+which에서 which는 생략이 불가능합니다.

12 , which = , and(but)+대명사 입니다.

14 나는 그것이 사실인지 아닌지 모르겠다. '~인지 아닌지'는 whether
또는 if를 사용합니다.

15 though, although: 비록 ~일지라도

16 moreover, in addition: 게다가

17 가정법 과거 완료 문장을 직설법 과거로 바꾼 문장입니다.

18 전치사(in)+which

19 what, 너의 손에 갖고 있는 것을(what) 나에게 보여줘.

20 the way=how=the way that

21 as soon as=On ~ing: ~하자마자

22 ⓐ가게에 언제(when) 가니? ⓑ숙제를 끝낼 때(when), 갈게요.

23 이것을 끝낼 수 있을지 아닌지, ~인지 아닌지의 의미를 가질 때는
whether 또는 if를 사용합니다.

24 ⓐ그가 어린 시절을 보낸 영국(장소) ⓑ그가 태어난 한국(장소), 장
소는 관계부사 where을 사용합니다.

25 the day when, 시간은 관계부사 when을 사용합니다.